D1413966

Shaker Cities of Peace, Love, and Union

Published in cooperation with

HANCOCK SHAKER VILLAGE, INC.

Deborah E. Burns

SHAKER CITIES of Peace, Love, and Union

A History of the Hancock Bishopric

UNIVERSITY PRESS OF NEW ENGLAND

Hanover and London

University Press of New England, Hanover, NH 03755
© 1993 by University Press of New England
Appendix © 1992 by Deborah E. Burns
Printed in the United States of America   5   4   3   2   1
CIP data appear at the end of the book

for Amy Bess

Living souls, let's be marching
On our journey to heaven
With our lamps trimmed and burning
With the oil of truth.
Let us join the heav'nly chorus
And unite with our parents.
They will lead us to heaven
In the path of righteousness.

Tyringham, 1853

Contents

Illustrations follow pp. 72 and 144.

Preface

This book is intended to be a narrative history of the Shaker societies at Hancock and Tyringham, Massachusetts, and Enfield, Connecticut, tracing their respective fortunes from the first contact with Believers to the communities' eventual closings. It is not meant to be a religious history of the Shakers; my desire has been to learn more about the individuals who joined the Society.

Nevertheless, the Shakers are part of American history, and American history was part of the Shakers. Even though the Shakers were a community apart, they experienced the same social and economic forces that shaped American society. For example, the decline of the Shakers in southern New England paralleled the decline of New England's agricultural base. The intriguing question is not why these three Shaker societies ended, but why they succeeded for so long, when other celebrated communal ventures dissolved within a decade. In a rushing, thrilling, fast-paced, opportunity-filled society such as America, what held people in these austere communities?

The answer is that Shakerism worked for some people, even as it failed, sometimes quite spectacularly, for others. Even with numerous scandals and apostasies during the mid-1800s, Shaker life, for many members, went on serenely. Most of all, I believe, members were held by the spiritual life, which runs like a river through Shaker history, sometimes raging, sometimes calm. Love bound members together in a life centered around religion and work, not around competition and greed. Always, despite dissension and strife, it is this love that long-time Shakers remember. For women, the Society had many other advantages as well: security, serenity, and the chance to achieve a leadership position or develop other talents.

One of my special interests in this history became the natural family within the Shaker society. The bonds of kinship were an important, though unacknowledged, part of the adhesive that held the communities together. In the first fifty years, when big, multigenerational families joined the Society en masse, members' commitment was deep and fervent; many children of such families grew up to become important leaders. Others, of course, did not stay, and I was able to pursue a few of these out into the world.

Regarding sources, much of the information on the early Shakers comes from Believers' own "testimonies," often made with the intention of attracting new converts and/or defending Mother Ann Lee against her critics. These are colorful, subjective reminiscences. I have used them because they carry their own truth: statements such as Rebecca Clark's, Julia Johnson's, and Elizabeth Wood's convey the flavor of Shaker life as a more objective account cannot. I have tried to balance them by drawing from newspaper reports and local histories, and from the accounts of hostile apostates and bewildered visitors.

ACKNOWLEDGMENTS

One of the wonderful surprises about this endeavor has been the generosity of the Shaker scholars I have met, many of whom have devoted their lives to the study of the Shakers, and who shared their insights with me as well as their documents. I especially wish to thank Jerry Grant at the Emma B. King Library at the Shaker Museum and Library, Old Chatham, New York; as well as E. Richard McKinstry and Beatrice K. Taylor at the Henry Francis du Pont Winterthur Museum; Paige Lilly and Leonard Brooks at the Shaker Library, the United Society of Shakers, Sabbathday Lake, Maine; Mary Ann Sanborn and Nancy Adams at the Shaker Library, Shaker Village, Inc., Canterbury, New Hampshire; Sarah McFarland at Sawyer Library and Sylvia B. Kennick and Lynne Fonteneau at the College Archives, Williams College, Williamstown, Massachusetts; and Ruth Degenhart at the Berkshire Athenaeum, Pittsfield, Massachusetts. All of these individuals and their staffs patiently retrieved endless piles of documents and generously shared their own expertise. It has been especially meaningful to do research in Shaker villages; the calm beauties of Sabbathday Lake, Canterbury, and Hancock pervade my memories of this project.

My deepest gratitude goes to the wonderful staff at Hancock Shaker Village, especially Robert F. W. Meader, Librarian, who made me feel like part of the family, and whose wit, courtesy, and deep knowledge of the Shakers made the hundreds of hours I spent in his domain always a delight. June Sprigg alerted me to essential issues and documents and reviewed parts of the manuscript at various stages; in addition, the superb insights contained in her many books were always an inspiration. Lawrence Yerdon deserves special thanks for steering this manuscript through its final stages.

I am especially indebted to those who have explored their own family or town histories and shared them with me, including Gary Leveille, Jean Helwig, Carolyn Canon, Eugenie Rudd Fawcett, Arnold B. Hale, Alice M. Hale, the late Marcia Eisenberg (Tyringham genealogist), Clinton Elliott, Fred A. Loring, Richard Steinert, and Helen Dodge. Equally helpful were those who shared items in their collections, especially George Kramer, Helen R. McGinnis, and the late Milton Sherman. In addition, Eugenie Rudd Fawcett and Mr. and Mrs. George Kramer allowed me to explore their Shaker-built homes, for which I thank them. I am also grateful to Gustave S. Nelson and the conferees at the 1990 Berkshire Shaker Seminar who heard excerpts from this work.

I depended for background on scholarly works by Priscilla J. Brewer, Daniel W. Patterson, Stephen J. Stein, Robley E. Whitson, June Sprigg, Edward Deming Andrews, and Theodore E. Johnson.

There are three individuals without whom, I can honestly say, I could not have produced this book. One is Magda Gabor-Hotchkiss, Associate Librarian at Hancock Shaker Village, who deserves an entire page of thanks. She generously shared her expertise in identifying dim faces in old photographs, cheerfully retrieved documents and unearthed pictures, endlessly discussed fine points of Shaker history—and became a dear friend in the process.

The second person is Stephen Paterwic, president of the Boston Area Shaker Studies Group. With his remarkable memory and great sensitivity toward the Shakers he answered dozens of questions, critiqued the manuscript at various stages, and shared a wealth of documents. Any remaining errors, of course, are my responsibility alone.

The third person is Amy Bess Miller, who gave me this project and has always been its heart and soul. Her creativity and her love of the Shakers have inspired this book from beginning to end, and to her it is lovingly and respectfully dedicated.

I would like to thank my family—my siblings, Mecca, Stewart, and David, for their support and interest in this book; and my parents, James MacGregor Burns and Janet Thompson Keep, who imparted to all of us a love of history. Finally, my deepest thanks go to my husband, Thomas P. McHugh, and my children, Sean and Tess, for keeping me rooted in the joyous present.

Shaker Cities of Peace,
Love, and Union

A Company of Angels

On May 19, 1774, a decrepit ship, the *Mariah*, departed Liverpool for New York, carrying a small, hopeful group of passengers who practiced a strange new religion. During the stormy three-month crossing the captain and crew must have marveled at the behavior of the six men and three women, who often danced, twirled, and trembled in wild ecstasy—they called it worship—on the ship's open deck. No less astonishing was the fact that their leader was a thirty-eight-year-old woman named Ann Lees, whom the others called "Mother."

Like thousands of others who had crossed the Atlantic Ocean before them, they carried with their scanty possessions the dream of religious freedom. Rejecting both the Church of England and the sober alternative of Quakerism, they believed that the Second Coming of Christ would occur within each individual, making that individual then capable of living a pure, celibate life on earth. Called Shaking Quakers or Shakers for their uninhibited style of worship, they had struggled for more than ten years to survive in teeming industrial England. They were hated for their unconventional behavior and beliefs and had been taunted, pelted with horse manure and mud, stoned, kicked, and beaten with clubs.

Recently, as persecution intensified and converts were slow to come, Mother Ann had envisioned speaking to rapt, upturned faces in a faraway land—America. James Whittaker, a devoted young follower, also had foreseen a great destiny: "I saw a large tree," he reported, "and every leaf thereof shone with such brightness, as made it appear like a burning torch, representing the Church of Christ." Convinced they could live as angels on earth, they could imagine no better staging ground for their great experiment than a country unsoiled by the sins of European civilization.[1]

Their challenge was to find a home and a following in the vast frontier of America. Although they never achieved their larger ambition, to convert the world, they found ready hearts in the backwoods of New England and New York—individual seekers who seemed to be waiting for the Shaker message. Over the next two centuries, paralleling the larger drama of the formation and growth of the United States, the Shakers would attempt to create their ideal society. Their message was powerful and timely enough that they attracted thousands of converts in twenty-four communities in ten different states.

Three of those communities, located in Hancock and Tyringham, Massachusetts, and Enfield, Connecticut, were gathered together as the Hancock Bishopric. Their history followed the general pattern of Shaker societies: the early, backbreaking, joyous years; the establishment of communities and sharing of property; the development of the famous Shaker industries; the peak agricultural period; the "Era of Manifestations," or "Mother Ann's Work," when a religious revival swept the Society; and the gradual decline.

Although each of the three communities was economically independent, there were many political and social ties. The two elders and two eldresses of the bishopric Ministry, for example, were carefully selected from all three societies, and they in turn appointed family leaders. Newcomers entering one community, particularly children, were moved to another in the bishopric if populations were imbalanced. Members of the different communities frequently exchanged visits, especially once the railroad made travel easy between West Pittsfield and Enfield, and similar values, rules, and customs would have made them feel as at home as at a cousin's house.

Despite the similarities, each community was unique. Members' different personalities, backgrounds, talents, and ambitions flavored the societies in which they lived. Crafts and industries varied. Although the communities were not planned but simply grew up on the farms of the original Believers, the situation of each village—its topography, its fertility, its proximity to a highway or railroad or to a settlement of "world's people"—deeply affected its history. Each community endured its own particular hardships, and each closed for its own particular reasons. Tyringham, for example, closed barely a century after the Shakers arrived in America, whereas Hancock survived until 1960, one of the longest-lasting communities.

Hancock, Tyringham, and Enfield were bright fruits on a single branch of the tree envisioned by James Whittaker. Like the other communities, the Cities of Peace, Love, and Union were experiments, attempts to create a heaven on earth. Though they have ended, these experiments cannot be termed a failure. The Shakers have survived for a remarkably long time amid a culture that has grown increasingly alien. They won the world's respect for their decency and productivity. In their history we find a joyous commitment to a shared spiritual quest, a harmonious communal life, equality for women, careful upbringing of children, peace, hard work, and patient craftsmanship.

These issues and others are still being explored by the Shakers and are of consuming interest to all of us today. Little could Whittaker or Mother Ann know, as they stood at the deck rail gazing hopefully toward America, that we would someday be looking as eagerly back at them.

When the *Mariah* docked in New York on August 6, 1774, her passengers disembarked into a land that was seething with new ideas—politically, religiously, and socially turbulent. Political tension was at its peak, not only between the colonies and the mother country but within America as well, between loyalists and rebels. Since 1765 the Stamp Act had taxed colonists on every newspaper or legal document. Certain items were forbidden to be manufactured in the colonies, and new tariff levies drained money back to England. These intensely unpopular laws were enforced by a standing army that the colonists were required to support.

In 1774 things were happening quickly. The previous December general resistance to a hefty tax on tea had culminated in the Boston Tea Party. The British considered this incident a throwing down of the gauntlet and closed the Port of Boston until reparation would be made. In turn, angry colonists had proposed a stoppage of all trade with England. A month after the little band of Shakers arrived, on September 5, 1774, the First Continental Congress met in Philadelphia, and eleven of the thirteen colonies—New York and Georgia were the exceptions—ratified an agreement to cease all imports of English goods immediately and all exports to British ports within a year.

Anti-English feeling was swelling. Colonists were arming themselves; newspapers were fiercely debating the issues. The American Revolution would soon begin in earnest. And on backcountry farms, in taverns on rural crossroads, in tiny hamlets far from the cities, the small farmers and laborers of New England also felt the revolutionary surge.

Rural America was in a religious turmoil as well, its citizens reeling from revival to revival with a spiritual hunger not satisfied by established churches. The Great Awakening of the 1740s had paralleled the English Shakers' disenchantment with established religion. Seeking a vital, ecstatic faith, many country people still felt that the Congregational church was too dry and theoretical in doctrine and too dominating in practice. Some became dissenters, particularly Baptists, demanding that each believer experience a conversion, a personal confrontation with God.

The Baptist faith drew thousands of converts yet generated more confict in its turn. A splinter group calling itself the Separate-Baptists broke off for a familiar reason: they felt the new Baptist religion had already become corrupted by respectability. The Separate-Baptists refused to baptize infants—because babies could not consciously accept God—or to pay the state taxes that supported Congregational churches. Compromises effected by the Warren Association in 1767 attempted to mend this split but consequently excluded many of the most radical Baptists. These radicals, or New Lights—among them Joseph and David Meacham and Valentine Rathbun—were ripe for Shakerism.

And so were the ordinary yeoman farmers who flocked to revival meetings. Many had come to eastern New York and western Massachusetts looking for cheap land in the mid-1700s, their households packed into horse-drawn, solid-wheeled farm carts. Their lives, like those of other colonists, were arduous as they toiled to clear land and eke out an existence on rough, stony fields and in rude log houses. For them, as for most of humanity, life was sheer hardship with incessant labor, and they nurtured no expectations for anything greater in this life. Searching, spiritually restless people, they endured harsh pioneer conditions and sought through the Spirit the joy that was rarely present in daily life.

Revival meetings promised entertainment at least and the possibility of supreme ecstasy, yet they often delivered great disappointment. Ardent apocalyptic expectations would lift believers to feverish heights and then swiftly yield to anxiety, doubt, discouragement, and finally, depression and lethargy, as the spirit of God seemed to be withdrawn from the participants and they were cast back into ordinary life. Yet the next meeting would draw them back again, hopeful and eager.

It was an exciting time, when heights of genius and creativity were reached and anything seemed possible. In this volatile political and religious climate the new American nation envisioned by revolutionaries seemed to many to be the destined backdrop for the Second Coming of Christ.

The little band of Shakers dispersed when they arrived in America but held fast to their dream. Ann Lee (the final *s* was dropped when she arrived in America) found work as a washerwoman in New York City, and before long she and her husband separated. The rest of the group—William Lee (Ann's brother), James Whittaker, John Hocknell and his son Richard, James Shepherd, Mary Partington, and Nancy Lees (Ann's niece)—went up the Hudson River and procured a wooded, swampy piece of land in Niskeyuna, in the wilderness just northwest of Albany.

In spring 1776, as the American Revolution began in earnest on the Lexington, Massachusetts, common, Ann Lee traveled up the Hudson River to join the other Shakers in Niskeyuna. The little working-class group from industrial England—unskilled, like so many other European immigrants, in agriculture or animal husbandry—would spend the next few years struggling to survive in the raw American wilderness.

While the Shakers were becoming established, a young man named Joseph Meacham, Jr., was undertaking a spiritual journey of his own. A member of an old, prominent Connecticut family and eldest son of the first Baptist preacher in Enfield, the young man had himself become a lay preacher in his father's church in 1773. Since then, however, he had become increasingly disturbed by dissent in the church, observing "those who professed to be Brethren, and followers of the Prince of Peace, destroying, ravaging and rending each other miserable as was in their power"; and he concluded that members of the congregation were no less sinful as Baptists than they had been as Congregationalists. In 1776 he left Enfield and embarked on a pilgrimage, seeking a lasting faith whose adherents were pure of heart and free from their sinful natures. After three years his path brought him to the Freewill Baptist Church in New Lebanon, New York, six miles west of the Massachusetts line.[2]

Meacham arrived in New Lebanon just in time to participate in the New Light Stir, a series of revivals that touched down like tornadoes in the hills along the New York–Massachusetts border. At the center of the tumult was the conviction that Christ's Second Coming was near at hand and that the Kingdom of Heaven would soon be established on earth. Eager settlers left the larger Congregational and Baptist communities and gathered into sects, one of which Meacham led in ecstatic daily meetings in New Lebanon. Trances, speaking in unknown tongues, prophecies, receiving spirits into one's body, and other such wonders were common fare as the settlers waited confidently for the radiant appearance of Christ.

When the summer of 1779 gave way to the fall and Christ did not appear, Meacham and his congregation were plunged into a crisis of faith. Confused by the prophetic signs they had perceived, they were still certain that something was happening, somewhere. The usual revivalistic cycle from ecstasy to despair seemed about to be played out yet again. At one point Meacham said he could not help the people, "for I cannot help myself."[3]

In desperation he and other leaders sought evidence of spiritual power and millennial "signs." They searched most urgently for what they considered the key sign: believers who lived pure lives, with a Christlike freedom from all committed sin.[4]

Once-high expectations were simultaneously faltering at Niskeyuna. There, emaciated Shaker men and women were hard at work clearing stumps, draining swamps, cutting channels through bogs, plugging slough-holes with dirt and sand, planting, raising buildings, and establishing small industries, barely scraping enough together to feed themselves—and daily expecting a flood of disciples.

Not a single soul, however, converted for years. Great doubts surfaced among Ann Lee's followers, but she herself remained supremely confident that their moment was yet to come. "O my dear children!" she urged them. "Hold fast, and be not discouraged. God has not sent us into this land in vain; but he has sent us to bring the gospel to this nation, who are deeply lost in sin; and there are great numbers who will embrace it, and the time draws nigh." Mother Ann may have intentionally kept a low profile as the Shakers built up their substance. She also prudently avoided drawing attention during the critical years when the American Revolution was being fought around Albany.

In the fall of 1779, Mother Ann instructed her followers to lay up extra stores. "We shall soon have company enough," she promised them, "to consume it all."[5]

The following March word began to filter to farmhouses and taverns that a peculiar new religion had been established at Niskeyuna. The news reached settlers tapping their maple trees and contemplating their spring plowing in the Taconic Range and the Berkshire Hills along the Massachusetts border, not forty miles east of Niskeyuna. Rumor was that the group, led by an inspired English prophetess, preached that the Second Coming had in fact already occurred.

Ministers and preachers, their spiritual antennae finely tuned, were the first to investigate. They were intrigued by the strange reports and by the notion that Armageddon might be an individual, not a global, experience. Yet there was an immediate problem: even though women preachers had participated in the New Light Stir, many male ministers were deeply skeptical that a female could exercise any spiritual power or claim any special knowledge of God.

Joseph Meacham first sent an associate, Calvin Harlow, to Niskeyuna. Harlow found himself strongly moved by the presence of Mother Ann and the elders, although he did not convert at that time. He asked Mother Ann about Paul's biblical prohibition of women elders in the Church, to which she replied:

The order of man, in the natural relation, is a figure of the order of God in the spiritual creation. As the order of nature requires a man and a woman to produce offspring; so, where they both stand in their proper order, the man is the first, and the woman the second in the government of the family. He is the father and she the mother; and all the children, both male and female, must be subject to their parents; and the woman, being second, must be subject to her husband, who is the first; but when the man is gone, the right of government belongs to the woman; So is the family of Christ.[6]

Her answer gave the first portrayal of the Shakers as a family, sanctioned by both natural and divine law, and of her own role in it. The image of the family would become the predominant metaphor for the structure and ideal of the United Society.

Meacham, impressed by Harlow's report, decided in May 1780 to go and see for himself. He and two companions (Amos Hammond, another Baptist elder, and Aaron Kibbee) went on horseback to the little settlement and spent a day there.

After a service of dance and song a dialogue took place. Young James Whittaker was spokesman; he said, "We have been laboring for years in the work of the regeneration. We have actually risen with Christ, and travel with him in the Resurrection."[7]

Meacham then asked the crucial question: "Are *you* perfect? Do *you* live without sin?"

"The Power of God," answered Whittaker, "revealed in this day, does enable souls to cease from sin; and we have received that power; we have actually left off committing sin, and we live in daily obedience to the will of God."

The visitors from New Lebanon learned that the Shakers believed in free will, that God was merciful, and that a final redemption was available for all. However, this redemption required a spiritual rebirth through confession of sins and an avowal of celibacy.

Meacham and his companions were electrified. Here was a concrete road to salvation, not a lot of vague theory. Celibacy was not a foreign idea to these American seekers: the Puritan conflict between flesh and spirit was a common theme, and they knew that the way to Heaven would not be easy. In addition, the ecstasy of Shaker worship, the clear, developed doctrine, and the radiant peace among the Believers must have had a profound effect.

This was the true beginning of the Shaker movement in America, when the little band from England, now ensconced in their small settlement in the woods, received the inquiring, seeking ministers from the Taconic hills. Meacham converted to Shakerism, and Mother Ann would later refer to him as her "first-born son" in America.

 CHAPTER ONE

"Living Souls,
Let's Be Marching!"

Twenty-five-year-old Captain Daniel Goodrich was the first of his large family to move onto what would later be Shaker lands, just west of Pittsfield, Massachusetts, in 1764. Along with him came his wife, the former Anna Baldwin (pregnant with their first son, Daniel Jr.), and their two small daughters. Berkshire County, with its thick forests, rushing streams, and hills holding marble outcrop and iron ore beds, had been the last part of Massachusetts to be settled, after the French and Indian wars had ended. Two years later Captain and Mrs. Goodrich were joined on the wild, rugged tract by three generations of family and friends. That June the General Court of Massachusetts had released the six-thousand-acre southern portion of the twenty-thousand-acre Plantation of Jericho to a group including Daniel; his father, Benjamin; three of his brothers; and nine other settlers: Jeremiah Osborne (or Osborn) and his son Hezekiah, married to Goodrich's eldest sister Abigail; Dudley and Eleazer (or Elizur) Deming; Hezekiah and Israel Talcot; Joshua Simons; Samuel Lamb; and Theophilus Bishop. Most of them, like the majority of Berkshire settlers, hailed from Connecticut.[1]

The Plantation of Jericho—the future town of Hancock—was a long, narrow rectangle stretching northward along the New York border, bisected by a precipitous, virtually impassable east-west spur of the Taconic Range. When the settlers arrived, the rectangle was broader than it is today; when the New York–Massachusetts line was established in 1787, Hancock lost some ground. The Mountain Tract, as the land granted to Goodrich and the others was called, occupied the broad valley and thickly forested hills in the southern end of the rectangle, quite remote from the town center developing to the north.[2]

For the next fifteen years the settlers labored to open up the dense forests of birch, beech, and maple where black bears, white-tailed deer, and gray wolves roamed. They cut the giant trees with double-bitted axes, built cabins with the logs, and planted fields of corn and wheat among the tree stumps.

Perhaps the Goodrich family was typical of the families who settled the Mountain Tract, many of whom later converted en masse to Shakerism. Benjamin Goodrich, the fifty-one-year-old patriarch, had followed his brother, Captain Charles Goodrich, one of the first settlers of Pittsfield, to the area from their family seat in prosperous Wethersfield, Connecticut, just south of Hartford. Benjamin joined his son Daniel on the Mountain Grant, settling his portion of the property with his wife, their twelve other children, and several grandchildren.

Although they would later respond to the Shaker message, these were not idle, dreamy people who drifted from one revival to the next. Like most frontier people they were independent, industrious, and frugal. The Goodriches, in particular, were an active, involved family who served as officers in their country's battles and in their town government. Captain Daniel Goodrich fought at the Siege of Quebec and was a deacon in the young Baptist Church under the ministerial charge of Valentine Rathbun of Pittsfield. Samuel Goodrich, the third son, would be killed in the revolutionary war.[3]

On July 4, 1776, the Plantation of Jericho was incorporated as the town of Hancock (named after John Hancock, president of the First Continental Congress and later governor of Massachusetts). In order to serve as a member of the town committee Daniel Goodrich made the roundabout trip west and north through New York and then east to the town meeting. Later he would serve as selectman and in 1778 was appointed a representative to the Massachusetts General Court. Others destined to become Shakers were also prominent in town government, concerned with such issues as control of roaming livestock, smallpox inoculation, and prohibition of horse racing; Hezekiah Osborne served as selectman and constable, and Eleazar Deming was on the first town committee and surveyor of highways.[4]

Every Sunday the Goodriches and their neighbors crowded into their carriages and farm wagons and traveled east a few miles to the home of a fiery Baptist preacher named Valentine Rathbun (or Rathbone). Rathbun had arrived in Pittsfield from Stonington, Connecticut, in 1770 with his wife, Tabitha, and nine of his twelve children, joining his brothers Daniel and Amos, who had bought farms in Richmond. He had settled just over the Pittsfield line from Hancock, establishing a water-powered fulling mill in the section of town later known as Barkersville. A devout Baptist, Rathbun was dissatisfied with Pittsfield's sole Congregational church and began holding Sunday meetings at his home. Soon several dozen neighbors gath-

ered there weekly to hear his powerful sermons. In 1772 he formally organized the first Pittsfield Baptist church, serving as preacher and elder.

During the next few years, as anti-British feeling swelled in Berkshire
County, Rathbun became a radical, outspoken leader and was elected to
Pittsfield's Committee of Inspection and Correspondence, which had
formed to take over governmental duties from British officials. He was also
appointed to the General Court of Massachusetts and in 1779 represented
Pittsfield at the state Constitutional Convention. By 1780, Rathbun was a
prominent citizen, an influential leader, a prosperous manufacturer, and
head of a thriving Baptist church. He was also a familiar figure in nearby
Hancock: Daniel Goodrich was an elder in his church, and Rathbun's
daughter Eunice had married Goodrich's brother Ezekiel.[5]

Like other local ministers, in June 1780, Rathbun heard of a remarkable
new religion arising near Albany. Rathbun's congregation urged him to go
and visit the Shakers and bring home a firsthand report, and he did so.
Upon his return he called a meeting in a large barn, no other building being
big enough to hold all of the curious people, "for they came from Pittsfield,
Richmond, and Hancock, and the barn was filled to overflowing insomuch
that they sat one upon another."[6]

He testified to the eager crowd:

According to your desires, I have been to see that people so much wondered at;
and I believe they are the people of God. I believe that it is the strange work, that
should come to pass in the last days. . . . I could as quickly speak against the Holy
Ghost as to speak against that people; they sing the song of the redeemed, they sing
the song that no man can learn; I could not learn their song any more than I could
track the birds in the air; they seemed like an innumerable company of angels, and
children of the first born, singing praises to the Heavenly Host.

He added that the Shakers had told him that when he found his "lot,"
or true position, he would become an elder. The Shakers may have perceived Rathbun's leadership ability, or they may have been slyly manipu-
lating him; at any rate, they won his immediate allegiance.

Rathbun, in turn, had a powerful effect on his audience in the crowded
barn, inspiring many who would become the first Hancock Shakers. A
number of listeners were carried away by excitement, including one
Walter Cook, who jumped up on a bench and began to screech, bowing
vigorously.

Amos Rathbun, Valentine's brother, became very agitated as well. He
managed to travel to Mother Ann in Niskeyuna and converted in her presence. He told her he would "sing aloud" of his salvation, to which Mother
Ann replied, "Amos, thou shalt sing bass in heaven."

Later, Amos Rathbun said,

Mother told me in the beginning that I must give up All, to find the pearl of great price, and I did, for her words ran through my soul like holy fire. I took father, mother, wife, and children, house and land, and all that was dear to me in this world, and put them in one scale, and my soul into the other, and I quick found out which balanced; my soul was my all, and obedience to Mother was my salvation and promise of eternal life. I have not had any more feeling to look back, after any of those things which I gave up, than I have to fill my bosom with glowing embers, I have laid hold of eternal life and I will live it though thousands fall by my side.[7]

Amos Rathbun's wife and children did not join with him, which caused him much heartache.

The eager members of Valentine Rathbun's audience had had certain experiences in common. Scraps of religious education had kindled their impressionable natures into a blaze of guilt and fear until they believed they were wallowing in sin and doomed to spend eternity in hell. Yet they could find no way out, no road to salvation. As one Believer wrote later:

When this testimony was first declared in America, there were many who had long been waiting for some Divine manifestation. . . . Their object was to find something that would not only convince the understanding, but purify the heart from dead works, and effectually deliver the soul from the bondage of a sinful nature. They could not build their hopes of salvation upon a transient ray of Divine light that affected the sense and feelings for a little moment, and then left them to wander in darkness and doubt till another momentary return of the same or something similar. Nay; they could not rest satisfied short of an enduring substance—a light that would continue to shine brighter and brighter till the perfect day—an essential reality that could not be doubted—that was as evident as the light of the sun on a clear day, and as indispensable to themselves as their existence.[8]

A critical spiritual dilemma was occurring, yet existing churches could supply no relief. If, however, respected local ministers such as Rathbun and Joseph Meacham were embracing Shakerism, their searching congregations needed no better example. The trickle of curious ministers to Niskeyuna turned into a torrent of excited laypeople, eager to know more about the signs and miracles, the gifts and ecstatic worship of the Shaker gospel.

Daniel Goodrich, Jr., for example, was only fourteen at the time of the 1779 New Light Stir, yet he was already suffering from a sense that he was "an enemy of God." To make matters worse, many of his friends seemed to have found salvation and rebirth through the revival while he was untouched. He attended meetings, prayed, and constantly questioned his friends about their experiences, yet he could not discover what he needed to do to be saved.[9]

When he was fifteen, he attended Rathbun's meeting in the barn. Finding that the charismatic Baptist minister had accepted Shakerism, the boy was quick to find his own way to Niskeyuna, with his sister and a company of friends. Particularly moved by the "solemn and heavenly" singing, which seemed to reach emotions too deep for words, he confessed his sins and became a lifelong Believer and leader. "I believed it to be the worship of the living God," he wrote later, "such as my ears had never heard, nor my soul felt before."[10]

Visitors came in hordes over the next few months, abandoning their corn patches to weeds and crows, letting their hay sit in the fields. As Mother Ann had predicted, the Shakers were glad of the extra stores they had laid up. It was a great union of families, several of which would form dynasties within Shaker leadership. Daniel Goodrich, Sr., his brother David and his entire family, their younger brothers Hezekiah and Jeremiah, John and Sarah Deming, and a number of their Hancock neighbors were early converts. Some of the visitors, like Hezekiah Hammond, Ebenezer Cooley, and Elizabeth Chauncey, were summoned to Niskeyuna by powerful dreams. Even the Marquis de Lafayette was said to have found his way to the Shaker community.[11]

The Town of Hancock had to appoint a committee to settle affairs with Hezekiah Osborne, then constable, "who on account of Shakers principals hath refused to collect taxes." Amos Hammond had to be excused for the same reason; Jeremiah Goodrich served for a year and then also withdrew; Valentine Rathbun himself resigned from the town and state committees on which he served.[12]

According to Shaker tradition, when visitors arrived at Niskeyuna they were greeted by Ann Lee and the elders as if they were expected. They might receive a simple meal, often served by Mother Ann herself, on a well-scrubbed wooden table. The meeting would begin in silence, followed by preaching and perhaps some dancing, and then Mother Ann, William Lee, or James Whittaker might sing. One of the elders would then approach each visitor and speak directly to him or her, answering questions or commenting on the person's spiritual state. During the visit the regular work of the settlement—farming, gardening, dairying—continued.

One Shaker sister later recalled spending eight days at Niskeyuna when she was eleven years old. "We had a little straw to lay on and cover over us," she remembered, "but we were so crowded that if I turned over all had to turn also." All visitors were put to work, the women sewing or spinning, the men chopping wood. Meetings lasted every night "until cock-crow," after which the group would sleep until sunrise. Breakfast and supper consisted of broth. This girl didn't mind the lack of sleep: "I felt anxious to see hear and learn all I could."[13]

Many young people made their way to Niskeyuna on foot or with a company of friends on horseback, driven by their desire for salvation. Reuben Rathbun, Valentine's son, had been terrified of Judgment Day from the time he could distinguish between right and wrong. Although he decided, while in his teens, to forswear all "carnal enjoyments" and to serve Jesus Christ, he found this vow impossible to keep. When he heard of the Shakers, and particularly of their commitment to celibacy, he too traveled to their little settlement. He too was deeply affected by Mother Ann's singing "a strange tune, with a mystical voice, in a mixture of words known and unknown which seemed to be a perfect charm." Convinced she and the Elders were "equal unto the angels," he confessed, ready to "take up the cross" against all sins.[14]

David Meacham of Enfield, Connecticut, had also been suffering concerning his "loss from God, especially in the actual gratifications of the lust of the flesh." He had heard of this "strange people near Albany" and knew that his brother Joseph had embraced their faith. Upon meeting them he too became fully convinced that Christ's second coming had occurred and confessed on his first evening in Niskeyuna.[15]

Mother Ann remarked that it was "a real gift of God" that he had come but warned him that he would encounter great opposition from his father. Sure enough, back in Enfield, Joseph Meacham, Sr., was vehemently opposed to his younger son's conversion and assembled a trio of ministers to speak with him and attempt to overthrow his faith. David was resolute, however, and even managed to persuade his father to open his mind to the Shakers.

Like Joseph Meacham, Samuel Johnson had spent his life searching for a way to live in the Spirit. He had been a deeply religious child even at age six. As a young man he received a degree in theology from Yale College, briefly taught the Indians of the Five Nations, and in 1777 was ordained the first Presbyterian minister in New Lebanon. His religious life was turbulent, however: after three years, with grave doubts about the established church, he moved with his wife and three children to West Stockbridge, Massachusetts, and plunged into the spiritual cauldron of the New Light Stir. When that revival waned he heard of the Shakers, and he and his wife, Elizabeth, went to hear Samuel Fitch speak. Convinced his spiritual quest was finally over, Johnson, though partly lame, walked to Niskeyuna the very next day. Mother Ann took one look at him and said, "James, take this man and let him open his mind"—words that resounded deep within the visitor. He confessed his sins to James Whittaker and remained with the Shakers a week. Soon his wife and children had joined with him.[16]

In June 1780 thirty-five-year-old Nathan Goodrich and his wife, thirty-year-old Hannah, left their five children at home in Hancock and went to Niskeyuna. Their initial reception was far from welcoming: Mary Partington greeted them from the doorway by shouting, "Strip off your pride and abominations! We know you, but you do not know us! We have men here that are not defiled with women, and women that are not defiled with men!" The next day Hannah inquired of Mother Ann about Nathan, and Mother Ann replied, "Let your husband alone—fastening your lust upon him!" Despite this harsh treatment, Hannah and Nathan were persuaded that these were indeed the people of God. After they joined the faith, Mother Ann showed them, especially Hannah, great love and charity.[17]

Nathan's younger brother, Elijur (or Elizur), a prosperous twenty-eight-year-old merchant, also became an early, ardent convert, although his new wife of six months, twenty-year-old Lucy Wright of Pittsfield, remained skeptical. The daughter of John and Martha Robbins Wright of Northampton, Massachusetts, and Wethersfield, Connecticut, Lucy had grown up just a mile and a half northeast of the Goodrich farm. Although she did not attend school, she had a lively curiosity and managed to educate herself by reading. Her mother died when Lucy was about eighteen.[18] Like so many others, Lucy had been swept up in the 1779 New Light Stir.

Although she and Elijur Goodrich were married in December 1779, they did not live as man and wife. According to a later Shaker historian, Elijur said that Lucy "was so beautiful and amiable that he could not bear to spoil her with the flesh; hence they lived uncommonly continent." Certainly, they had no children.[19]

The following June they went to Niskeyuna to see the Shakers. In contrast to her enthusiastic husband, Lucy hung back. Elijur Goodrich later recalled that he confided in Mother Ann, saying "that [Lucy] was connected with a high proud people, and it was doubtful in my mind whether she ever would believe and obey the gospel." Mother Ann responded, "Take faith, Lucy may be gained to the gospel, and if you gain her it will be equal to gaining a nation," evidently seeing in the young woman's serene strength great potential for leadership.[20]

After she and Elijur dissolved their marriage, she succeeded in converting her father (a former deacon), her brother John, and most of her "high proud" family; she would become Mother Ann's most trusted associate, a magnificent organizer, and eventually, Mother herself after Ann's death.

Ann Lee was now at the height of her personal charismatic power. With just a few words or a song, it was said, she could transform the mood of an entire assembly from deep despair to rapture. Yet she refused to be deified. If her followers kneeled to her, she would kneel with them, saying, "It is not me you love, but it is God in me." She herself waited on her visitors, saying, "I am among you as one that serveth." She gave up her own bed to visitors, sleeping on the bare floor with no blanket and only a folded garment for a pillow, in winter as well as summer. And at the table she ate the scraps others left. "It is good enough for me," she would say, "for it is the blessing of God and must not be lost." She preached prudence and economy so that enough would be left over for those in need.[21]

There were many small children, Believer Samuel Johnson noted later, who, by a few words from Mother Ann, received "impressions of goodness which governed them through life." Young girls were particularly affected by Mother Ann, and she and the elders spent a good deal of time talking with curious children, explaining the Shaker beliefs. Thankful E. Goodrich, the ten-year-old granddaughter of Valentine Rathbun and niece of Captain Daniel Goodrich, first went to Niskeyuna in 1781 and thought the Shakers looked "lovelier" than anything she had ever seen. "Mother called me her Child," she remembered later, "and said, that I might love and embrace her, I did so, and her smel seemed pure heavenly and angelic." Thankful cast her lot with the Shakers, confessing her childish sins to Father James Whittaker.[22]

"He then taught me the way of repentance," she later wrote, "how to shun the snares of sin, to be honest chaste and modest, in all my words and ways, and I felt his heart searching power, and spirit, as much as my little soul was able to bear, together with his everlasting charity and love; Then I could weep and rejoice, with my Heavenly parents, and join in their solemn sound and Heavenly songs, which had no end."

Zipporah Cary grew up in Cheshire, just north of Pittsfield, and in 1781 attended several Shaker meetings at the home of Squire Joseph Bennett, who had converted with his family. The girl was deeply moved as she held Bennett's infant granddaughter and watched the child's mother dance joyously. Zipporah's father was an abusive drunkard, but her mother converted and finally the girl did as well, to the dismay of her Baptist and Quaker friends.[23]

When Olive Miller of nearby Hinsdale, Massachusetts, was twelve or thirteen, she participated in an awakening and became terrified that she would go to hell. None of the preachers she heard seemed to offer hope. At age fourteen, in 1780, she heard from her parents about Mother Ann and the Shakers

... that they had found a way whereby souls could live pure lives, free from sin in every form. I was anxious to go and see them, about the middle of February I started with my father and mother and seven or eight others for Watervliet. The snow was going off, and it was exceeding bad traveling, but we were so desirous to go that we traveled on foot more than half the way. . . . In the evening I rode at three miles, in company with Elder John Farrington, to Mother's house which was small but many had gathered there to see and hear. I had a comfortable lodging that night with my mother on a bed upon the floor, and in the same room with blessed Mother Ann and Mary Partington who also lay upon the floor.

I saw Father William and Father James at this time, and heard them preach the gospel of salvation. I found I must confess my sins, yea, everything that was wrong and forsake them forever: by doing this, and bearing a daily cross, I could find the acceptance of God, but in no other way. This I freely and faithfully did, with the determination to live a pure life the remainder of my days, let what would come.

Olive Miller visited Mother Ann and the elders several times after that, noting that they were loving, kind, and very charitable but "powerful, keen and sharp against evil."[24]

No sooner had word spread about the little group of Shakers than persecution began. It started out mildly enough; children would pour out of roadside shacks along the route between New Lebanon and Niskeyuna, jeering "Shaker! Shaker!" when they saw the sober wagons roll by. Soon, however, the Believers were contending not only with mocking children and hostile neighbors but with bitter backsliders as well.[25]

Valentine Rathbun, initially buoyed by visions of becoming a Shaker elder, turned against the faith after a few months when a leadership position failed to materialize. He may have disagreed with the Shakers on dogma; more likely, he had difficulty subduing his strong personality. His sons Valentine and Reuben and his daughter Eunice (married to Daniel Goodrich's brother Ezekiel), as well as several grandchildren, remained faithful members, but he himself became one of the Shakers' most vocal—and violent—enemies.

The Shakers also faced hostility from local authorities. Members of the political and religious establishment were stunned by the Shakers' success in winning converts. A New Lebanon justice of the peace, Samuel Jones, made the following statement many years later:

[The rise of the Shakers] commenced shortly after the New Light meetings were set up where the utmost wildness and irregularity both in Doctrine and conduct had been encouraged by the leaders of the sect—Ann Lee and her confederates at that time resided near Albany, and hearing of the new sect at New Lebanon some of the company came and taking advantage of the Infatuated minds of those New Lights who were athirst for something new and strange they quickly led them into their Mystery of Inequity and their increase for some time was very rapid. The consequences was the destruction of many families; the ties of affection between Husbands and wifes parents and children must be dissolved according to their creed and as far as their baneful Influence extended it was so.[26]

One bafflement that quickly divided onlookers into two camps, entrancing some and repelling others, was the dancing. The Shaker dance looked to nonbelievers like an orgiastic frenzy completely foreign to any religious exercise they had ever known. Yet for those who had shaken off the Congregationalist and Baptist decorum and been through the fire of a revival, the Shaker dance may have been a main attraction of the sect. They would have recognized the manifestations and perceived in the worship an ecstasy worth experiencing for themselves.

Valentine Rathbun described a Shaker meeting at Niskeyuna:

They begin by sitting down, and shaking their heads, in a violent manner, turning their heads half round, so that their face looks over each shoulder, their eyes being shut; while they are thus shaking, one will begin to sing some odd tune, without words or rule; after a while another will strike in; and then another; and after a while they all fall in, and make a strange charm. . . . Some singing without words, and some with an unknown tongue or mutter, and some with a mixture of English: the mother, so called minds to strike such notes as make a concord, and so form the charm. When they leave off singing, they drop off, one by one, as oddly as they come on. . . .

When they meet together for their worship, they fall a groaning and trembling, and every one acts alone for himself; one will fall prostrate on the floor, another on his knees and his head in his hands; another will be muttering over articulate sounds, which neither they nor any body else understand. Some will be singing, each one his own tune; some without words, in an Indian tune, some sing jig tunes, some tunes of their own making, in an unknown mutter, which they call new tongues; some will be dancing, drumming on the floor with their feet, as though a pair of drumsticks were beating a ruff on a drum-head; others will be agonizing, as though they were in great pain; others jumping up and down; others fluttering over somebody, and talking to them; others will be shooing and hissing evil spirits out of the house, till the different tunes, groaning, jumping, dancing, druming, laughing, talking and fluttering, shooing and hissing, makes a perfect bedlam; this they call the worship of God.[27]

As if the dancing were not upsetting enough, the Believers were portrayed as traitors to the country; these were revolutionary times, after all, and this group from the hated mother country preached pacifism. Rumors circulated that Ann Lee had come over from England with General Burgoyne's army and that she was a "camp woman," plotting against the liberation of the country.[28]

The Albany Committee of Safety grew suspicious about the continual movement of people, goods, and stock in and out of Niskeyuna. David Darrow of New Lebanon, worried that the little Shaker community had so little food and was continually giving away what it had, drove "nine fat wethers" to Niskeyuna in July 1780. He and a couple of other Shaker farmers were seized and taken before a justice of the peace.[29]

Joseph Meacham and James Hocknell arrived and declared with Darrow that they refused to do military duty. All three were committed to prison without a trial, but this was not enough. Mother Ann, William Lee, and James Whittaker were taken to Albany for questioning. After a short examination the Shakers were charged with treason and committed to prison in the old fort just above town, the usual place for Tories and prisoners of war.[30]

Others in the New Lebanon area were dragged out of meetings. Samuel Johnson, the former Presbyterian minister, was on his knees at a meeting at Dr. Isaac Harlow's house when he was seized and carried to the home of the aforementioned justice of the peace, Samuel Jones, and a leader of the opposition to the Shakers. Johnson claimed he had been very active in supporting his country's rebellion until a vision convinced him people could not follow Christ and simultaneously tolerate war and fighting. He was imprisoned in the jail of the old City Hall. Alone with three children, his wife petitioned for his freedom. Evidently Johnson's brother finally got him released on a plea of insanity.[31]

These events gave the faith a tremendous boost of publicity and sympathy. Many Americans were distressed by the government-sanctioned persecution, considering that the American Revolution was a fight for, among other things, religious freedom. Others were struck by the similarity of Mother Ann to Jesus. The jailed leaders preached their beliefs through the prison gates and converted dozens, including Joseph and David Meacham's skeptical father, Joseph, Sr.

In November 1780, the male prisoners were released. Ann Lee was finally set free in early December on one hundred pounds bail and made a joyful return to Niskeyuna.[32]

The little settlement at Niskeyuna had by now matured. The Shaker theology was well defined, and the beginnings of a communal economy were in place. The rough, boggy woods, so painstakingly cleared and drained, had become thriving gardens. Now there were many visitors to Niskeyuna and new converts almost every day. And Mother Ann had won strong supporters, including Joseph Meacham, Calvin Harlow, Elijur and Daniel Goodrich, and Samuel Fitch. Lucy Wright, who till then still lived with her husband, moved to Niskeyuna in 1781, upon Mother Ann's request, to take charge of the sisters' affairs.

But the spirit of opposition was still alive. In December 1780, just six months after his first enthusiastic account of the Shakers, Valentine Rathbun published a twenty-four-page pamphlet titled "Some Brief Hints, of a religious scheme, taught and propagated by a Number of Europeans, living in a Place called Nisqueunia, in the state of New-York," which charged the Shakers with treason and papacy and enjoyed at least seven printings in two years. At the Pittsfield town meeting in March 1781, Rathbun moved that a committee be appointed to devise "some measures to take with those people known as Shakers." A few weeks later the committee declared "they had reason to apprehend that those people called Shakers are, in many instances, irregular and disorderly in their conduct and conversation, if not guilty of some high crimes and misdemeanors" and recommended that the grand jurors "inquire into all the conduct and practices of said people which are contrary to law, and make due presentment thereof, particularly all blasphemies, adulteries, fornications, breaches of sabbath, and all other breaches of law, which they may have been guilty of." Furthermore, the committee urged "that all tithing men and other persons use their best endeavors according to law, to suppress all disorders and breaches of the peace of every kind; and also direct the town clerk to inform the commanders at Albany to help prevent correspondence and intercourse between people in Niskeyuna called Shakers and some of this town and county disposed to embrace their erroneous opinion."[33]

Nevertheless, the wave of pro-Shaker sentiment that followed her release from prison, the maturity of the community at Niskeyuna, and the steady inflow of converts from distant places persuaded Ann Lee that it was time to take her message eastward on a missionary tour. In May 1781, scarcely six months after her release from prison, a group of nine set out from Niskeyuna on horseback and in wagons to try to transform the heart of New England.

CHAPTER TWO

"The Path of Righteousness"

On a fine June morning in 1781 ten-year-old Elizabeth Wood was picking strawberries by the side of the road near the Meacham home in Enfield, Connecticut, when she heard the creak and rumble of an approaching wagon. She later said it instantly occurred to her that Mother Ann Lee was coming, even though no one was expecting her and Elizabeth herself, who thought the Shaker leader was some kind of a witch, had never met her.[1]

The little girl's intuition was correct: Mother Ann was indeed coming down the road, accompanied by a number of Shaker elders. Elizabeth pulled down the bars of the gate to let the wagon through and followed the group to the house. Ann Lee called, "Where is the old man?"—referring to "Grandfather" Joseph Meacham, Sr., who had visited the Shakers in prison and there converted. He came to the door and let the party in, and the woman took off her outer things and called for some water with which to wash.

"After dinner," Elizabeth Wood remembered later, "Mother walked into a room and sat down by herself. I went in and kneeled down before her and told her I had called her a witch and wished she was shot with a piece of silver. What made you call me so said she was it because you have heared others say so. I told her I did not know. Well it was, said she and I can forgive you and pray God to forgive you. Get up, child." Mother Ann went on to ask Elizabeth about her parents and told her a great many things about them "which I knew was revealed to her by the gift of God." Elizabeth became a Shaker and remained faithful until her death at age ninety-six in the Church Family at Enfield.

Ann Lee and the elders stayed in Enfield for a number of days. Many people visited, curious to converse with the Shakers, and a number converted; yet much hostility surfaced as well. A group of town selectmen came and advised Mother Ann and the elders to leave, and after a week they did so, continuing on their journey uneventfully.[2]

The group traveled north into Massachusetts, bound for the town of Harvard, which Ann Lee would make her center of operations for the next two years. There she founded the communities of Harvard and Shirley and took the initial steps for the founding of the four Shaker societies in New Hampshire and Maine. She returned to Enfield in late February 1782.

Hearing of Ann Lee's presence a second time, that March two hundred men gathered at the Meacham house, not to accept or even to learn about this disturbing new religion but to make sure it didn't take root in Enfield. The mob was led by one Jonathan Bush, captain of the militia, who ordered Mother Ann to leave within an hour or she would be carried off by force. This time she decided to comply. Elder James Whittaker announced to Captain Bush and his followers, "We came to this place peaceably, but since you have judged yourselves unworthy of the gospel we will go to some other place."[3]

The mob trailed after the small group of Shakers, heading west toward Lovejoy's ferry. On the way, Mother Ann and her group felt themselves to be surrounded by angels, "which so strengthened and encouraged them that they broke forth in heavenly songs . . . with great power of God while their wicked persecutors, who understood none of these things, followed on, in gloomy silence."[4]

In a village on the way to the river an abusive and threatening group gathered. Lieutenant Elijah Jones, an American officer in Colonel Sheldon's regiment of dragoons, was passing by and noticed the disturbance. Curious, he rode up and observed the unruly crowd tormenting their victims, who patiently tolerated every taunt and insult. The young officer took up a position by Mother Ann's carriage, determined to prevent harm and further abuse. As he escorted Ann Lee safely onto the ferry, he assured her she had nothing to fear. Mother Ann often mentioned this incident later, saying, "God sent that young man there for my protection."

The third and last time that Ann Lee came to Enfield, in the early fall of 1782, a mob again collected and followed her as she passed through the neighboring towns of Stafford and Somers. Entering the Meacham house, she took off her outer things and emerged again, this time with eleven-year-old Elizabeth Wood. When the crowd thronged around her, Ann Lee lifted her arms and said, "Stand back and let me come." The crowd parted, and the woman and girl walked calmly through, evidently soothing it by their serene, courageous presence. They passed around the house to the back and there ascended the porch stairs.[5]

Just as they reached the top of the stairs, the crowd seemed to awaken as if from a trance. Someone shouted, and the mob rushed for the steps.

David Meacham leaped for the stairs, blocked them, and ordered the crowd to stay back. One fellow tried to pass between his legs, but Meacham caught him tightly with his knees and spanked him soundly.

"It sounded pretty smart," recalled Elizabeth Wood, who told this story with pleasure throughout her long life in the Church Family, "as the chap had on a pair of leather britches."

> The rest of the company were more pleased than mad, they haw hawed and laughed heartily and began to disperse, but in the meantime they caught Molly Partington the one who rode with Mother and thought it was the old elect lady sure enough, and they draged her along and put her onto a horse and one man got on to the same horse behind her to hold her on. David M. left the other man and went and halled her off of the horse and they collard David and pulled his ears till the blood ran down his shirt sleeves.

The town constable, John Booth, intervened at this point and demanded that the rioters either settle their differences peaceably with David Meacham or stand trial. Although Meacham asked only that the rioters confess their actions before their own churches, the men refused, went to trial, and were found guilty.[6]

Unlike Hancock, Enfield had been an established community for generations; citizens of Salem, Massachusetts, had settled it in 1681, one hundred years prior to Ann Lee's visit. The town was then part of Springfield, not being annexed to Connecticut until 1752. The township was generally good, level land, except for the "elevated and romantic borders of the Connecticut [River]," wrote a historian in 1819, and the soil was mostly a light, sandy, fertile loam. Forests of walnut, oak, chestnut, butternut, and yellow pine provided ample building materials; yet there were also some "fine plains." The town was renowned for its substantial plow-making and carpet-weaving businesses, along with its busy grain mills, fulling mills, carding machines, a powder mill, a forge, three tanneries, and five distilleries. A vigorous trade with the southern states was in place in the early nineteenth century; in 1810, $20,000 worth of plows were sent to the southern states.[7]

Joseph Meacham, Sr., was of the third generation of Meachams in Enfield; his father, grandfather, and great-grandfather had all been weavers and fullers. Originally a Congregationalist, he may have participated in the Great Awakening, and he probably heard Jonathan Edwards give a famous sermon in 1741 in the town of Enfield: "Sinners in the Hands of an Angry God." Meacham later became the first Baptist preacher in Enfield, establishing a small church and society of Baptists in the northeastern part of town. The names of Joseph Sr. and his sons David, Joseph Jr., and Moses all appear in petitions to the General Assembly of Connecticut as Baptists in May 1757, asking for relief from the taxes required to support the Congregational church.[8]

Enfield had experienced a great religious awakening in 1777 and three years later had received word of a group of people near Albany who practiced a strange new religion. Many in the area, particularly Joseph Meacham, Sr., were initially deeply prejudiced against the Shakers. "It was said their leader was a witch," recalled one resident, "that their religion was witchcraft, and was dreadful and terrible beyond expression."[9]

Nevertheless, Meacham's second son, David, soon converted, following his older brother Joseph into the faith. David Meacham was a respected landholder in Enfield, an elder in the Baptist church, and a former constable and tax collector for the town. As a leading citizen, his conversion to Shakerism in the summer of 1780 must have deeply affected his fellow townspeople.

It certainly made an impact on his father, who now had one son professing Shakerism at home in Enfield and the other imprisoned in Albany for his beliefs. He decided to investigate; he traveled to Albany and heard the testimony through the prison gates. When he came home, he was a Believer himself and seemed "to have something in him which he did not possess before," as one who knew him recalled. Like Valentine Rathbun in Hancock, here was a respected minister confirming the truth of the Shaker gospel. He and David Meacham became the foundation stones of the Shaker faith in Enfield. The senior Meacham's remarkable spiritual journey had taken him from Congregationalism through Baptism to Shakerism, in which faith he died in 1794 at the age of eighty-two.[10]

In the early months of 1781, Joseph Meacham, Jr., visited Enfield a number of times with Samuel Fitch, laying the groundwork for Mother Ann's first visit. Converts came from all over the southern Connecticut River valley: Samuel Eaton, Samuel Parker, Eliphalet Comstock, Nathan Tiffany, Justus Markham, Jehiel Markham, Asa Allen, Ezekiel Slate, Daniel Wood, James Pease, Lot Pease, Timothy Pease, Elijah Billings, Joseph Fairbanks, and their families.

The persecution, however, now took a new form. In June 1782 the selectmen of the towns of Enfield and Somers appointed overseers to take charge of all of the business of the above-mentioned men, claiming that they were not responsible to manage their property. The order read:

... the subscribers select of the town of Somers Being Informed that Nathan Tiffany and Daniel Wood Jr. of Somers hath for some time past spent their time to no good porpose so that it is sopost that they are wasting their Estates ... whereupon it is considered and orderd by us the subscribers that Mr. Ebenezer Spencer Jun. of Somers shall be an Overseer to Nathan Tiffany and Daniel Wood Jr., to advise and order [them] in the management of their Business from time to time During the pleasher of the Slectmen . . . [and they are] herby ordered and directed to Render an Account once in Every four weeks to his Overseer how he spends his time etc. and wee do now order that no Person whatsoever Shall make any Bargain or Contract with [them] without the Consent of his Overseer.[11]

In August, however, the Shakers petitioned the Superior Court at Hartford and won release from such overseers by showing they were well able to take care of themselves.

Ann Lee never visited Tyringham, Massachusetts, which occupies a lovely valley just south of Lee and was the scene of some of the harshest persecution of the Shakers. William Lee and James Whittaker went to the village in 1782 to encourage the fledgling group of Believers; that same year the town appointed a committee to "keep out of town all persons called Shaking Quakers."

The valley had been opened to settlement in 1735, purchased from the Stockbridge Indians by Colonels Ephraim Williams and Nahum Wood to build a road between Boston and Albany. Settlers soon arrived and erected mills along the little streams that poured down the mountain walls to join the Hop Brook, and more came after the fall of Quebec and the end of the French and Indian Wars in 1759.

The town of Tyringham was incorporated in 1762. The Hop Brook was then still a swamp that flooded from hillside to hillside in spring. Wild hop vines twisted around trees in the valley, and the hillsides were covered with virgin forests of maple, oak, and pine.

At the end of the revolutionary war many families moved into Tyringham, and settlers began to drain the valley bottomland. Yet there was already a steady movement westward from Tyringham, like that from so many other small New England villages, as young people departed to seek their fortunes elsewhere.[12]

"A remarkable place was chosen for this village," wrote Eldresses Anna White and Leila Taylor in 1904 of the Tyringham Shakers' site. "The country is mountainous and the mountain rises several hundred feet above the buildings, while the valley in which was found their best tillage is many hundred feet below. Some of the houses, entered from the roadway were two stories in front and four stories in the rear, being built against the side of the mountain." Indeed, the particular challenges of this Shaker community's location—its steepness and its proximity to world's people—would significantly affect its history.

The three Allen brothers were the first Believers. Joshua, Abel, and William Allen had come from Coventry, Connecticut between 1774 and 1779 (judging from where and when their children were born). They may have had relatives in Tyringham; an Asa and a Joseph Allen are both mentioned in early town records. Local farmers William Clark, Elijah Fay, and Dr. Henry Herrick, all men in their thirties and forties from prominent families, soon decided to join the three brothers, and the group began to worship together at each other's houses. William Clark's one-and-a-half-story, twin-chimneyed cottage, perched on the mountainside looking eastward across the sweep of the Hop Valley, became the center of activity and the nucleus of the Shaker community.[13]

It also became the focus of brutal persecution. Once, when the group had assembled to worship, a boisterous mob gathered and began taunting them. William Clark was grabbed by the hair when he was on his knees, dragged outside, and there whipped with a cat-o'-nine-tails. Others tried to protect him and also were beaten.[14]

Thanks to a neighbor, the worshipers had some warning the next time a riotous mob—"several Enemies from the other side of the hollow"—was on its way, and they barred the door with a large fire shovel as a brace. The mob managed to batter down the door and hurled the shovel directly into the assembly, breaking the thumb of one of the sisters. The meeting was ended, "which was often the case." According to one version, however, Brother Thomas Patten "was taken with the Power of God, and went out among them and with a female voice began to sing verry pritty to them putting his face up to one and then to another of the enemy which so softened their feelings they soon left. . . . Brother Thomas was no natural singer."[15]

The hostility, however, only intensified. One time a mob came and, finding the door barred, went into the woods and cut "an Indian ladder being a pole with the limbs cut off at some length from the body." They clambered up on the roof carrying a large door, which they placed atop the chimney, evidently intending either to smoke the Shakers out of the house or to make them suffocate. When the brothers and sisters inside opened the windows for relief the mob threw rocks and wood chips at them. "But very *meraculus*," one early Shaker historian wrote, "as it was a very still and calm evening the Dore was taken from the Chimney and saled with rapitidy in to the thickest part of the Mob, which frightened them so much that they went off again."[16]

Even visitors were not safe. Samuel Fitch of Richmond, who was by now a member of the Shaker leadership, came to preach to the Believers. When word spread that he was at Clark's house, a group of hostile neighbors came and seized him, dragging him about a mile and a half away. There the group "had a commity appointed to inflict such Punishment as they should think Propper." That punishment consisted of whipping Fitch out of town. "He went home in such a bloody and bruised situation that even his own folks did not know him."[17]

The committee appointed by the town proudly reported in 1783 that it had "proceeded so far as to whip one strolling Shaker who refused to leave the town." However, Shaker stories tended to be shaped over generations into parables, and this one was no exception. The wielder of the whip was said to have developed three cancers on his right arm and died in great agony.[18]

James Whittaker later wrote his parents in England from "Parts, near Albany," about such punishment: "[For preaching the Shaker gospel] I have been imprisoned, beaten, mocked, calumniated &C, and have been pursued by cruel and desperate mobs night and day. And once last summer I was whipped in the most cruel manner, being stripped naked, and my hands tied up, being streched up above my head. However, God hath preserved me, in a wonderful manner."[19]

As elsewhere, much of the fierce hostility in Tyringham revolved around the Shaker dance. Ignoring the Believers' fervent commitment to celibacy, local people speculated that at the height of religious frenzy the Shakers danced naked or engaged in other licentious behavior. Certainly, there is no reliable record of such occurrences; if they did happen as experiments in the early days, they were very uncommon and uncharacteristic of the Shakers.[20]

The town was also concerned about the Believers' great stock of provisions, that visitors coming from out of town would eat everything up without the town committee's knowledge. A committeeman went to check on the Shakers' supplies; a favorite Shaker story maintains that in less than two years he returned as a pauper to William Clark's house with a bag under his arm to beg a few potatoes for his starving family. All of the members of the hostile town committee endured similar impoverishment, according to Shaker legend, some selling their farms and going west, a few staying and eventually coming to the Shakers and apologizing for their wicked behavior.

In the meantime, however, the town passed several laws: one prohibiting the local miller from grinding any grain for the Shakers, another forbidding the blacksmith to do any work for them, undoubtedly speeding the community's isolation and self-reliance.[21]

Despite such torment, the little sect continued to grow. The Shakers were soon joined by Abisha Stanley and James Pratt, friends of Thomas Patten from Belchertown, Massachusetts, which Mother Ann had visited on her missionary tour in spring 1783.

Mother Ann's tour of New England lasted more than two years. In August 1783 she arrived in Hancock, where an enthusiastic and devoted Shaker community awaited her—along with a vehement and well-organized opposition.

Mother Ann's sojourn at Daniel Goodrich's house seemed to Hannah Fuller Goodrich, she later recalled, like one long, joyous revival meeting, with visitors coming from far away and meetings going on all day and all night. On August 3, the Sabbath, many nonbelievers attended the meeting—some interested, some merely curious, and some openly hostile to the Shakers. The meeting began in silence, as usual, with the Believers grouped around Ann Lee. Mother Ann might have sung in her clear, sweet voice, or one of the little group of English Believers that accompanied her might have described how the Kingdom of Heaven could exist inside each person. A current of joy might have passed through the group. Then participants would have begun to respond to the powerful workings of God upon them—dancing, singing, trembling, shouting, leaping, speaking in strange languages, prophesying. If she looked around, Hannah might have seen many friends and neighbors: her family by marriage, the Goodriches; the Talcotts from up the road; friends of her own age such as Valentine Rathbun, Jr., John and Sarah Deming, and Rebecca and Mary Clark. Before long, however, the restless crowd of onlookers grew unruly and aggressive, sneering at the worshipers, then threatening and even physically harassing some of them till the meeting was abandoned.[22]

Again the following day a great crowd of spectators gathered in the yard, many plaguing and pestering the Believers. The leader of the hostile crowd was none other than Valentine Rathbun, Sr. He and his followers entered the house and began to taunt Mother Ann and the elders, shouting that they were deceivers and false prophets.

Valentine Jr., arriving at this moment, was shocked at his father's behavior and language. He drove the old man from the house, angrily scolding him: "I think it is a shame for a man of God, and a minister of the gospel, as you profess to be, to come here at the head of a mob, to abuse the innocent people of God."

Inflamed by this rebuke from his own son, Valentine Sr. clambered up on a mounting block in the yard and began to rain blows upon the young man's head with his stout hickory staff. With blood streaming down his face, Valentine Jr. wrestled the staff away from his father and flung it away.

The rest of the mob continued to jeer and shout. Mother Ann's face, so dear to her followers, was tired and strained, Hannah noticed, and she realized that the past two years of travel, fraught with similar scenes of violence, had worn her out. Hannah and another sister went out and attempted to soothe the uproarious crowd so that Mother Ann could slip unnoticed out a back door and into a waiting carriage. She drove to the home of

Samuel Fitch in nearby Richmond. Once she was safely gone, the elders joined the sisters talking to the crowd, and then they all followed their leader to Richmond.

There, after another unruly scene, Ann Lee and several of the Shaker elders were arrested on charges of blasphemy and disorderly conduct. They appeared before the Board of Justices of the Peace in the Richmond meetinghouse the next day, and their commitment to their faith impressed the judges.

Samuel Fitch, however, apparently could not leave well enough alone. He stood up and began to sermonize, warning the judges: "Take head what you do to these people [the Believers]; for they are God's anointed ones, whom he hath sent to America."

The speech evidently irritated the judges, and they withdrew to discuss what they should do with the Shakers: "for although they appeared to be conscientious, and acted upon religious principles; yet they deluded the people, and disturbed the inhabitants, and they must be taken care of, or they would turn the world upside down."

The judges finally decided to fine Mother Ann and the elders $20 for disturbing the peace and ordered them to leave the state. The Believers immediately put forth the money, but they decided among themselves "to obey God rather than man." Mother Ann and the elders returned to Hancock to stay with Nathan and Hannah Goodrich and to continue preaching to large, enthusiastic crowds there.

Meanwhile, Samuel and Dyer Fitch and Elijur Goodrich, listed as living in Richmond, were ordered to give bonds for their good behavior. They refused, however, insisting that if they did so they might forfeit their right to worship God in their own way. They were then committed to the Barrington jail to be tried by the county court.

Ann Lee traveled to Barrington with a sizable party to visit the brethren in jail there—after all, Elijur Goodrich and Samuel Fitch had visited her in jail three years earlier. Among her traveling companions was Jonathan Slosson of West Stockbridge, who begged her to visit his parents, staunch Believers, on the way back to Hancock. She did so, staying from Saturday through Monday.

A favorite Shaker legend arose in regard to Mother Ann's sojourn with the Slosson family. So many Believers and curious spectators gathered at the little house that weekend, coming from New Lebanon, Hancock, and elsewhere, that the meeting had to be held in the yard. Shaker tradition holds that Slosson and his family fed more than two hundred people during the weekend, and the one hundred horses he turned into his six-acre cow pasture grazed it bare. After his company had left, his neighbors taunted him, asking how he would graze his four cows on his depleted pasture. "Trust in God," Slosson replied calmly.[23]

The following Saturday his pasture was said to be ankle-deep in blossoming white clover, so abundant that he let his neighbors graze their horses and cows there. His own cows were said to have furnished a prodigious quantity of butter and cheese that week.

The tavernkeeper next door said to Slosson, "How is it? I keep tavern, and have pay for all I dispose of; and yet I can but just get along: You have much more company than I do, and entertain them upon free cost, and yet you always have a fulness." The man didn't understand, but he did become very friendly to the Shakers for the rest of his life.

The period in Hancock and Richmond was a joyous time for the local Shakers. Believers thronged there from other places, receiving spiritual sustenance from the elders and from one another. The meetings continued nonstop, round the clock, until one Believer said, "We could hardly distinguish the days of the week; for every day felt like sabbath."[24]

But their persecutors had not forgotten them. During one large worship service at Hannah and Nathan Goodrich's house a crowd of unruly men rode up to the door. Mother Ann went out and spoke to them, bidding them to depart. When the men defied her, she raised her hand and commanded, with great authority, "Draw back, I say, or I'll smite the horse and his rider!"

Shaker legend holds that the horses responded instantly. They ran backward the ten rods' distance from the house to the road, their riders unable to control them. Once on the road, they turned and started docilely for home.[25]

After Mother Ann had spent a week at Nathan and Hannah's, a large mob gathered, headed by Valentine Rathbun and a neighbor named Aaron Baker. Like drunken madmen, the mob shouted and threatened, ordering the Shaker elders to leave. Ann Lee and William Lee, deciding that it was finally time to move on, assured the crowd that they would leave the next morning before ten o'clock. When its request was so easily met, the mob was divided, milling around aimlessly; some wanted to use violence anyway, others not. One man even grabbed and held Elder James Whittaker until others insisted he release him.[26]

True to their word, the next day, Saturday, August 23, 1783, Ann Lee and the elders and a large company of Believers set off from Nathan and Hannah Goodrich's to visit New Lebanon. They stopped for their midday meal at Israel Talcott's house, on the mountain west of Hancock, where Abigail Talcott was cooking a small pot of meat and vegetables over the fire for her little family. When Ann Lee informed her that she must provide dinner for

the group, Abigail replied, "Then I must boil more meat and sauce."
Mother Ann responded, "Nay, there is plenty." To Abigail's astonishment,
the little pot was said to have held enough for the company of almost forty
people.[27]

After Ann Lee's return to Niskeyuna in the early fall of 1783, she was
worn out, exhausted, drained from years of travel, struggle, laborings. To
her followers she seemed to have grown weaker, possibly because of the
physical sufferings and persecution she had endured.

Her brother William died the following summer (on July 21, 1784), and
after this she visibly declined, knowing she was going. "Brother William is
gone, and it will soon be said of me that I am gone, too." She'd often
murmur, "Well, I am coming soon." Her ten years in America had been
extraordinarily fruitful: she had attracted hundreds of converts and established Shaker communities throughout the Northeast.

As she lost strength, she shared a vision of the future of the United Society of Believers. "The time will come when the Church will be gathered
into order," she said, "and then it will be known who are good believers.
But that is not my work; it is Joseph Meacham's work: my work is nearly
done."[28]

In the seven weeks after her brother's death, Ann Lee grew weaker and
weaker. She asked Lucy Wright to sit by her and take care of her. Finally,
on September 8, between midnight and 1 o'clock A.M., she died. Her last
words were "I see Brother William coming, in a golden chariot, to take me
home."

CHAPTER THREE

Creating a Community Apart

A shock rippled through the larger Shaker community upon Mother Ann's passing. Some Believers, despite everything she said, expected her to live forever and were greatly disillusioned by her death. Others fell away when James Whittaker succeeded to the leadership, instead of Joseph Meacham or John Partington. "This to be sure was a very trying time to believers; it being so contrary from what was first expected," wrote Reuben Rathbun.[1]

Whittaker had turned from an earnest boy into a passionate, forceful exhorter and a visionary in his own right. According to Rathbun, who took several journeys with him, Father James was harsh toward the enemies of the Shakers yet very tender toward children and those he loved.

Whittaker is credited[2] with being the first Shaker leader to envision a communal life for the Believers, in a letter from Enfield dated February 25, 1782, to Josiah Talcott, Sr., of Hancock. In rather abrasive terms this letter urges Talcott, a carpenter by trade, to use his large piece of land, to farm it and not leave it idle.

Thou art idle and slothful [he wrote], whereby thy land layes unimproved and pretty much waste; from whence arises want, and is a great burden to the poor man that dwells in the house not far from thee. This is abominable in the Sight of God, and will surely bring upon thee want and poverty, as well as the wrath of God in hell. . . . Thy women with thee are also idle, hatchers of cockatrice eggs and breeders of lust and abominable filthiness, as well as covenant breakers. . . . I charge thee before God to mend thy ways. First rouse up thy senses, shake off thy sloth and idleness. And as the time of plowing and seeding is approaching, get thy farm in readiness. Neglect no means; see that thou are not wanting in anything: get thee out upon thy land and view what is wanting and what must be done first, what next, and so on in order. . . . Make your women turn out and mortify their lusts, and they will find health as well to their bodies as to their souls.

And when you have done all you can towards seeding your land for the present season, set yourselves faithfully to put your whole place in order. For you have land enough to maintain three families or more, well improved.

Whittaker went on to warn Talcott that God might take his land from him if he did not obey. Talcott did begin to farm, greatly prospered, and died a faithful Believer at the age of eighty-one.[3] Whittaker's unswerving conviction (some said fanaticism) may have been the crucial element that saw the Shakers through the uncertain period following Ann Lee's death. The faith was certainly vigorous a year later when, on October 15, 1785, the first meetinghouse was raised at New Lebanon, ordered by Whittaker.

During the mid-1780s the Shakers at Hancock continued to hold their own meetings, and the band grew larger. On August 30, 1786, they laid the foundations for a Hancock meetinghouse, where the local farmers could gather and worship. With its gambrel roof, dormer windows, and separate entrances for brethren and sisters, the building was similar to the meetinghouse at New Lebanon and a fine example of the future pattern of Shaker meetinghouses. It was framed by Moses Johnson, a New Hampshire builder who joined the Shakers and left a striking legacy in the nine meetinghouses he constructed. A Quaker visitor later described the building: "Their meeting-house for religious worship at Hancock, is of beautiful workmanship, painted inside a glossy Prussian blue, the steps at the door are hewn out of a solid block of white marble, and from the neatness of every thing one would suppose the whole house was washed between every meeting day."[4]

The meetinghouse was forty-four feet by thirty-two feet and painted white, the color reserved for the church in a Shaker community. Downstairs was the large meeting room with movable (not built-in, according to Warder) benches, wooden pegs marching around the walls, green-blue woodwork, and plenty of space for uninhibited worship. The second floor contained the rooms of the ministry: two elders and two eldresses.

The Enfield Shakers constructed their first meetinghouse that same year, and its builder, judging by certain structural similarities, also may have been Moses Johnson. The following July it held the funeral services for Father James Whittaker, who died at David Meacham's home in Enfield at the age of thirty-seven while on a tour of Connecticut with Reuben Rathbun and was buried in the Shaker cemetery just up the road from the church. Whittaker had always been held in special esteem at Enfield; Church Family members proudly claimed that he hand-dug the first well at that location. Many non-Shakers attended his funeral.

After James Whittaker's death, Joseph Meacham became leader; and as Mother Ann had predicted, it was he and the other American leaders who formally gathered and structured the society of Believers. Despite or per-haps because of the great enthusiasm for Shakerism at this point, chaos governed several of the communities, with power plays, rivalry, and sharp disagreement simmering between leaders.

In a remarkable move, Meacham elevated Lucy Wright from her position in charge of the sisters' affairs to share the eldership with him, becoming "Mother." Since Mother Ann's death, all power had been held by men, as in the world. Other leaders, notably Calvin Harlow, supported Meacham's action. A celibate and sexually segregated world like this one would, after all, require a female hierarchy to parallel the male one.[5]

Yet recalling the early reluctance to accept Mother Ann, some Shakers did not find it easy to accept Lucy Wright's leadership, burdened as they were with the worldly—and biblical—notion that women should remain servile to men. Reuben Rathbun, though he hailed Meacham as "a man greatly beloved and respected by all the people," was not happy with the appointment of Lucy Wright. "[A]s to their parents," he wrote later, "it was doubtless without any difficulty they acknowledged Elder Joseph to be their father in the Gospel; but as to a mother, it was such a new thing and so unexpected that there was something of a labor before the matter was finished." Rathbun refused to call Lucy Wright by name, instead consis-tently referring to her (and to Eldress Sarah Harrison) as "she that was called our mother."[6]

In her defense, Wright's supporters pointed out that although wives had little status in the Bible, virgins were highly esteemed and played a leading role in the primitive church. Perhaps Lucy Wright's "stainless" life with Elijur Goodrich, in addition to her obvious intelligence and organizational skill, eventually won her the confidence of the membership. She would go on to become one of the most important leaders in Shaker history.[7]

Meacham and Wright realized that to live the ideal of the primitive Chris-tian church, to follow the path of greater light, required that they separate themselves from the world and live communally. Their ideal society would be both church and community. This was possible, however, only through the abolition of carnal relations between the sexes, which not only distracted Believers from their main focus on God but also led to pride, jealousy, lust, and many other ills. "Bearing the cross"—the experience of self-denial in general and celibacy in particular—was in itself an important spiritual exercise.

In September 1787, the two leaders invited all who had embraced the faith and wished to live "as angels on earth" to gather together at New Lebanon, where the meetinghouse awaited them and land had been do-nated. That fall dozens of Believers came, camping out in barns and huts. On Christmas Day they sat down together for their first communal meal.

Among them was David Meacham, who had left Enfield that year after his wife and sixteen-year-old son both died of consumption and were buried in the Shaker cemetery.

Jonathan Clark left a record of what life was like in the first Shaker communities. Despite the joy of living together in a community consecrated to their faith, the members endured extreme tribulations, partly because of a famine in the area. Their waking hours in summertime were still spent draining swamps, planting, sowing grain, making hay, and harvesting. They slept on the floor, fifteen to a room, some without even a blanket. On the Sabbath they generally fasted because they weren't working. They looked like skeletons, Clark wrote; they could work, but they could not run.

At last the crop began to ripen. "We began to live better," wrote Clark. Slowly, they prospered, and their strength increased. Father Joseph urged them to have faith, saying the time would come when their children would have plenty to give away. Indeed, in ten years that prediction came true.[8]

In 1788, Meacham began to structure the New Lebanon community in a manner that would serve as a model for all of the other Shaker societies. This was the first example of the superb organization that would keep the Shakers united even when the revivalistic fervor ebbed. He established two primary principles: first, that "all true Church order and Law . . . is given by revelation" and second, that "order and union are necessary for the health and prosperity of the Church." In effect, this meant that all rules laid down by the elders were to be considered to have come directly from God, and were thus incontestable. It was probably at this point that obedience became foremost among the Shaker virtues.[9]

The overall governance of the United Society of Shakers was based on the model of the family set up by Ann Lee in her original justification of her leadership to Calvin Harlow. Meacham clustered the communities into bishoprics of two or three, to be governed by a Father and a Mother, assisted by an elder and an eldress. Elders and eldresses under them led individual families. In recognition of the different skills required for different offices, elders were appointed to take charge of spiritual matters and the community's internal problems; deacons or trustees were given control over work, finances, and dealings with the world; and caretakers had responsibility for the Children's Order.

Each community was to consist of several of these distinct families, which were self-supporting and self-organized and located from a half-mile to several miles apart. The Church Family, the geographic hub and spiritual nucleus of each community, was presided over by an Elder Brother, an Elder Sister, and an assisting elder and eldress. The other families were arranged around the Church Family, sometimes in a rough cross, often making up North, South, East, West, and Second or Middle families. Later leaders would set up novitiate or "gathering" orders to accommodate new members.

In 1790, Joseph Meacham gathered the Hancock, Tyringham, and Enfield societies into the Second Bishopric (the First, or Mother's, Bishopric consisting of Watervliet and New Lebanon) and began to organize the Hancock Shakers after the New Lebanon model. The Hancock and Tyringham societies were geographically close, and it was natural to link them together. Enfield was farther away—two full days' travel in 1790—and could almost as easily have been gathered with the communities in Harvard and Shirley, Massachusetts. We can speculate that it became part of the Hancock Bishopric because of Enfield's many historic and familial ties to Hancock, New Lebanon, and Watervliet. Not only the Meachams but also the Goodriches, the Demings, and many others had connections to the Hartford area. Settlers from all over Connecticut, in fact, had moved up the winding Housatonic Valley to Berkshire County, and there was much interaction.

In 1790 the Hancock society was already a devout and industrious little community. That year it erected the earliest section of the machine shop, one of the first large communal buildings, across the road from the meetinghouse on what had been Daniel and Anna Goodrich's farm. Hancock land had been deeded over to the Shakers from, for example, Hezekiah Hammond and Calvin Harlow of New Lebanon and Daniel Goodrich's uncle, nonmember Charles Goodrich, between January 1787 and 1789.[10]

Now the members were anxious to take the next step, to live together in a community, for they understood that they would make much greater spiritual progress once they were in "full Church relation." Meacham sent three elders from New Lebanon to examine the group of Hancock Believers and ascertain whether they were ready to embark upon their stern path. Elder Henry Clough, Meacham's talented assistant in the Ministry and a former New Light preacher from New Hampshire, was the youngest of the three at age thirty-six. According to his biographer, during the first two meetings held with the Hancock Believers he said not a word. At these initial meetings many participants perceived that something seemed wrong: people spoke, but a curious reserve possessed the group, a mysterious tension holding everyone back.

When finally requested to speak at a third meeting, Clough declared that someone in the assembly was hiding a secret sin, making the Hancock Believers unready and ineligible for admission. The other elders and the congregation were stunned, and when the ministers retired to their room in the meetinghouse, they admonished Clough for discouraging the people.

A knock on the door interrupted them, and one of the brethren entered and painfully confessed a hidden sin. Then, one by one, many more Believers came in and revealed hitherto undisclosed transgressions.

After that cathartic afternoon the Hancock community was considered ready to become part of the larger Society. Clough's evident rapport with the Believers made him feel obligated to become elder at Hancock, a position he was reluctant to take on in exchange for his post as second in the overall Ministry. Father Joseph advised him to seek someone else able to take the eldership, and if he could not, to accept it himself. Clough interviewed several of the brethren. At last, when he spoke with Calvin Harlow (called "only a common but much esteemed member of the Church"), he felt a great sense of relief; he knew he had found the right person for the job.[11]

Mother Ann had once predicted that Harlow, one of the first Americans to come and meet her in Niskeyuna, would become important. She had said to James Whittaker, "O the bright glories I see for Calvin! I see him stand with his people like a Bishop, ministering the gifts of God." She added, however, in a typical example of her reverence for manual labor, that "the scriptures say a man shall eat his bread by the sweat of his brow. Go then and tell Calvin that he must gain a gift in hand labor, before he can find his lot, and order of his people." Calvin had done so, learning to work as a farmer. He was distinguished throughout his career as elder for his modesty and diligence.[12]

On December 17, 1790, Father Calvin Harlow arrived at Hancock to take charge of the Believers, with two Hancock brethren he had selected to be his helpers, Jeremiah Goodrich, tenth son of Benjamin Goodrich, and Reuben Harrison, originally from Richmond. The Hancock Shakers were immensely satisfied with the choice of Harlow and with the now-formalized family union: "I can truly say I have felt my soul joined to them," wrote Daniel Goodrich, Sr., "as sensibly as I ever felt heat or cold. Yea, I feel joined to them in the bonds of everlasting love and union."[13]

Christmas had been the date of the first communal meal at New Lebanon in 1787; now, in 1790, it marked the formal beginning of the Hancock community. Father Calvin explained the meaning of the celebration: it should be observed as a holy day on which no manual labor should be done, a day devoted to God. For decades it would remain a day of fasting, expiation of sins, and reconciliation, second only in the Shaker calendar to the birthday of Mother Ann on February 29.[14]

In daily talks or "ministrations," Father Calvin issued a number of orders regarding temporal things—"to labour against a light sense and spirit, to be faithful in buiseness and not be slow in our movements, like people worn out with the flesh." He also urged the members to keep their relation to work and to the people of God at New Lebanon, to be faithful with their hands and do their work as though they were doing it for God; and not to hurt each other's feelings but to work to fortify one another.

He preached on a variety of subjects, tailoring his words to the needs of the youthful community. At some meetings he taught prudence and care for health; at others he warned against "a light carnal empty sense," saying it was as dangerous as a serpent's sting and as poisonous as the asp. Occasionally, he goaded his congregation into competition with the Believers at New Lebanon, who "loved and esteemed each other better than themselves, and strove to make everyone happy, and fleshly affections had no place there; and . . . it ought to be so here."[15]

Joseph Meacham presided over the formal gathering of the Hancock Church Family on January 14, 1791. Sarah Harrison, originally from Richmond, came from New Lebanon to serve as Mother, with Hannah Goodrich as her helper. That month, twenty brethren and twenty sisters gathered; over the next year the number would increase to more than ninety.

In 1790 or 1791 the first dwelling house, southwest of the machine shop, was erected. Harlow and Harrison organized the living and working quarters so that the sexes were separated—brethren and sisters lived in different areas of the dwelling house, worked and ate separately, and worshiped in separate parts of the meetinghouse. The communal life augured well for the economic and physical survival of Shakers and their principles. Until then some married couples, such as Elijur Goodrich and Lucy Wright, had continued to live alone together, attempting to follow Shaker principles. It was certainly easier for a man and woman to "bear the cross" if they lived in a large communal household, where women lived on one side of the building and men on the other.[16]

Rebecca Clark, daughter of William Clark of Tyringham, left a vivid description of daily life in the Hancock community as the Believers embarked on their grand experiment:

In the year 1791, at the age of 21, I was gathered into the Church at Hancock, Mass. The purpose of our coming together, was for a greater privilege in the gospel, than we could enjoy in small families. There were nearly a hundred in the family where I lived. When the shell was sounded (a token to rise in the morning) we all quickly rose; and we had but fifteen minutes to dress and get ready for meeting. Fourteen of us slept in one room. When we arose, some packed the beds one on another; some swept the room; others got water to wash in. After our morning meeting, we went to our several employments. Some to getting breakfast for the brethren, as they ate first. Our buildings were small; and we had to eat and live accordingly. We worked diligently, early and late, and lived sparingly. Our beds, bedding, and clothing that we brought with us, we all divided among the members of the family, as equally as could be. We had but few feather beds, our beds were mostly straw; and we made them on the floor. Many of us slept three on one bed; and when we washed our bedding, we had to dry it the same day, and put it on at night. We were all much engaged to build buildings, and to raise provisions, and gather a substance to live on. While the brethren were building, the Sisters worked much out of doors to help the brethren. The remainder of the time were diligent in spinning, weaving, etc. etc. We manufactured our own clothing for many years; even our caps and handkerchiefs we spun and wove for a number of years.

Our food was very scanty, but what we had we ate with thankful hearts. For breakfast and supper, we lived mostly upon bean porridge and water porridge. Monday morning we had a little weak tea, and once a week a small piece of cheese. Wheat bread was very scarce; and when we had butter it was spread on our bread before we came to the table. Our bread was made chiefly of rye and Indian meal mixed together. Our dinners were generally boiled. Once in a while we had a little milk, but this was a great rarity. When I look back to those days, and then to the fulness with which we are blessed, it fills me with thankfulness.[17]

That March, Daniel Goodrich, Sr., wrote a letter to Father Joseph, stating his satisfaction with the Hancock community: "I believe, of all men, I have the greatest reason to be thankful to God and the Church, for the unmerited charity I daily receive. I can truly say I feel thankful, and fully satisfied in every sense, in relation to our present ministration, and beg their charity, while I learn to do well."[18]

The Hancock Church Family, now with meetinghouse, dwelling house, machine shop, and probably other work buildings, was established on the Goodrich farm. The Second Family was also gathered in January 1791, on the property of John Deming in West Pittsfield. Within two years two more families would be gathered into the Hancock society: the West Family on the Talcott farm in 1792 and the East Family (which eventually became the novitiate order) on the Bryington land in West Pittsfield in October 1793. Later branch families were the North and South families.[19]

Many Hancock and Pittsfield residents were calling themselves dissenters by 1789 and refusing to pay taxes to support the Congregational church. They included John Deming, Daniel Goodrich, Hezekiah Osborne, Josiah Talcott, Joshua Birch, Rufus Cogswell, Dr. Shadrach Hurlbert, Samuel Phelps, and Ephraim Welch. To their number should be added Israel Miner, who in 1790 claimed he "never heard Mr. Allen [the Congregational minister], and can teach Mr. Allen, and thinks he ought not to pay his rates to him, and is a Shaker as much as anything."[20]

For the most part these early Shakers were upstanding citizens, the original families of Pittsfield being well represented in the Demings and Goodriches. Another was William Pepperill Williams, son of an early Pittsfield settler and judge, distant cousin of a signer of the Declaration of Independence. Williams joined with his wife and children and became an elder.

In 1791 the Hancock Believers verbally agreed to consecrate their property and services in a "united inheritance." They would commit this agreement or covenant to writing in 1796, basing it on a similar document executed in New Lebanon the previous year. The lots, or positions, of the Hancock eldership were not assigned until 1792, although the temporal order (deacons and trustees) was established during this first winter, indicating that financial organization was deemed a more critical need as the community gathered. Daniel Goodrich, Sr., became Deacon of the Church Family, soon joined by his son, Daniel Jr., and Calvin Cogswell.

As early as April 1789, many converts had dedicated their possessions to the cause, emulating the community at New Lebanon, where a communal economy was already in effect. Meacham felt that such a system was essential for Shakers, that money and individual possessions—and the greed and envy they could generate—might be even more dangerous to the Society than cohabitation of the sexes.

There was great variation, after all, in the value of the possessions brought into the community. Some of the new members at Hancock were far wealthier than others; many were virtually destitute. The net of extended families throughout the community guarded both the equity and the cohesion of the group. The Talcotts, for example, were well off and noted for bringing in the community's first silver spoons. James Talcott contributed a horse, a year-old steer, three sheep, two lambs, a feather bed, two barrels of cider, bushels of oats, wheat, and rye, two large pewter platters, three spoons, and quantities of cheese and butter, "the whole of the above account computed at 38/7/6." Stephen Slosson, on the other hand, brought just his joiner's tools, and his brother Eliphalet contributed a small iron pot. John Deming donated a quantity of leather: "4 sides soalleather 5 sleigh whips 1 side upper leather 1 calfskin 2 sides upper leather etc." Reuben Rathbun contributed a span of horses and a wagon. Joshua and Louise Burch Torye brought in a feather bed, two chairs, a platter, five plates, two new pails, a cheese, a bacon, and a pair of irons—probably all they could fit in their wagon when they came from Stonington, Connecticut. From Nathan Goodrich came fifteen sheep and three yearling calves "for the support of his children."[21]

In early March 1791, after teaching his congregation "a medium between a light sensation and falling too low, which he called the straight and narrow way," Calvin Harlow left with Daniel Goodrich, Jr., and Reuben Harrison to visit the societies in Enfield and Tyringham.

That year Moses Johnson built the Enfield community's second meetinghouse on land given for the purpose by David Meacham, and the first was moved a short distance and occupied as a shop. The first dwelling house of the Church Family was built about two to three rods southwest of the old Meacham house. Originally constructed with a gambrel roof, it was later enlarged and made upright.[22]

The Church Family at Enfield was formally gathered in 1792, with Eliphalet Comstock, Daniel Goodrich, Jr., Mary Wood, and Ruth Pease as elders. Father Calvin examined the young people and selected nine of them, including eighteen-year-old Elizabeth Wood, to go into the Church Family. Three times, Sister Elizabeth later remembered, he asked her, "Will you be subject to every gift that is or may be felt for you?" and three times she answered, "Yea, Father, I will."[23]

The community grew rapidly, and families spread out from the center. The Believers at Enfield and Somers commissioned Amaziah Clark and Daniel Wood to collect a second family into the order, and in 1794 the Second, or North, Family began to be gathered under elders Amaziah Clark and Elisha Allen, eldresses Lucy Markham and Ruth Farrington, and trustee Daniel Wood. The South Family was established in 1795 under Elder Elias Pease to embrace the Young Believers of the Church Family; the East Family began the following year and consisted of the Young Believers of the North Family. In 1796 fifty-one men and women signed the first Church Covenant in Enfield.

In 1792 the Tyringham Shakers united their farms and properties to become a Shaker society. In 1797 they signed their own covenant, which was revised in 1800. The list of signers includes the original families: the William Clark family, the three Allen brothers and their families, Dr. Henry Herrick and his three children, Elijah Fay and his family, the large family of Abisha Stanley, brothers Thomas and Asa Patten and their wives, James Pratt and his daughter Zeruah. Other families—the Culvers, the Bigelows, and others—augmented the ranks.[24]

William Clark's mountainside farm became the heart of the Church Family, and the William Allen farm became the Shaker North Family, perhaps incorporating some of the Henry Herrick farm as well. Evidently, Tyringham's intense hostility toward the Shakers had run its course: the town records of 1796 show the sum of $18.94 appropriated as a salary for William Clark, as "the Shaker minister."[25]

A new generation, whose members had accepted the faith as children, came into its own during the 1790s as the first group of American leaders aged. Father Calvin's health was declining by 1792, and he informed the Believers that he would no longer be able to give a daily ministration, that instead they must gather to the elders appointed in different orders and families. "This was a trying time and a grievous word to many," wrote Daniel Goodrich; nevertheless, it strengthened the lower echelons of leadership.[26]

In 1792 the elders were chosen at Hancock: Reuben Rathbun and Jonathan Southwick at the Church Family, and John Deming and John Talcott, respectively, at the Second and West families. According to Rathbun, the elders' function was "to stand between their parents and the rest of the family with whom they lived—they were to receive the word and counsel from their parents, and communicate the same to the rest of the family— the family were to look to the Elders, and to them only, for every gift of God they received; and likewise the Elders to the parents."[27]

Hannah Goodrich was called from her native Hancock in 1793, leaving her position as Sarah Harrison's helper to become first eldress in the New Hampshire ministry at Canterbury. Her place as second in the female line in the Hancock ministry was filled by Rebecca Slosson and shortly thereafter by Cassandana (Dana) Goodrich, Hannah's thirty-three-year-old niece and the daughter of Daniel Goodrich, Sr.

In the last two years of Father Calvin's life he was plagued with painful consumption of the kidneys, and his assistant, Jeremiah Goodrich, virtually held the community together until Harlow's death on December 20, 1795, at the age of forty-two. Father Calvin had been well loved for his mildness and his kindness to young people. In Enfield he once asked Elizabeth Wood to sing for the worshipers, since she was greatly talented. Yet the young woman, paralyzed with fright, found she could not utter a note for days. Finally, on the Sabbath, Harlow said gently, "Elizabeth, you are like the servant we read of, who said, I go, but went not. Now will you sing." "Yea, Father," she said, "I will." His calm belief in her enabled her to sing alone that afternoon, joyously, for the entire assembly.[28]

Elder Nathaniel Deming, who had been second in the Ministry for two years, succeeded to Father Calvin's position. Because Jeremiah Goodrich moved to the New Lebanon society, his brother Daniel came back from Enfield and became Deming's assistant. Certain family names were already dominating the leadership; this would characterize the Shaker communities for the next century. The Goodriches, for example, were called the "royal family," because so many of their members achieved leadership positions. Like the Goodriches, Nathaniel Deming and his family—his father, John Deming, Sr., a revolutionary war veteran from Wethersfield, Connecticut; his mother, Sarah Robbins Deming; and his six siblings—had been among the first converts to Shakerism in early 1780 and remained prominent in the leadership ranks. John Deming, Sr., led the Second Family until he died in 1829, and Nathaniel's younger brother William served for many years as elder in the Church Family. (Sarah Deming may have been the cousin of Lucy Wright's mother Martha; they had the same maiden name and both hailed from Wethersfield.) In Enfield as well, certain families that had joined en masse, such as the Terry, Farrington, Tiffany, and Allen families, provided many if not most of the early leaders.[29]

Father Joseph Meacham died at age fifty-five at Enfield in August 1796, just two years after his eighty-six-year-old father, and he specifically passed the Ministry to Lucy Wright, saying, "Thou, tho' of the weaker sex, . . . will be the Elder or first born after my departure." Sarah Harrison had been stricken with a feverish malady the previous spring, and she died on September 19, 1796, just thirty-six years old, having kept up her visits to Enfield and Tyringham until the end. Her place as female head of the Hancock ministry was taken by her helper, Cassandana Goodrich, also thirty-six.[30]

That so many leaders died at such early ages may be explained by the fact that times were still hard for the fledgling communities. Work was incessant and backbreaking for both men and women as they struggled to make a communal home for themselves. Food was still scarce. The weather did not cooperate: the short New England summer could send temperatures soaring into the nineties or could alternate parching droughts with suffocating humidity and drenching rains. Winters were cold and long, with snow lingering on the ground for seven months in some years. The soil in Hancock and Tyringham, as in much of New England, was thin and stony; Tyringham's steep hillside site, although magnificent, faced east and so lost hours of precious afternoon sunshine.

As if leadership changes and the struggle for sheer survival were not enough, Valentine Rathbun produced another bitter article about the Shakers in 1797. To his original grudges he could now add criticism of Shaker communalism: "When I consider . . . the awful effects of that diabolical scheme in parting men and their wives, . . . in monopolizing wealth to themselves in the most fraudulent way, &c. I believe it to be my duty to caution and warn people against such lying imposters." He reported gloatingly that the Hancock and New Lebanon Shakers were "on the decline, their old people being dead and dying, and their young people leaving them."[31]

Yet the spirit of conviction and resolution was highest at this time when the communities were struggling to survive. Already the Shakers were committing themselves to excellence of products and services, sensing that the entire Society and its beliefs would be judged harshly if one Shaker-made item were shoddy or ill-made. Father Calvin, who had evidently taken to heart Mother Ann's esteem for the products of manual labor, articulated this in a letter to Deacon Daniel Goodrich, Sr.: "I believe that the regulation of the trades that are in this Branch of the Church, belongs to thee. See that every thing is done well in every branch; and that nothing goes out, without it is done well or in the best manner."[32]

By the mid-1790s the Shaker doctrine had matured considerably from its early days in England. The worship service still began in silence and then gave way to singing, dancing, shaking, shouting, leaping, speaking in unknown tongues, and prophesying. But since the first gathering at New Lebanon in 1787 the dance had become more formalized and regular, with men dancing on one side and women on the other. Russell Haskell, a nineteenth-century Shaker historian and elder from Enfield, called this dance the "Back Manner" and said it was performed in ranks. First the dancers or laborers would go forth in a "kind of hitching step," turning and returning to their point of origin, making the broad scrubbed planks of the meetinghouse floor thunder mightily. After repeating this a few times the dancers would perform "some kind of shuffle" in place or skip back and forth without turning. The other commonly performed dance, introduced at Enfield in 1789, was called by Haskell the "Skipping Manner," in which the dancers would skip three steps, turn, return three steps, turn, and then shuffle in place.[33]

Angelic music was a constant part of Believers' lives—heard upon rising, before and after meals, and during meetings. Hummed without words or with strange syllables, songs drew the Believers together; music also reached deeper wells of feeling and spirituality than could mere speeches. Lucy Wright and Daniel Goodrich, Jr., were just two of the many who responded to song when the preaching of the elders at Niskeyuna failed to move them. The singing of Mother Ann plumbed the depths of Goodrich's soul: "I felt as though I had got among the heavenly hosts, and had no right there; for I had neither part nor lot in it. I cried aloud, in distress of soul; for I believed it to be the worship of the living God, such as my ears had never heard, nor my soul felt before." Father James Whittaker created a number of early songs, many with words, including one of the most beloved, "In Yonder's Valley."[34]

Dancing, singing, and the other manifestations known as the Gifts of God were deeply significant to the Shakers. They were considered messages or impulses from heaven, and their forms ranged from spontaneous methods of worship (such as the "laughing gift") to rigid codes of social behavior.

Increasingly, however, such gifts were controlled or guided by the elders. Although the religion was still personal, experiential, and spontaneous, the communal life seemed to require a strict order, a clear hierarchy, and absolute obedience in order to remain stable. Just as the once-freewheeling individual manifestations were evolving into formal, patterned, collectively performed dances, so the experience of God became less personal and spontaneous and more uniform and ritualistic. Some members found the life becoming too stifling; others, like Reuben Rathbun, found it impossible to submit to authority.

Rathbun had been zealous and obedient under Father Calvin and had been rewarded with the powerful position of Elder Brother in the Hancock

Church Family. His disaffection with the Society may have begun when Father Joseph chose Lucy Wright to serve with him in the lead ministry, an appointment Rathbun never seemed wholly to accept. When Meacham died and Wright was named sole leader, Rathbun became increasingly dissatisfied with what he considered to be conflicting messages coming from the Shaker leadership. Mother Lucy's failure to elevate Henry Clough to the top post of the lead ministry rankled him, even though Clough himself faithfully supported her decision.[35]

Rathbun was even more disturbed by the selection of Nathaniel Deming and Cassandana Goodrich to head the Hancock ministry. Daniel Goodrich, Sr., who was, of course, delighted by the choice of his natural daughter and a young man he had known all his life, wrote: "To them we look with all confidence, as many of us have been acquainted with them from their youth to the present time, and know they have ever been true to the cause, submissive and obedient to their teachers. . . . And for their faithfulness we willingly, yea, thankfully receive them as our spiritual leaders, believing them fully competant in their abilities as well as their spiritual travel."[36]

Rathbun, in contrast, possibly disappointed that the ministry eldership had gone to the younger pair and not to him, claimed that Deming and Goodrich were not true to the teachings of Ann Lee and the other "parents." "There seemed to be that faith required of me, in relation to them, that I was not able to obtain, without further understanding, it appeared to me, as well as to a number of others, that in order to believe and receive, what they told me I must reject, what we had been taught by our own parents, and count them as deceivers and imposters."[37]

Shaker historian Calvin Green, recording the official version sixty years later, claimed that "[Rathbun] was a very haughty and self-important person, and having never subdued his self-exalted spirit by mortification and humiliation, . . . he aspired to the leadership of the Society by self-appointment and subtility." In this he seems to have resembled his father, Valentine.[38]

Thwarted ambition was not, of course, one of Rathbun's stated reasons for his increasing vexation with the Society: he had specific practical and theological complaints. He found that even after fifteen years as a Believer he could not completely eradicate his carnal desires, and he blamed the religion for promising that he might. He felt that too many Shakers were not living as shining examples but were excessively vengeful toward the world—that, for example, they didn't care if a cow wandered into a neighbor's grain if the neighbor was a non-Shaker. He charged that the Believers were not educating their children in humanitarian principles and that those who left were completely wild, unequipped to survive in the world. He claimed that backsliders were not treated fairly when they departed from the community. He no longer believed that the Shaker Society was a heaven on earth or a New Jerusalem; there was plenty of sorrow, pain, and death, he felt. And he had become convinced that the Second Coming of Christ had not occurred because when it did, it would be evident and incontestable, and he did not feel the world had changed since the arrival of the Shakers. To make matters worse, his father, Valentine, had been working on him for years, attempting to persuade him to leave the faith and return to the Baptist church, pressure the younger man resisted as late as 1796.

In contrast to his father's diatribes, however, many of Rathbun's observations about the Society seem thoughtful and perceptive. His alienation could not have been unique and might be seen as marking an end to the Shaker "honeymoon." The Ministry's insistence on obedience was inevitably changing the tone of the Society from that of the exuberant early years, and it undoubtedly turned away other potential leaders who were brilliant but idiosyncratic—a problem that would continue to haunt the Believers. Rathbun's sense of ambivalence and conflicting messages may have reflected the changes in the Society as it underwent the same kind of "institutionalism" that the Congregational and Baptist churches had been accused of earlier in the century. Significantly, this formalization began after Ann Lee's death, when the Society began to be governed by men.[39]

Rathbun's discontent with both spiritual teachings and temporal practices grew during the last years of the 1790s. Jonathan Southwick, his helper, or second, in the Church Family eldership, supported the appointments of Deming and Goodrich, creating a rift among the Believers. Historian Green later claimed that Rathbun tried to turn the younger generation away from the leadership by insinuating that there was no need for things to be so strict, that they could live "after the fashions and customs of the world" and still find eternal life.

The job of straightening out the situation fell to Henry Clough. He arrived from New Lebanon in the early summer of 1799 and called a meeting of the Hancock Believers. Taking Jonathan Southwick by the arm, he walked to one side of the room and asked all those who felt "in union" with Southwick to come over with them. A great mass of Believers did so. Seeing how very few stayed behind with him, Rathbun is said to have flung himself on the floor, admitted his wrongs, and relinquished his eldership.

The entire Society was stunned by the crisis; Mother Lucy Wright compared Rathbun to a drowning man. Southwick was appointed as the new Elder Brother, and great pains were taken to isolate Rathbun. He left on July 24, 1799, with Sister Elizabeth Deming, natural sister to Nathaniel, and subsequently married her.

Like his father, Reuben became a bitter enemy to the Believers, and the following year he published a detailed "exposé" that not only described the events leading up to his departure but also charged Mother Ann with frequent drunkenness and violent behavior and charged the Shakers with licentiousness. In response to accusations that he had had an unseemly relationship with Elizabeth Deming while an elder, he said that he had never noticed the difference between men and women while in the Society, despite his admitted difficulty in bearing the cross against the flesh.[40] Reuben and Elizabeth Rathbun moved to Marcellus, New York, in 1800 or 1801; by then they had a son. Valentine, Sr., who had closed his church in 1798, soon joined them. Reuben was killed by a falling tree in 1807, at the age of forty-seven. His father lived to the age of ninety.

Certainly the Rathbuns' experience was not unique. Although many people came to the Shakers during the 1790s, many also departed, partly because of the arduous living conditions. The Shaker communities experienced a steady outflow. Among those who left was John Deming, Jr., who married a Shaker sister and moved west to Burlington, New York, where he died in 1791. His brother Adin, married to the former Martha Phelps, followed him out the next year with an ox team and farming tools.[41]

The communities were beginning to take on the look of villages, with the first of the large communal buildings going up. Farms had been deeded over by the Goodrich, Talcott, and Deming families in Hancock; the Allens, Clarks, and Herricks in Tyringham; the Meachams, Markhams, Woods, Billingses, Peases, and Munsells in Enfield.[42]

The appearance of the Hancock Shakers' substantial machine shop in 1790 indicates that that community was already pooling its resources and labor. Here the brethren would carry on heavy mill work, operating lathes, cutting and planing lumber, and making metal parts. An elaborate and ingenious waterpower system was soon set up, centering on the machine shop. Water traveled from the stream north of the village through iron pipes and, during one period, a hollowed-out tree trunk to feed an overshot wheel in the basement. From there the water was distributed to other locations in the village—the barns and stables, the washing rooms, the mill that sawed firewood—and eventually to the fields to water the animals. The sisters began using the western portion of the building as a washhouse around 1800.

By 1795 the Hancock sisters operated a dairy, which became so successful that twenty years later the three buildings comprising it were considered inadequate. The dairy was enlarged after 1820, when the roof was lifted to add a weaving loft.[43]

Sometime in the late 1790s the Brethren's Shop was raised. Here they may have practiced any number of trades: coopering, tinsmithing, broom and brush making, oval and round box making, clockmaking, harness making, shoemaking, chair and cabinetmaking, button making, engraving of headstones, or the manufacture of yarn swifts for winding yarn, wire-toothed cards for carding wool, spinning wheels and reels, and smoking pipes and stems. Other specialized shops housed other activities; the Shakers believed that people needed a variety of tasks to keep them happy.[44]

A garden seed house, where seeds were dried and packaged, was in place to the west of the machine shop by 1800. This young industry must certainly have benefited from the extension of the turnpike west from Pittsfield to the New York state line in 1798.

At Enfield, the Church Family had erected its first dwelling house in 1792 and a dairy house three years later. The North Family's first dwelling appeared in 1794; the South Family's, a year later; and the East Family's, in 1796.

Tyringham's mountainside site was also being transformed into a tidy little community. Moses Johnson, builder of the Hancock and Enfield meetinghouses, as well as those at other New England Shaker societies, may have built the 1792 Tyringham meetinghouse as well. The Shaker cemetery had already been established across the road and down the slope; the earliest of its ninety-nine graves is dated 1790.

Between 1792 and 1800 the Tyringham Shakers built their great red ox barn on the hillside below the road through the village. This massive structure already shows some of the elements—massive size, efficient and innovative organization—that would characterize Shaker buildings. An overhead ramp, supported by massive timbers and iron tie rods, enters the hayloft from the road, to allow direct unloading of haywagons into the mow. The cattle were kept on the main floor, reached by driving under the overhead ramp. The lowest floor, of stone, was for box stalls and manure and led directly to a stone-walled yard.

The Tyringham Shakers built their large (sixty-five by thirty feet) four-story dwelling house next to William Clark's house around 1800. The first story contained a spacious communal dining room and a kitchen with an immense marble sink cut out of a single block and an oven reaching from the floor to the ceiling. Upstairs were living quarters. The building was especially noted for its hand-forged iron details, particularly the thirty-four-inch door hinges and the iron posts on the outside stairs.[45]

By the turn of the century, the communities in the Second Bishopric had achieved a certain stability, with a mature theology and a relatively secure physical and social environment. Despite the enmity of backsliders, the members' spiritual fervor was high, their leaders were well in control, their communal economies were in place, their productivity was starting to win them the respect of the world, and converts were flooding in.

And finally, there was enough food so that they had extra to give away, fulfilling a prophecy made by Father Joseph Meacham during the hungry years of the late 1780s. On November 7, 1798, during a severe epidemic in New York City, the New Lebanon, Hancock, Watervliet, and Tyringham societies dispatched twenty-seven wagons to that city loaded with provisions, together with $300 in cash.[46]

CHAPTER FOUR

"On Earth 'Tis a Heaven":
Years of Fervor

Dearest home above others of fathers and mothers
Of brothers and sisters whose love cannot fail
On earth 'tis a heaven by Providence given
And on its rich bounties my soul does regale.
—Enfield, 1886

An elated Daniel Goodrich wrote David Meacham in 1806: "I am persuaded it must be a matter of consolation to you all to here of the welfare of our beloved brethren in every part of our or the Lord's dominion, at every place to the Eastward our very neer and deer friends appear to be under the blessing of God in things pertaining to this Life and the Life which is to come."[1]

The years between 1800 and 1820, presided over by Lucy Wright, were the golden age of the United Society of Believers and of Hancock, Tyringham, and Enfield in particular, a heady time with a purity of religious fervor that would never be equaled by future generations. At the same time the hard work and frugality of the eighteenth century were paying off in temporal prosperity. As a consequence, the communities were growing: by 1803, there were five families established at Hancock, containing a total of 142 people, a little more than half of whom (76 persons) resided in the Church Family. By 1820 the number would swell to 317, growing faster than at any other time in the community's history until it reached its peak of 338 in 1830. A revised covenant, or "constitution," was drawn up in 1801 to clarify the financial relationship between the individual and the Society.[2]

The next thirty to forty years would see great stability in the eldership. This was true both of the Ministry—Nathaniel Deming and Cassandana Goodrich would serve well into the 1840s—and the individual families of the three communities. One reason for the stability was that so many leaders of this generation were linked by blood, as, for example, in Enfield, members of the Allen, Wood, and Terry families; natural sisters Mitta and Agnes Munsell; Amaziah Clark and his son, Amaziah, Jr. (See Appendix.)

Although the population of the town of Tyringham decreased by half between 1800 and 1850, the little Shaker village on the mountainside was growing. Membership rose from fifty-three in 1800 to ninety-two in 1820 (the high point in that society was ninety-three in 1850). The community enlarged its landholdings to more than 1,500 acres, extending from the top of their mountain east to the Tyringham Main Road and from the Lee town line south to the little hamlet of Jerusalem. Of the two prosperous families, located three-quarters of a mile apart, the Church Family had the larger number of communal buildings—the meetinghouse, the large dwelling house, the great red ox barn, and various shops and outbuildings. A third family developed, but was gone by 1837. In 1823 the Church Family built its office (sometimes called the elders' dwelling), a handsome, two-and-a-half-story brick Federal-style building, with marble lintels, water courses, and date stone. With its basement kitchen, long dining room, and dormitories above, it was used as both an office and a residence.[3]

Construction was progressing at all of the societies, with the families pooling their labor. An Enfield builder recorded his busy activities in 1810 and 1811: raising a cider mill, digging the "suller," raising the store at the North Family in 1810, and building an addition to the South House in 1811 by lifting the roof and then framing, clapboarding, and plastering the walls of a third story and rebuilding the chimney. The following year the North Family dwelling received the same treatment, indicating the pace at which the community was growing.[4]

The Enfield Church Family had joined with the North and East families to construct an industrial complex centering around a triphammer dam beginning in 1803. A granary and a sawmill went up at the Church Family in 1807, followed in 1810 by an office and a brethren's shop. The next decade saw the erection of barns, blacksmith and nurse shops, washhouses, wagon houses, mills to produce cider, grain, and lumber—seven work buildings at the Church Family alone and five at the South Family. Yet the expansion was not just industrial; the North Family put up dwelling houses in 1813 and 1821. In 1823 the third meetinghouse was built.

At Hancock, meanwhile, the East Family put up seven farm or industrial buildings between 1808 and 1818, including a seed house, a dairy, a tannery, and a fulling shop. A map of Church Family, Hancock, drawn in 1820 (see illustration) shows thirty-four buildings in the Church Family alone, including the meetinghouse; two substantial dwelling houses; the office; a schoolhouse; separate shops for brethren, sisters, elders, and the Ministry; the machine shop; a nurse's shop; a dye shop; a tan shop; a blacksmith shop; a hatter's shop; a cider house; and four large barns. By that year the farm at the Hancock society was productive enough that "bounteous meals" were served to the hundreds of Shakers there, and an "abundant surplus" was sold to outside markets. One traveler in the 1820s considered the farm "the finest in the Berkshires, more prosperous now, perhaps, than any others in the county." Because of this fast growth and prosperity, the Church Family felt its buildings had become inadequate, the garden house and the tannery being particularly cramped.[5]

The thriving dairy business, however, was in direst need of expansion, especially after a fire in February 1825 consumed one of the cattle barns and the surviving cattle had to be driven through a blizzard to the East and South family barns. The following year, curious neighbors and passersby watched the Believers construct a most remarkable building to replace it.

The "Round Stone Barn" was not the first barn in America to be built in a circular design; even George Washington had a sixteen-sided barn, built in 1793. But the Shakers' barn was large, ingeniously designed, and truly round, built on a scale possible only because of their communal economy and large farm. With its yard-thick stone walls, ninety-foot diameter, ring of fifty-two cows facing an immense central haymow supplied from above, circular track for haywagons on the upper floor, and conical roof crowning all, the barn became a famous landmark and a model of efficiency for master barn builders, especially suitable for large farms out west.

As Eric Sloane has pointed out, it was constructed so that many people could work together without getting in one another's way. Each floor has a ground-level entrance; the main floor has entrances for the cattle, and on the upper floor twenty-four hay wagons could enter and pass abreast in a complete circle, depositing their loads in the mow before exiting. The cows' body heat, held in the barn by the massive walls, kept the structure from freezing. At the center of the mow a ventilating shaft, said to be as stout in diameter as the mast of a ship, carried the dense steam from the hay up and out of the building.[6]

The local farmers and other observers were impressed. As a reporter for the *New York Farmer* wrote, "The great rule of domestic economy, '*a place for every thing, and every thing in its place*,' is no where more strikingly exemplified—and tho' they make no pretensions to the fine arts, and have little of what is called taste, yet all their arrangements, and the products of their labor, exhibit the proofs of thoroughness, permanency, utility, and substantial comfort."[7]

Elder William Deming and Daniel Goodrich, Jr., are thought to have designed the barn, although the Shakers shunned awarding credit to any particular individual. The builder was obviously extremely talented at engineering and knew that a circle would enclose the greatest space with the least amount of wall. The form seems well suited to the Shakers, who considered circles a symbol of perfection and used that shape in their boxes, hats, drawer pulls, rugs, baskets, and dances.

To build the structure the Shakers hired outside labor, boarding the ma-sons and paying them $500 apiece. Herman Melville read this later in his copy of *A History of Berkshire County* and scrawled in the margin, "Amazing." The builders used limestone and granite hauled in from the fields and chestnut for the interior woodwork and the spokes supporting the roof. The total cost of the building was $10,000, an enormous sum for the time.

Accompanying the physical expansion was a gradual relaxation of local hostility toward the Believers. As early as 1808, Thomas Allen, Congregational minister in Pittsfield, described the Shakers as "a very harmless, innocent people, good citizens, and honest, industrious, peaceable members of society. They are good farmers and artists, and offer nothing for sale that is deceptive. As a body of people, their morals are good, they are very charitable to the poor, and are sincere and upright in their religion, and deserve not the charge of hypocrisy in particular more than other class of christians." The Reverend Mr. Allen decided that "Roman catholic methodists" was the best way to describe the Shakers.[8]

The Enfield society was also winning the admiration of its neighbors. According to one account,

> . . . Notwithstanding the absurd tenets of the Shakers, they are, in many respects, an exemplary and worthy people. Their religious principles necessarily affect the order of their Societies, by producing an entire separation of the men from the women; yet their communities present the most striking evidences of regularity and decorum. Their buildings are remarkably neat and convenient, and every thing appears a model of order and economy. They are characterised by a striking simplicity and plainness of manners, and are sober, industrious, and economical. They are skilful mechanics, and excellent farmers and gardeners. But what is more than all this, they are a community of "honest men."[9]

The same authors also praised the Enfield Society's "excellent tract of land," by now comprising more than one thousand acres and under "the highest state of cultivation." The Shaker village was portrayed as a wealthy and flourishing community, inhabited by master horticulturists, mechanics, and craftspeople, "their wares are justly esteemed, being always good and free from all deception."

The Believers certainly looked neat and trim in a costume similar to that of the Quakers. The sisters wore high-waisted, box-pleated dresses, with a net cap or bonnet, an apron, and a kerchief knotted modestly across the bosom. The brethren wore smocks for work and, at other times, long coats, waistcoats, breeches, and wide-brimmed palm-leaf hats.[10]

The Shakers had won the world's respect through their reliably excellent products, their honest and sober demeanor, and their generosity in times of crisis. A report from Hudson, New York, in the *Pittsfield Sun* of November 28, 1803, stated:

On Thursday morning last, between eight and nine o'clock, 73 waggons arrived in this city from New Lebanon loaded with different kinds of provisions which is a donation from the Societies of Shakers in New Lebanon and Hancock, to the sufferers by the late terrible epidemic in New York. The following are the quantities of provisions which they shipped from there to New York, viz. 853 lb. of Pork, 1951 lb. of Beef, 1746 lb. mutton, 1685 lb. rye flour, 52 bushels rye, 24 do. beans, 179 do. potatoes, 34 do. carrots, 2 do. beets, 2 do. dried apples. Besides these provisions the two Societies made up 300 dollars in specie, which is also to be presented to the poor of New York. Would not the more wealthy part of the community do well to imitate this most noble example of the Shakers?

The report ended with an exhortation to the reader to "go and do likewise." The receiving clerk for the City of New York deemed this "a very liberal donation," and the Believers received a letter of thanks from Governor De Witt Clinton.[11]

There were many examples of similar generosity and neighborliness and other times when the Shakers donated their labor to local projects. In June 1824, for example, forty brethren and fifteen teams helped level Pittsfield's East Street and improve the public square, for which they received special thanks from the newspaper. William Cargill of Tyringham recalled that the Shakers did his family's haying one August—and did a first-class job, too—when his father was stricken with typhoid fever.[12]

Another reason for the decline in hostility toward the Shakers can be traced in a daybook kept by Enfield trustee Joseph Fairbanks from 1799 to 1804. The Shaker community had become an important resource for local citizens, a place where a farmer could always obtain needed goods or services, honest prices, and friendly advice. The following jobs were done by the Shakers for world's people between 1799 and 1809: boring beams, mending a mill, sharpening plow irons, mending chains and a pitchfork, shoeing horses, mending a hay knife and a butcher knife, mending a wagon wheel, and making a crane, as well as other blacksmithing and ironmongering. Among the goods sold were barrels of cider, quarts of brandy, bushels of rye, rails, bushels of potatoes, a wagon body, a small coffin, a stove, a pump, six chairs with white oak bottoms, a hooping barrel, nails, a horse collar, a horse yoke, leather, a loom, peaches, wheat flower, seed wheat, hay, beef, cheese, pork, seed corn, a dozen pigeons, a quart of molasses, a dozen candles, mutton, and tobacco. In exchange the Shakers took money, labor, or barter such as food, livestock, raw materials, or finished goods—timber, cheese, a tub of nails, two hundred barrel hoop poles, a set of clock weights, two cows, four turkeys, some white oak logs, three dogs, a quarter of veal, a calfskin.[13]

Barter was the preferred way to even up a bill at the time because money was scarce and banks were not well trusted. When anyone paid in paper money, the Shakers would record carefully the serial number of the bill and the name of the bank that issued it, as, for example, "Had of Elez Forbes, Somers, April 28, 1804, one 5 dollar bill Merchants Bank NY No. 3129 Aug. 4, 1805."[14]

Frequently, as was the custom in the larger economy, the local farmers were given credit for months on end. Some would eventually work off their debts to the Shakers, as shown through meticulous records. A neighbor named Samuel King, for example, seems to have purchased many of his provisions from the Enfield Church family—nine hundred pounds of hay, a quart of molasses, pork, wheat flour, brandy, cheese, candles, rye, wheat kernels, an ax, a pound of tobacco, cheese, and beef. He worked off his debt in thirty-seven days by breaking flax and cutting and splitting wood. Others paid by tending cattle or helping at haying time. And still others may in desperation have mortgaged their land to the Shakers.[15]

Despite their desire for a world apart, therefore, these nineteenth-century Shaker societies were not isolated but were functioning cogs in the larger community around them. Although they did not vote until well into the twentieth century, they paid taxes, assisted their neighbors, and took in and cared for the orphaned and the infirm. Their mills, forges, tanneries, and schools served the non-Shakers nearby. Later they would run the post office and assist at the train station, which would, as often as not, be called "Shakers." Everywhere they lived their presence enriched their community with their handsome, immaculate farms and their superb products.[16]

The growing interconnectedness between the Shakers and the neighboring farmers was both a curse and a blessing. Although the Shakers benefited from the steady local market for their goods and services, their worldly success drew new members interested only in material benefits. And the more daily contact the Believers had with the world, the more its free and easy ways impressed the younger and less committed members.

Berkshire County was the launching point for a good deal of missionary activity at the turn of the century, partly because of its position at the edge of the settled world and partly because of its well-established churches. In 1798 county clerics and laypersons organized the country's first home mission society, its task being to carry the gospel to central New York. Eight years later some Williams College students got caught in a thunderstorm during a prayer meeting in a field near the college campus. While sheltering under a haystack, they founded the American Foreign Missions society.[17]

Beyond the secure little world of the communities, Shaker missionary activities were also in full swing in the first decade of the century. Far from being removed and remote, awaiting converts, the Believers would send talented speakers throughout the East, to wherever the fire of a revival had been ignited. There they knew they would find people who had tried several religions, endured several revivals, and always, eventually, become discouraged about their chances for salvation. These people would often say they were looking for preachers who were living inspired lives. In the Shakers, many would find what they were seeking.

In Pittsford, Vermont, for example, in 1801 a revival began when an eerie, inexplicable light appeared over the house of James Wicker. Many local farmers hastily joined the Methodists, but one, Justus Brewster, wrote to the Shakers at New Lebanon expressing his disappointment in the preachers of that denomination. Brothers Issachar Bates and Benjamin Youngs traveled to Pittsford and deeply impressed Brewster, not to mention his nine-year-old daughter Sally, who thought they "looked just like Jesus Christ." The Brewster family, along with about twenty other Pittsford residents, ended up converting and following Bates and Youngs back to the Society. Sally Brewster renamed herself Cassandana after Mother Cassandana Goodrich and succeeded her as first eldress in the Hancock Ministry many years later.[18]

Similar proselytizing triumphs, and the boost they gave the ongoing communities, led to the pursuit of the most ambitious missionary attempts ever undertaken by Shakers, authorized by Lucy Wright: the establishment of seven communities out west (four in Ohio, one in Indiana, and two in Kentucky). The Believers in the East had heard about huge, frenzied camp meetings occurring on the western frontier, and they remembered a prophecy of Mother Ann's: "The next opening of the gospel will be in the south West, but I shall not live to see it."[19]

The Hancock Society contributed $100 to the proposed missionary effort. Brothers Bates, Youngs, and John Meacham walked to Ohio in 1805 to participate and there won into the sect, among others, Presbyterian minister Richard McNemar, who brought most of his congregation along with him. Others followed. Many eastern leaders went west to help direct and organize the new communities, including David Meacham, who became an elder in Ohio.

Back home, the Society was charged with excitement by these developments. Daniel Goodrich, Sr., wrote David Meacham in Ohio in 1806: "I have had great desire to Live for many years to hear and see what is Now manifested at Ohio and in adjacent places, for which my heart is Glad; I can truly say with confidence I feel more Interested in this Work . . . than I ever did in all the Kingdoms of this World."[20]

The happy, thriving bishopric was devastated in 1813 when a disastrous typhus epidemic struck the Hancock community, taking fourteen lives. Until that year the Shakers had used a burial ground at the West Family, probably originally that of the Talcott family; now the number and frequency of deaths made it necessary to establish a new cemetery across the road from the Trustees' Office.

The Ministry lamented:

... to have the most turbulent and mortal Disease which was ever known begin among the breathren and sisters, and strike at the Vitals of the Church and Tare away its strong Foundation Pillars so that in the course of a little more than a month 14 of our beloved Brethren and Sisters have been carried off, and many of them such as were the very flower of the People in this place and such as have been good and faithful believers from first to last. Brother Willard [Allen] (36), Sister Sarah Deming [Father Nathaniel's natural sister, as well as their mother] (43), in the prime of life, both Elders in the Church and full of the gifts of God both in Public and Private, should be taken away from us, has been a matter of great Enquiry among many, and how to account for it, we are unable, only that God seeth not as Man seeth and when ever he feels to chastise his people he sees and knows what is for their good.[21]

Perhaps the hidden good to the Shakers was this: tragic as the epidemic was throughout the area, it nevertheless served to bring new members into the fold. Several Believers later wrote that it was while hovering near death during this terrible illness that they became receptive to the Shaker message. Lucy Davis, for example, wrote in 1843 that she had been stricken with the "epidemic feavor" in 1813 at the age of twelve, and it had been thought she would die. Hell seemed to gape before her, and she begged her visitors, young and old alike, to kneel by her bed and pray for her. She promised God she would lead a better life if she recovered. She did get well, and though she immediately forgot her promise, she remembered it when she encountered the Shakers three years later. She confessed and renounced the world and lived in the Enfield society until her death at age seventy-two.[22]

Another young woman, Betsey Haskell, wrote poignantly of her ambivalence regarding the Shakers:

I visited the Shakers in the year 1810, when in the 22nd year of my age. While there, a spirit of conviction fell upon me, and I felt unprepared to die. The way and means of salvation were clearly set before me, at this time inexpressible were my feelings.

I returned home with a heavy and aching heart, the thought of being a Shaker was altogether insupportable. I sought all means which ingenuity could devise to extricate myself. For I felt as though I was linked into a chain that was harder to break than iron.

When she fell sick with typhus a few years later, she "made solemn promises and thought if God would see fit to spare my life I would be in truth a believer." Like Lucy Davis, she remained in the Enfield Society for the rest of her long life.[23]

An 1817 revival or "stir" in Savoy, Massachusetts, drew Calvin Green to investigate. He established a Shaker society there, but it proved difficult to control from New Lebanon. When brethren were found lounging in doorways wearing nothing but their shirts and when members continued to carry on with their "old mates," the New Lebanon ministry took steps to close the society in 1821. Many members moved to Hancock.[24]

Despite the influx of new converts, the seed of the future membership decline was already planted. The times had changed, after all: the newcomers had not for the most part undergone the kind of spiritual quest common three or four decades earlier, nor had they known the powerful personalities of Mother Ann and the first elders. The Shaker societies they were entering had changed as well: now they were settled and solid, with a more staid worship and more rigid regulations, far from the struggling, buffeted, ecstatic communities of the early days. And as Priscilla J. Brewer has pointed out, a demographic weakness was already present: the growing percentage of unconverted children required spiritual training from adults, but fewer members were of a suitable age to serve as teachers and role models. By 1820, more than a quarter of the members at Hancock were under sixteen; at Enfield the percentage was even higher.[25]

Some critics of the Shakers had targeted their inadequate education of their children. Reuben Rathbun, for example, charged that the Society's children did not receive any education in "humanitarian principles" and that those who subsequently left for the world were wild, unruly, and uncivilized. In fact, unlike the area's distinguished private schools—Williams College, Lenox Academy, Pittsfield's Young Ladies' Institute, the Berkshire Medical Institution, and many others—the public schools throughout Berkshire County were of poor quality for many years. This was due primarily to lack of public financial support, despite the Massachusetts Education Act of 1789, which required that towns of fifty families support a common school for six months of the year. Horace Mann, the champion of free public education and secretary of the Massachusetts Board of Education, remarked in 1839 that "to make an impression on Berkshire in regard to schools is like attempting to batter down Gibraltar with one's fist." Indeed, the education of their children was an ongoing challenge for the Shakers.[26]

The Hancock Shaker school, established soon after 1791, was made a separate school district in 1800, and in 1817 it became a public school for world's children and Believers. A separate school was built at the East Family to accommodate the children there, who were actually residents of West Pittsfield.

Sometime between 1820 and 1830 a new school, for twenty-five students, was built at the Church Family. The children entered through the west door (the door on the east side being reserved for the teacher) into a little cloak-room, hung their coats and caps on the wooden pegs, and perhaps dropped a couple of logs into the woodbox. Then they filed into the schoolroom, with its fixed wooden benches and desks, raised platform for the teacher's desk, and big pot-bellied stove in front.

As in other New England schools the curriculum stressed moral instruc-tion and practical training. In early years teaching the gospel would be con-sidered sufficient "book learning." In addition, the boys were taught mechanical skills and crafts, and the girls learned domestic arts—spinning, weaving, carding, and sewing—often by the apprentice system.

Seth Youngs Wells, elder of the Second Family at Watervliet, had been head of the first instituted city school in Albany, New York, before he con-verted to Shakerism along with his entire family. In 1821, Mother Lucy Wright, concerned about the quality of Shaker education, assigned him to supervise Shaker schools, which he did with great skill until his death in 1845.[27]

Wells had a benign and visionary attitude toward schooling. He believed that children should love their teachers, "for if scholars can not love their teachers, they will not love their school, and consequently are in no situ-ation to learn much by their instructions." He further believed that the school's role was twofold: to teach and to occupy children's restless minds. He felt it was important to make teaching methods varied and interesting to keep the pupils' minds alert.[28]

Punishment's purpose, Wells believed, was to reform. He instructed against use of the rod except "in cases of extreme necessity when all milder means have failed." He thought teachers should fashion discipline accord-ing to the individual child because different tactics would work with dif-ferent people.

Wells's curriculum stressed the practical: the three R's, grammar, and public speaking. Numbers, he maintained, should initially be taught with small counters, like beans or corn kernels, not with figures, to help the child understand quantities. By 1833 thirteen-year-old Jane Osborne of the Han-cock Church Family was computing with both American ("federal") money and British sterling. Reading was taught by using pictures of objects with their names printed below. The alphabet, grammar, penmanship, oral read-ing, and correct speech were all emphasized. History, on the other hand, with its "confusion of wars, contentions, frauds, crimes and villainies of almost every description," was not stressed. Nor were the sciences or ge-ography, the latter being taught just by globes and maps, not by books.[29]

Guiding Wells's educational philosophy was his Shaker perspective. School subjects, he believed, served higher moral and religious purposes. Grammar and public speaking were necessary so that people could express themselves well, for example, in their accounts of heavenly "visitations." Music was taught by 1833 because it was such an important vehicle for heavenly messages. "Our great object," wrote Wells, "should be to make good Believers of [children brought in] . . . , that they may become useful and honorable members in the house of God."[30]

As elsewhere in the county, the boys attended school in the winter, the girls in the summer. When other public schools changed this schedule, however, so that boys and girls could attend together, the Shakers maintained the segregated system.

Except for this schedule the school was well respected in the community. The town of Hancock pointed to it as a model school, praising the good discipline, neat schoolrooms, and clean textbooks. An 1839 Pittsfield School Committee report commented:

The school in the Shaker district has been taught with great fidelity and system and has been a pattern of regularity, quietness, and good behavior. The improvement in all the classes has been uniform and good, but not as great as in other schools. The probable reason for this circumstance is to be found in the fact that the scholars receive only about three months schooling a year. The boys are taught in the winter and the girls in the summer. With larger schools we might easily anticipate an amount of improvement here fully equal to any within the circle of experience.[31]

Diarists visiting from other communities later in the century would comment on the schools in Hancock, Tyringham, and Enfield. An 1846 visitor particularly praised Tyringham, marveling that this very small community had such a well-taught, well-equipped school. Enfield, on the other hand, had no separate school building until midcentury; and after a school was erected it burned down in 1870. The community held classes in a wing of the Church Family dwelling. Its students, however, excelled in singing.[32]

The boys attended school in wintertime so that they could help the farmers with their strenuous outdoor work during the growing season. In the Tyringham Shaker Society, an energetic, hardworking community during the early years of the century, the farming calendar matched that of the non-Shaker yeomen of the area. The farmers toiled in a frigid April, sowing wheat, flax, and oats, mending fences, trimming apple trees, and planting onions. In May they planted corn and beans and set out apple trees, washed and sheared sheep, and planted potatoes. June was devoted to weeding and half-hilling the corn, hoeing carrots, and breaking up the fallow. In July the brethren hoed the potatoes and then began haying, and in August they reaped and harvested the English grain. September was a particularly busy time, as they simultaneously harvested and prepared for winter: they sowed rye, mowed the rowen, went out after timber, separated the ewes and the lambs, cleaned the cucumber seeds, cut corn, spread flax, "whipped off " the flax seed, laid the winter logway, pulled beans, and gathered apples. In October they dug potatoes; cleaned the flax seed; gathered corn, pumpkins, turnips, chestnuts, and carrots; and plowed the orchard. In November they turned the flax, got out dung, heaped up slabs, made fences and aqueducts, plowed out water courses, killed the fat cattle, threshed the oats with horses, killed hogs, and sawed stove wood. December was devoted to threshing wheat and cutting timber, logs, and stove wood. In January the brethren threshed oats, cut timber, drew wood from far distances, planed wagon spokes, cut logs, began seed-peddling voyages, and drew stove wood logs for the next year's stock. February and March were occupied with drawing and sawing wood, until mid-March, when they began "to fix for sugaring."[33]

Maple sugaring was a big business for the Tyringham Shakers, as for their worldly neighbors, and especially valued since it provided income during a lean time of year. The area had been known for its fine maple trees by Native Americans, who were said to have camped every winter on Camp Brook to tap the trees there. Local legend holds that it was in Tyringham that white settlers first learned to make maple sugar. One farmer might tap 1,000 to 1,500 trees in what was considered "the year's first harvest."[34]

Although molasses was readily available, shipped from West Indian sugar plantations, many antislavery Northerners cautioned against consuming a product that so directly supported slavery. "Make your own sugar" advised the *Farmer's Almanac* in 1803, "and send not to the Indies for it. Feast not on the toil, pain, and misery of the wretched."

The Shakers were described by a visitor from Harvard in 1846 as having a grand maple orchard: "the stately towering and majestic trees rose to a dizzy height and by far the largest size I ever saw entirely clear of underbrush." By that year the Tyringham Shakers were making a ton of maple syrup and sugar annually at the North Family alone, "and I could not learn that they bought any West India goods at either of the families," wrote the visitor. Sugaring was one of their largest industries: they had built sugar houses and furnaces both at the North Family and on the side of the mountain above the Church Family, amid a "great maple orchard." There were three sugar camps in the spring, containing altogether five thousand trees.[35]

The Shakers' drive toward self-sufficiency was not motivated solely by religious separatism, nor was it unique to them; every rural New England community of the 1790s and early 1800s had to be a complete little world with gristmill, tannery, saw mill, forge and, where possible, marble quarry. Mirroring the larger society around them, the Shakers began in the first two decades of the new century to specialize in certain industries, particularly the manufacture of brooms, tubs, pails, nails, furniture, cloth, and leather and the cultivation of garden seeds and medicinal herbs. At first these products simply served the individual communities' own needs, but the Shakers' efficiency of production and their use and development of labor-saving devices soon allowed them to produce an excess to sell to the world. But although the world's people quickly came to appreciate the quality and reliability of Shaker goods, the communities did not produce just for "export." The primary market for their products was the Society itself.

Transportation was improving rapidly in the early 1800s, boosting trade and small industry throughout the region. By 1807 a hard road stretched west from Pittsfield through the Hancock Shaker community and 250 miles into New York State. Within five years the Pittsfield–Albany highway was an all-weather macadam, one of America's earliest paved highways.[36]

The Shaker villages bustled with activity. From the open windows of the little shops on a summer afternoon could be heard the rasp of saws, the clank of turning lathes, the soft conversation of the sisters at their looms weaving cloth from flax and wool raised on the surrounding fields. In the machine shops the brethren may have made wagons and wagon parts; in the blacksmith shops they probably manufactured a miscellany of goods including wrought and cut nails, door latches and hinges, knife blades, ox yokes, saws, plow irons, scythes, axes, shovels, frying pans, and tailors' scissors. Even as humble an item as a soup ladle or a boot scraper received a graceful treatment in wrought iron. The fine workmanship in iron at Tyringham and Hancock—the exquisitely wrought railings at dwelling entrances; the hardware on doors; the arches in kitchens, laundries, and dairies; and the stoves—indicate how expert the Believers were at this craft. The brethren made the wooden patterns for stoves and other cast-iron items in their shops and then cast them. The tinwork was also of excellent quality, producing tin measures, ceiling fixtures, candle sconces, patterns used in making oval boxes, and, at Enfield, templates used for quilting.[37]

Perhaps no other industry was as suited to the Shakers as broom making, an activity carried on both at Hancock and at Tyringham as well as elsewhere in New England. Brooms and brushes, applied vigorously, maintained the polished, shining appearance that became typical of Shaker villages. The Shakers are credited with inventing the flat broom, which soon replaced the common circular broom and its antecedents, brooms of birch twigs or hemlock tips. Shaker brooms and brushes came in all sizes and shapes and for all purposes—long, flat, or round brooms; dust mops; ceiling brooms; broom-corn brushes; horse brushes; clothes brushes; scrubbing brushes; and paintbrushes. Broom corn had been grown in Shaker gardens since its introduction at Watervliet in 1791 and was now a major money crop throughout New England. In their shops the Believers combed the seed from the broom fiber, turned the soft maple broom handles on a foot-lathe, and tied on the broom twine.[38]

Shops were constructed to house different trades such as leather tanning and hatting. Hats, made from felt, wool, or beaver's fur, were an early product of many Shaker communities, but the business became concentrated at Hancock during the first quarter of the nineteenth century. The price of a hat ranged from four shillings for a felt hat in 1789 to six dollars for a fur hat in 1828.

Visible in the 1820 map of the Hancock Church Family is a small "tan house" just west of the office. In 1835 a new and much more substantial tannery was erected, on the earlier site of a cider house. All three stories of the building accommodated the thriving leather industry, furnishing leather for Shaker shoemakers, harnessmakers, and hatters. The hides were first soaked and leached in large cypress vats in the basement. The brethren would then hoist them to the floor above, where they scraped the hides and then hung or spread them out in the attic to dry. This was a most lucrative operation for many years, until commercial tanneries arose in the 1860s.[39]

The Shakers made all of their own furniture from an early date. Rejecting the ornate flutings and massive lion's feet of the neoclassical and Empire styles, they lightened and refined the strong, simple designs of colonial America. And rather than using imported mahogany, they created tables and chairs out of their own maple and later birch, cherry, and butternut. Each community's chairs had certain identifying marks—Enfield's rocking chairs, for example, made under the supervision of Philip Burlingame, were distinguished by the tall oval pommels atop their straight back posts and by their mushroom-shaped handholds.[40]

The Hancock society produced its fine furniture solely for its own use during the first decades of the nineteenth century. According to Eldress Caroline Helfrich, the West Family, under David Terry, was the center of the craft—appropriately so because Josiah Talcott, the original owner of that land and an elder of that family, had been a skilled carpenter. The Hancock Shakers' early skill in carpentry also can be seen in the fine workmanship on the balustrades, newels, paneling, and built-in cupboards in the brick dwelling.[41]

The Enfield community, meanwhile, was developing its own school of carpentry. Among the Shakers at Enfield lived a superb craftsman named Abner Allen (or Alley). According to recent discoveries by Jerry V. Grant and Douglas R. Allen, one trademark of Enfield's fine furniture was the tapered drawer side, designed to help the drawer slide easily in and out. Grove Wright, a later Hancock carpenter and elder, modified this feature in his furniture, the only similar known example of the tapered drawer side. Grant and Allen hypothesize that either Wright learned to do this at Enfield or Abner Allen visited Hancock and taught him the skill.[42]

The chair-making industry became concentrated at other communities by midcentury, as indicated by purchase orders. In 1853 the Hancock Ministry bought two small rocking chairs for $5 and six "setting" chairs for $15 from the New Lebanon South Family; the following year Jefferson White of Enfield ordered a quantity of chairs from Grove Blanchard of Harvard.[43]

The printing industry was in gear by the second decade of the century, with Hancock printer Josiah Talcott, Jr., producing two major Shaker works: *Millennial Praises* (1812), a hymn book, and twenty copies of the first edition of *Testimonies of the Life, Character, Revelations and Doctrines of Our Ever Blessed Mother Ann Lee, and the Elders with Her* (1816).

Articles made for sale at Hancock included wagons, plows, leather, hats, cards, measures, boxes, wire sieves, flax combs, wagons, plows, rails, woodenware, brooms, and brushes. There was much coopersware at Hancock as well—tubs, pails, sieves, cheese hoops, dry measures, keelers, churns, dippers, and pottles. The Church Family specialized in table swifts, adjustable reels for winding yarn.

Women's work was not valued to the same degree as men's, but as in any farm-based community, it was a vital part of the Shakers' self-sufficiency. Often expert in the domestic arts before they joined the Society, the sisters spun, wove, and dyed cloth; dipped candles; made cheese; and preserved the fruits of garden, vineyard, and orchard. They produced and sold palm-leaf bonnets, cloaks, baskets, knitted goods, and preserves in the office and store, in addition to the work they did in the weave shops, dairy, sewing rooms, kitchen, and washhouse. The community also carried on the domestic industries typical of any farm of the time: putting up dried apples; making applesauce, vinegar, dried sweet corn, and maple sugar; and making soap, linseed oil, and lamp oil.[44]

During the 1820s a second story was added to the Hancock sisters' dairy to accommodate the growing weaving industry. Here the sisters created everything from handkerchiefs to horse blankets, using frame looms, tape looms, and wool and flax wheels. Weaving was a valuable and satisfying skill, and the opportunity to learn it might not have been available to a young woman in the world in the 1820s. By the 1840s the sisters were producing a prodigious amount, as recorded by Hancock's Jane Osborne:

[1844] I commenced weaving in the spring loom, wove 39 yards of fullcloth 5 yds flannel 22 do cottons and worsted in the hand loom.
    [1845] I wove 35 yds of tow diaper 15 yds of forty 66 yds drab fullcloth 60 yds white flannel, 7 yds butternut worsted for panteloons wove with a wale 21 yds blue and white pocket handkerchiefs 40 in number the first I ever wove, three quarter

wide with two borders of five blue stripes w and 14 white threads between the borders . . . whole amount 257 yds.[45]

Every community of the time required mills, and Hancock had quickly erected grist-, saw-, and fulling mills. About a half-mile north of the Church Family a mill straddling the brook became the hub of a small industrial complex, and in 1819 "a little family" was set up in a North House there and "appear to be doing very well." The Hancock North Family sisters wove, dyed, and manufactured cloth, possibly also dyeing and fulling woolen cloth woven by women of neighboring farms and the sisters of the Tyringham society. Upstream from the mill the Shakers built a stone dam with a gate that could be raised or lowered by a system of rack-and-pinion gearing. The waterwheel there was said to have been one of the first turbine wheels in this country, replacing the usual overshot or undershot type.[46]

During the trade embargo brought on by the War of 1812 Pittsfield grew into an important textile center. A few miles east of the Shakers, Daniel Stearns had purchased and expanded Valentine Rathbun's old fulling mill. In 1823 the Shakers bought water privileges on a stream below the Stearns factory, where they erected a dam and, the following year, a two-story wooden gristmill. This they originally intended for their own use, but it quickly expanded to serve the public as well for nearly a century.[47]

In Tyringham the Church Family purchased one hundred acres of land about a half-mile down Jerusalem Road in April 1826, from Thomas and Hannah Garfield for the sum of $2,650. There they installed a South House near a spring, which they dammed in 1830 to make a seven-acre pond. This pond became the nucleus of the Church Family's industrial complex, which featured a gristmill, a sawmill, a planing mill, a small iron furnace, a forge, and, possibly, a triphammer. The Shakers' blacksmith and tool shop there became a busy center where Believers and world's people could exchange news while their horses and oxen were shod, nails were made, and stoves were cast.[48]

The Tyringham North Family built a similar type of dam around the same time, but that one operated differently. A dry-laid stone and earth dam, it was the lowest in a series of at least three dams that collected water from several hillside springs, creating several small basins.

The Believers in Tyringham were actively engaged in industries typical of the Shakers: the seed business on a large scale, broom making, manufacture of ox yokes and ax helves, and rake making, a major industry of the town of Tyringham. They also bought a gristmill in West Stockbridge that had been built in 1805 by E. W. Thayer. In 1833 or 1834 they built a workshop behind the Church Family dwelling, and sometime between 1820 and 1834 they put up the "Cobbler's Workshop." The North Family built the dairy and weave house in 1833, combining the two major sisters' activities under one roof, as had been successfully done in Hancock.

The Enfield community also had grown in size and industry. A new West Family had been established in 1818 under Elder Erastus Webster and Eldress Clarissa Ely. By 1827, Enfield had a new office, several imposing new barns, the South Family washhouse, a new sawmill, a dry house for drying corn and apples, a seed house, a distillery, and a system of aqueducts to transport water. As early as 1803 the East Family had begun work on the triphammer dam. This became a joint enterprise with the Church and North families, featuring a triphammer and forge where the Shakers made ax heads, shovel blades, and later in the century, lead pipe.[49]

The Society's property was rapidly increasing, as members deeded over their land. In Tyringham a spate of deeds in 1801 show substantial acreage being given by Dr. Henry Herrick (more than 150 acres), Abel Allen (20 acres), Nathan Culver (40 acres), Thomas Patten (70 acres), and William Clark (26 acres), always "for $1 and for the love and good will that I have and do bear unto the Church and community called Shakers in . . . Tyringham."[50] Between 1807 and 1819 additional property came into Shaker ownership from Herrick, Patten, Timothy Bigelow, Daniel Fay, Freeman Stanley, and Leonard Allen.[51] In Hancock as well, land was deeded over by many members in the first few decades of the century, including Daniel and Anna Goodrich, Josiah Talcott, the Deming family, the Cogswell families, John Wright, Jonathan Southwick, and numerous others, but these were generally for a price ranging from $333 for twenty-three acres to $2,000 for sixty acres.[52] And Lucy Wright's father, John Wright, and his neighbor Joshua Boynton deeded over property that would become a lucrative iron mine.[53]

The Shaker leadership encouraged individual members to develop their own expertise in a particular craft. Many members may have brought into the communities skills reflecting different regional styles. A restoration of the Hancock dairy/weave house in the 1960s uncovered five different types of joints used in connecting joists to sills and plates, indicating that five different Shaker carpenters had brought their individual, probably regional, building techniques to the job of adding a weaving loft. In other cases a master craftsman would train a generation of workers and develop a distinctive community style, while still creating products that were recognizably "Shaker."

Most members had certain areas of responsibility. Calvin Ely of Enfield, for example, wrote in his diary on all subjects—meetings, gardening, community comings and goings, deaths, illnesses, and so on—but claimed as his primary functions woodworking and tanning. Tanning was probably his responsibility alone, and he "barked" and then seasoned an enormous quantity of sheep skins, calf skins, and horsehide, fashioning sole leather, upper leather, and harness leather.[54]

His days, however, were spent in a great variety of tasks, indicating that, for an energetic person, Shaker life would have been rich and stimulating. Among his activities were framing, sawing timber for chair rungs, turning chair rungs and whip handles, making cider brandy, piling wood, painting Elder Nathaniel's wagon, plowing "my watermilion yard," planting potatoes, haying, painting sashes, husking corn, killing hogs, threshing rye, mending brass kettles, building a clock case, making shoes, laying an aqueduct, plowing the doveyard, cradling buckwheat, clearing an orchard, capturing bees, and packing seeds. He made a foot stove for two sisters and helped them cut and dry hog suet, and another time, "I gave all the sisters some flag [candy] well drest and got many thanks." He invented a "regulator to raise and lower the head of a sick person," and when the elderly sister for whom he made it died, as a woodworker he was given the responsibility of building her coffin.

The farms were producing abundantly. One September day Ely carried "200-weight" of watermelons up to the North Family and brought back 2½ bushels of peaches. The Church Family watermelons seem to have been locally considered an irresistible delicacy: in September sixteen watermelons were stolen out of the garden. Jacob and Peregrin Wood followed the thieves' wagon tracks to their den, "which greatly frightened them and in the evening they came and made restitution and confest the fact." The very next day, however, more thieves were discovered among the watermelons.

Ely's life was happy and content, balanced between vigorous work, hearty companionship, and the regular inspiration of the Sunday meetings. He commented on the gray mare foaling, the orchard in full bloom, and the first summer supper of cucumbers, baked potatoes, and codfish. On June 30, 1814, he wrote: "the beas swormed we had a Terrable hoozah to keep them from going off." His productivity and joy in life seem all the more remarkable because he was suffering from an ulcer in his side that would kill him the following April at the age of thirty-five.[55]

In the Tyringham Shaker community in 1818, twenty-nine-year-old Grove Wright (born January 17, 1789) was also busy, sowing wheat, flax, and oats; mending fences; pruning apple trees; washing and shearing sheep; planting potatoes; pulling beans; killing hogs; and performing the myriad of other tasks of a New England farmer. Wright, son of Mother Lucy's brother John, was born in Pittsfield and had joined the Hancock community with his parents when he was three years old.

At the age of nine he was transferred to the Boys' Order in Tyringham. There, in addition to farming, he learned from Thomas Patten the basics of carpentry, the trade he would follow for his entire life, beginning by planing wagon spokes; making cart axles, shingles, and plows (200 of the latter in 1818); constructing workbenches; and putting up work buildings. In 1815 he and the other brethren built a horse barn below the office, framing the building over a period of two weeks, raising it on June 13, covering and shingling it for three weeks, and then boarding the barn and finishing the stalls.[56]

The Hancock ministry—and perhaps his aunt, Mother Lucy—evidently noticed his steady nature and his dedication to Shaker principles, for in 1818 he was called from relative obscurity to become Second Elder in the ministry, assisting Elder Nathaniel Deming. This was a giant step for the young man, yet he took it in stride (his diary notes only "Grove Wright came to Hancock to live") and was a deeply loved and highly valued leader for forty-two years.

His letters and diaries over those four decades reveal a man who was never dogmatic but who had a personal, deeply felt spirituality. He was warm and jovial, devoted to the community, and capable both of inspiring his followers and of sustaining lifelong friendships with other elders, particularly Ministry elders Thomas Damon of Hancock and Grove Blanchard of Harvard. A talented carpenter, he may have worked as a master joiner on the built-in cabinets in the 1830 brick dwelling, and he produced other lovely pieces as well. He specialized in wooden pails and table swifts, continuing to produce at a prodigious rate into his sixties even while afflicted with a debilitating skin disease. One observer called him "diffident," and indeed he was a humble man, often closing his letters with a wry comment about his untidy "scrall" and unorthodox spelling. He once added a postscript with a box of swifts sent to Grove Blanchard: "There is so much grease on this sheet that I feel ashamed to send, but you will make allowance knowing who it is from."[57]

He lamented the multitude of apostasies at midcentury yet without the bitterness exhibited by other diarists. An optimist, he preferred to dwell on the hopeful signs within the Society, such as a particularly rapturous meeting. His writings abound with comments on farming activities, noting, for example, that the brethren planted white onions in a patch north of the brook or that they set out a young orchard north of the Ministry Shop, reflecting the knowledge and skill that dated from his Tyringham days. He commented on snow conditions and shooting stars—and regularly recorded when in April he first heard the spring frogs "peap."[58]

In 1818, the year Grove Wright assumed his ministerial duties, a visiting Quaker from Philadelphia named W. S. Warder described the Hancock community to Welsh social reformer Robert Owen, who was gathering information prior to founding a cooperative community in America. Warder was struck by the harmony of the village, the efficiency of its layout, the honesty of the Believers, and their scrupulous tidiness.

"On noticing the extreme neatness of the street through the village," he wrote, "no chip or stone being to be seen [sic], one of the brethren said, that the 'Sisters . . . when they walk out pick up every thing of the kind, for they delight in cleanliness.'" Warder described the ingenious water system, in which the small stream that descended the mountain north of the village powered a threshing mill, a fanning mill, and a corn or gristmill before passing under the road and arriving at the overshot wheel in the basement of the machine shop. The street through the village was sixty or seventy feet wide, he wrote, with the houses between fifty and one hundred feet apart. Fifty to sixty persons, he said, lived in a two-story, sixty-foot-square dwelling house.

Warder also left a detailed description of the Shaker Sabbath meeting of the time:

They walk in regular procession to the meeting [he wrote], and having no appointed preacher, an exhortation is delivered by one of the elders or of the brethren. There are no fixed seats or pews in the meeting-house, but only moveable benches. They enter, the men at one door and the women at the other. The floor being quite clean, they all kneel to a silent prayer, on the right knee. They then rise and form in regular columns, the men on one side and the women on the other. Several men and women then commence a tune, while every other person dances, keeping time admirably, for at least half an hour. The men and women, facing each other, advance and recede a few steps alternately, through the performance. When dancing is over, the seats are placed and an exhortation begins;—after sitting a short time, they rise and join in singing a hymn; then they take their seats, and another exhortation follows, that generally concludes the meeting. Sometimes they sing and dance a second time; perhaps it may depend upon the temperature of the weather:—in the hottest season the men usually take off their coats, and hang them with their hats on a row of wooden pins. After meeting they return in great order to their dwellings and partake of a cold dinner, as they do not cook on that day."[59]

The Shaker meetings were now attracting crowds of spectators and a regular stream of converts. Diary entries describe meetings in detail, reflecting the spiritual excitement of the time, a far cry from the cursory line common fifty years later: "Meeting as usual." The writers' spiritual life was naturally and easily combined with the life of work, indicating the degree of health and integrity the community was enjoying. This harmony might be partly attributed to Lucy Wright's influence. Until her death in early 1821 at Watervliet, she welcomed the expression of joy in services.

"We all attended meeting at the meetinghouse," wrote Enfield's Calvin Ely in 1815, "and there was a large concourse of spectators and considerable speaking. In the afternoon we all sung and danced and claped hands with the Ministry."[60]

Frequently, the speaking turned against the unconverted observers: "We all attended to the meetinghouse. Brother Daniel Goodrich spoke to the world very sharply reproached them of their stupidity."

The Ministry sometimes introduced a new form of worship. "July 11 Sab. In the afternoon North and East Famalys met with us at the meetinghouse. Elder Nathaniel and those with him attended with us and we had an entire new manner of meeting forming a wheel in a wheel and moving round in the butifulest manner."[61]

With the circular dance, described above by Calvin Ely, the Shakers reached a new height of creativity. A small group of singers formed an inner circle. Around them marched a circle of sisters and around them, in the opposite direction, a circle of brothers. To onlookers this great wheel of motion was a most inspiring sight. Many of the new dances were so complicated that they required rehearsals during the week to prepare for the Sabbath.

Although the dance continued to become more formal and regulated, new elements such as hand gestures were continually introduced to keep the maneuvers from becoming dull, justified by the elders' direct line of communication with the angels. "When Mother Lucy gave us the gift of motioning with our hands she spoak the following words," wrote one Believer in 1815. "This is a beautiful gift it feels like a great increase it is heavenly fruit it is angels' food the angels make the same motions the angels are all around us we need not think we are alone our good brethren and sisters that have left the body make the same motions in their times of rejoicing and I do not know but that is all the time."[62]

Shaker music also had changed from the early days, when chants and songs without words were deemed the best way to communicate with God. During the Kentucky Revival, Shaker missionaries had written hymns, which travelers brought back to the Northeast. First these were sung at union meetings, and then, in 1806, they began to appear in worship services. Many were printed as individual leaflets by community printers. *The Millennial Praises,* published at Hancock in 1813, set down the words of many of the hymns that circulated through the Society. Soon afterward a unique and fairly efficient type of musical notation evolved, using letters instead of a staff and notes, and this allowed the different Shaker communities to enjoy the same hymns. Only simple, a cappella, unison singing was permitted.[63]

Sometimes during meeting, the elders' attention would turn to the earthly lives of the Believers. "Elder Nathaniel used often to remind us of our duty in temporal things as well as spiritual," wrote Deacon Daniel Goodrich, Sr., before his death in February 1816. "We have a duty to do with our hands. This our ever blessed Mother and the Elders with her ever taught us. Their testimony was your hands to work and your hearts to God." Sly reminders of the exemplary behavior at New Lebanon followed, to prod Believers into higher paths. "This same living testimony is still maintained at New Lebanon where we are to look for our lead and pattern, and I fear if we do not wake up, we shall fall behind and loose sight of those before us."[64]

Elder Nathaniel would remind his listeners that, because the Believers' land and buildings were consecrated, the members should enter buildings in "the fear of God and not like the children of the world, stamping our feet, not even minding whether clean or dirty, slamming doors, laughing and talking loud. Hanging on the banisters and railings, leaning against the walls or resting on the window benches."

"These things ought not to be," he would continue. "But all ought to come in still, walk on their toes, and have no loud boisterous talking or laughing in any part of the House." He urged his listeners to partake of food with thanks, saying "Mother could eat the leavings of visitors and say, 'This is good enough for me.'"[65]

He would encourage everyone to feel responsibility for his or her job: "if it is no more than taking care of a hen, be faithful in that." He criticized "things out of order—gates shacklering [*sic*], doors up on our barns and outbuildings broken and hanging by one hinge, windows broken and not repaired. These things ought not to be. How can we expect a blessing in this careless state?"

Eldress Dana, for her part, focused on the sisters. She might scold the children and young people for chattering from the moment of rising all day long "till they talk every gift of God out of their souls and when they come into meeting they are both dead and lifeless. Then they wonder why they do not feel the gifts of God; and think the lack is in the Elders."

Domestic economy was of great importance. Eldress Dana advised the sisters to cut their cloth carefully and

to be prudent even if we had to piece a little more to save, for it was our hard earnings, and we ought to be careful and not be lavish or wasteful. And in making our clothes, we ought to be prudent and saving of our threads, and sew that which was proper and not make too free use of silk for it was costly and did not ought to be used where thread would do. And in mending our clothes she was very particular. She taught us to mend them in season, and not let them go till it would take double the time, cloth and thread to repair them that it would if we had done them in season.

She also urged the sisters to mend the brothers' clothes in due time and not let them go ragged and dirty, saying,

. . . in the fall when they have done wearing their summer clothes clean them and put them away for the next spring; and so in the spring for the next winter.

And in your kitchens you ought to be clean and neat about all your work: be prudent and saving. Be attentive and cook and season your victuals well. You may cook many good things and all be tasteless, while poorer and coarser victuals can be made good by proper care and knowledge.

The daily life of a typical Believer had by now assumed a formal pattern. The family might rise at four thirty in summer or five o'clock in winter, by the sound of a bell; eat breakfast one and a half hours later, dine at noon, and sup at six P.M.—except for Sunday, when they rose and breakfasted a half hour later, dined lightly at twelve, and supped at four. Brothers and sisters ate separately, in silence, after a silent kneeling grace. After the meal all rose together at a signal from the first elder, knelt, and then left the room quietly, going directly to their labor. The elders decided who would do what work, although specific skills or talents were encouraged by giving the person more responsibility and autonomy in that field.[66]

Four evenings of the week individual families would gather to worship and dance in the meeting rooms in family dwellings. Small "union meetings" were held on the other evenings as a way to allow members of the opposite sex to spend supervised time together, perhaps indicating that their segregated lives were proving difficult for young men and women. Individual members were paired with a partner of the opposite sex and the same age, and several of these pairs, of different ages, would be assigned to each union meeting. The two ranks of brethren and sisters sat facing each other on the straight-backed Shaker chairs, conversing on prescribed topics, reading aloud, or singing. Each pair constituted a mutually helpful unit beyond the union meeting as well; the sister would be expected to take care of the brother's clothing, and he would tend to her particular needs.[67]

Originally devised by Father Joseph Meacham, the union meetings were a creative and moderately effective approach to the inevitable frustrations surfacing in a strictly celibate world. But they could not halt the erosion of values and loss of membership that would occur in the next few decades.

Bearing Fruit

Ye faithful souls, unite and sing,
The precious fruits the seasons bring,
On the true gospel field!
Now in this great redeeming year,
We see the second crop appear,
And every grain, in the full ear
A hundred fold does yield.

In every perfect seed, we see
Two distant parts in one agree
To yield a perfect growth;
And while we stand between the two
The seasons past we can review
And what this seed has passed through
Till ripen'd in them both.
—"The Seasons," *Millennial Praises,*
Hancock, 1813

With his sober costume, broad-brimmed hat, and one-horse wagon, the Shaker seed peddler was a familiar sight on the back roads of New England by the early nineteenth century. His customers grew used to seeing him kneel in quiet prayer by his wagon or sit alone with a frugal meal in a public house. They looked forward to his visits and his unique, high-quality products, particularly the seeds. The wooden Shaker seed-boxes, which served as display cases as well as shipping boxes, sat prominently among the jars of horehound candy, wheels of local cheese, and other paraphernalia of every general store counter.

The Watervliet Shakers had started systematically growing seeds in their two-acre garden around 1790, supervised by Joseph Turner, probably selling to local farmers whatever was left over after their own use. Local response was good enough that in 1795 the New Lebanon Shakers sold onion, beet, carrot, cucumber, and summer squash seeds and the following year added radishes, turnips, and cabbages. In 1800 they sold more than $1,000 worth of seeds—indicating, at just a few cents per ounce, that this was already a thriving business. Before long the other communities followed suit, Enfield beginning to sell seeds on a large scale in 1802.[1]

Other seed houses, such as that of David Landreth & Son of Philadel-

Church Family, Hancock, view from the south, undated. (Collection of Charles Flint.)

Church Family, Hancock, view toward brick dwelling from trustees' office, 1835. (Hancock Shaker Village, Pittsfield, Mass.)

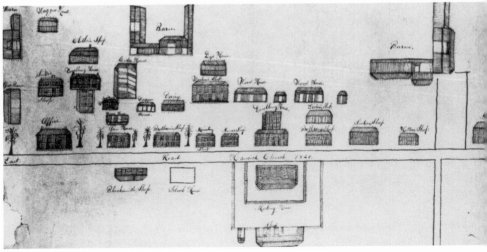

Map of Church Family, Hancock, drawn in 1820. (Hancock Shaker Village, Pittsfield, Mass.)

Church Family, Hancock, 1890s. Ira Lawson is fourth from left in back row; Frances Hall is third from right in second row. (The Shaker Museum, Old Chatham, N.Y.)

Left: Interior of round barn, Hancock, 1935–36. (Photo by Noel Vicentini, Index of American Design, WPA Federal Art Project.) *Below:* Round barn, Church Family, Hancock, around 1900. (The Shaker Museum, Old Chatham, N.Y.)

Dwelling (left), and shop and laundry (right), East Family, Hancock (West Pittsfield), 1903. (Hancock Shaker Village, Pittsfield, Mass.)

View toward west, East Family, Hancock (West Pittsfield), with Second Family visible in distance. (The Shaker Museum, Old Chatham, N.Y.)

Elder Richard Van Deusen, 1870s, prominent at both Tyringham and Enfield. (Hancock Shaker Village, Pittsfield, Mass.)

phia, had existed previously, but the Shakers succeeded thanks to their diligent labor; their clean, methodical habits; and their scrupulous insistence on quality. In addition, times were changing. Farmers had formerly produced their own seeds and swapped the excess with their neighbors; now, as more people moved into the rural areas of New England and New York, demand for clean, reliable seeds increased rapidly. City people, meanwhile, bought the Shakers' kitchen vegetables, packed every week into oxcarts and carried to market in Pittsfield, Albany, Hartford, and Springfield.

At first the Shakers sold seeds they purchased as well as those they produced. Before long, however, they found that seed not grown under their strict supervision and high standards was of poorer quality. In 1819 the Hancock, New Lebanon, and Watervliet societies drew up an agreement stating:

We, the undersigned, having for sometime past felt a concern, lest there should come loss upon the joint interest, and dishonor upon the gospel, by purchasing seeds of the world, and mixing them with ours for sale; and having duly considered the matter, we are confident that it is best to leave off the practice, and we do hereby covenant and agree that we will not, hereafter, put up, or sell, any seeds to the world which are not raised among believers (excepting melon seeds). New Lebanon, April 13, 1819.[2]

The concern for the reputation of the community and its impact on potential converts had become a policy that governed every Shaker industry; every first-rate seed sold to the world planted respect for the Society. The exception made for melons is interesting, however, considering the local fame of the Enfield watermelons.

Enfield, Hancock, and Tyringham all became active producers of seed, supervised by the garden deacons. Enfield became an outstanding center of seed production, with one hundred acres devoted entirely to the raising of seeds at midcentury, and that community's master seedsman, Jefferson White, even recruited members of other societies to grow seed for him on their own acreage. Much of Enfield's pre–Civil War trade was to the Deep South. Interestingly, the area of the lower Connecticut Valley where Enfield is situated was known for commercial seed production, particularly of fine onion seeds, as early as 1750. Onion seeds were among the most popular— and lucrative—varieties of seed grown in the three societies of the Hancock bishopric, in the early days costing a few pennies more per packet than any other variety. The onion, after all, was New England's second most important export vegetable (after potatoes), with as many as nine hundred bushels produced per acre.[3]

As early as 1817, non-Shaker retailers took out advertisements for Shaker seeds in local newspapers. On page 1 of *The Hampden Federalist* of May 1, 1817, for example, the Frost and Brewer company stated: "Garden Seeds—

of the last year's growth—from the Hancock and Enfield Gardens, a general assortment just received." The Sterns and Edwards company of Springfield also advertised having "received a general assortment of GARDEN SEEDS, from the Shakers of last year's growth."[4]

The Enfield society claimed in one of its ten catalogs that it offered "Pure Vegetable Extracts and Shaker Garden Seeds, Raised, Prepared and Put Up in the Most Careful Manner. . . . First Established in 1802, being the Oldest Seed Establishment in the United States." In the 1850s alone the community released seven broadsides, advertising an extensive variety of seeds.[5]

The Tyringham Shakers produced a broadside catalog in 1826, listing twenty-six varieties of seeds for sale. This community's most prominent building was the five-story seed house, built in 1854 and attached to the office, where the Shakers dried and packaged the flower, herb, and vegetable seeds grown in the gardens below. A freight elevator—a manually operated wheel hoist—carried heavy loads of seeds from cellar to cupola. Built into the walls of the building's attic were storage bins with sliding lids, as well as "numberless little cupboards and excellently made drawers, principally for the reception of seeds." One visitor glowingly described looking from the building's wide veranda across an "immense seed garden" and "beautiful smooth fields in front of us" with several smaller buildings for drying and storing the seeds, including a drying shed with furnace for drying seeds.[6]

Tyringham's seed house also contained a printing press for printing labels. To encourage retail sales in smaller quantities, the Shakers packaged their seeds in paper seed packets or envelopes instead of in the usual bulky cloth bags or wooden barrels. Printing presses such as the one in Tyringham churned out thousands of envelopes in eight sizes: pound bag size, bean size, beet size, onion size, cucumber size, cucumber long size, radish size, and lettuce size. On each envelope appeared the name of the seed variety and brief directions for planting—as well as, prominently, the Shaker name. Individual customers learned to recognize and demand the Shaker "seal of quality," and thanks to the convenient small packets they bought and tried out a variety of seeds they might otherwise never have sampled.[7]

Other seed-related inventions demonstrated the characteristic Shaker ingenuity. A chisel for cutting seed packets was invented, and machines were developed or improved to help clean different varieties of seed. And inevitably, the simple seed lists of the 1820s became the elaborate catalogs of the 1850s, complete with planting instructions and recipes.[8]

Hancock's expanding seed business, as illustrated in its catalogs, was typical of the other societies' enterprises. In 1813, Hancock produced the first of ten broadside seed lists. In 1821 a catalog titled "Garden Seeds Raised at Hancock and put up in Papers with the Retail Price Printed on Them FOR

SALE" included forty-eight types of seeds—four varieties of peas, three varieties of beets, watermelon, muskmelon, eight different herbs, and so on. Seed packets sold for 4 or 6 cents each, except for peas, which were 10 cents per packet, and onions, which were 12½ cents each, until the 1830s, when all prices were fixed at 6 cents each. By 1824 the number of seeds listed had risen to fifty-one and in 1839 to an impressive sixty-nine. By that year the Shakers had expanded their line to include twelve varieties of peas, including sugar peas with edible pods; nine varieties of beets; nineteen types of melons, including "rusty-coat muskmelon" and "nutmeg muskmelon"; fifteen herbs; and more exotic items, such as green globe artichokes and cayenne peppers.[9]

According to the *Pittsfield Sun,* in 1834 there were three families at Hancock, comprising three hundred individuals and holding seven hundred acres of land. "The land is not of the best description," commented the writer, "being cold, wet, and unfavorable to [grain], and their attention is mainly directed to the cultivation of grass and garden seeds, and the keeping of cows and sheep. Their first purpose is for their own supply. They raise the best they can, and they eat the best they raise." The writer evidently had no idea how lucrative was the cultivation of garden seeds.[10]

The business of developing new seed varieties was pursued energetically, and Shaker growers experimented with different techniques of propagation as well as with the latest agricultural methods, such as grinding bones for fertilizer. Their interest may have been stimulated by the annual Berkshire Agricultural Fair, launched in 1810 in Pittsfield by Elkanah Watson, where farmers could view each other's products and learn new ways to plow and fertilize. A "Gardeners' Manual," written by Charles Crossman of the New Lebanon society, first appeared in 1836 to provide gardeners with "some practical information relative to the raising and management of those valuable kitchen vegetables which are considered the most useful and important in a family." Jefferson White bought three thousand copies of this manual and resold them to his customers under his own name.[11]

Seed production and packaging was a major activity that took up the entire Shaker year. In a flurry of activity every January the entire community would prepare for the departure of the seedsmen on their travels, the sisters putting up great quantities of seeds in bags and envelopes while the brethren printed labels. In January, 1855 Carsondana Benton and Amelia Lyman in Enfield cut 2,500 seed bags—about 100 a day—which then were folded and pasted in an efficient assembly-line procedure. In mid- or late January the seedsmen, including Jefferson White, Joseph Patten, Lorenzo Brooks, Michael McCue, and Phidelio Collins, would embark on their routes, dropping off at each country store the rectangular wooden seed box, its compartments stuffed with seed packets. At the end of the summer the salesmen would return to the stores to collect the money for seeds sold, giving the dealer his share of the profits. At that time they would pick up all unsold seeds and take their first orders for the following year.[12]

Shaker gardeners would be out in the fields in early spring, preparing hotbeds of straw and manure, nursing seedlings along, and transplanting young plants and biennials into the gardens. Summer was a time of special vigilance, when the gardeners thwarted bird and insect competitors by applying lime, ashes, tobacco juice, and kerosene. Many hours were spent cultivating and weeding. "With the gardners," wrote one tired worker in 1844, "it is weed weed hoe hoe because the weeds grow very fast."[13]

Harvesting, by hand, began in late June with the first salsify seeds, followed in July and August by cole and root vegetables. In 1820 Hancock grew twenty-six pounds of fine carrot seed, filling 832 packets. Bean, cucumber, corn, and squash seeds were harvested in September, and finally, in October, the last crops came in—tomatoes, peppers, pumpkins, and asparagus. Harvesting was followed by threshing. In October the sisters began preparing the next year's seeds, a task that might involve pounding out pepper seed, cleaning and grinding onion seed, or squeezing and washing the seeds out of yellow tomatoes. In November they put up flower seeds in boxes, often engaging in friendly contests as they papered and packed. As an example of the quantities involved, in the year 1842, 122,900 seed bags were produced in Hancock alone.[14]

By the late 1830s, Hancock seed salesmen ranged throughout New York State, Massachusetts, Connecticut, and into the Midwest, traveling on the network of turnpikes and canals that now covered the region. By far the most important was the "Western Route," extending to Columbus and Burlington, Ohio, from which the Shakers received $4,599.10 in orders in 1839 alone. Shipments were sent "up the [Erie] Canal" or in wagons carrying seed boxes, a retail chest of seed envelopes, brooms, and other Shaker products. Next most profitable were the western New York routes, such as the Ramapo Route (through Newburgh, Saugerties, Catskill, New Paltz, Woodstock, etc.) and the Coxackie and Columbiaville Route, with shipments being made by ox- or horse-drawn wagon or by the Erie Canal. Seeds went down the Hudson River on the "New York Route" to New Rochelle, Brooklyn, Staten Island, Hackensack, Jamaica, and other destinations. Other routes were the Westfield Route, the Mountain Towns Route, the Fishkill Route, the Norwalk Route, and the Northampton Route, as well as the circuit of eager merchants in Pittsfield. Every year the orders grew: account books indicate that the same dealers increased their orders year after year.[15]

Early on, however, the Shakers found they were competing against themselves, with salesmen from different societies often covering overlapping territory. Brother Morrell Baker of Watervliet wrote the following to Hancock's Deacon Daniel Goodrich on December 22, 1822:

> . . . [W]e were obliged to seek ways and means to get our livelyhood and prety soon commenced the business of raising gardening seeds. There being none among the other societys of believers at that time who thought it worth commencing, or at least were not under the necessity to do it. All this time we vended our Seeds throughout the State we live in. But our Lebanon Brethren in a few years perceiving it was becoming profitable and that we were not able to supply the call for Seeds commenced the business. This we had no objection too, because they first entered into this agreement not to sell any Seeds this side of the North [Hudson] river. But soon our Brethren at Hancock followed, and not only they but till our Brethren towards the east did likewise, so that in a short time the business become so extensive, that our Lebanon Brethren were under the necessity to cross the river (but not without our consent and full union first). The brethren at Hancock soon followed, so that now through our liberality of giving in we almost compeled to give ells and some prety long ones too. Our Lebanon Brethren, on the north, on the South, on the east and on the west of us. And our Hancock Brethren a breadth through our whole state more than three hundred miles long so that at present we are confined to less than one fifth part of the state we live in and have no right to sell one seed in the state you live in nor any other state to the east of it. . . . I had almost like to forgot to state that we sold all the seeds we could in our limits proscribed to us, and you and our Lebanon Brethren sell 5 times as many seeds as we do and I believe it would not be much out of the way to say 7.[16]

One reason for the Shakers' success was their talented seedsmen, and an outstanding example was Jefferson White of the Enfield Church Family. The seedsmen were chosen with special care: not only must they exhibit a great talent both at horticulture and at business, but they also had to be steady, committed Believers who could withstand the temptations of the great cities.

Thomas Jefferson White was born on January 10, 1805, and arrived at Enfield at the age of four (June 6, 1809). When he was only twenty-seven, he was appointed deacon; and under his direction the Enfield seed industry flourished, becoming a five-figure business by his retirement in 1857. He was known for his shrewdness and enterprise, exacting full payment even for goods sold to other Shaker communities. One time he received a poorly cleaned quantity of onion seed from Elder Nathan Freeman of Alfred, Maine, which was to be exchanged for Enfield cucumber seed, and he wrote the following note: "We had to cleanse over the onion seed. It did not appear to waste but little in cleaning, still when we weighed it, all that we could make it weight was 62 1/2 lbs instead of 68 lb as measured. We have therefore weighted you out 63 lb. Early Short cucumber to go against the 62 1/2 lbs of red onion." White did add to the box a bundle of Issabella Grape Vines "altho we do not think you will succeed well with them, you are we think to far north" and "a small paper of purple Oval Egg Plant growth of 1848." In the next order White asked specifically that it "be clean seed, well sifted, and the false heads picked out."[17]

Complementing White's talent in business was a spiritual gift: he was also the leading spiritual instrument in the Enfield community. During the exuberant years of Mother Ann's work, he dominated that community's worship services by interpreting "orders" from divine spirits.

The vigorous seed business, and its profits, inevitably attracted the attention of ne'er-do-wells. On the night of February 16, 1839, Elder Grove Wright wrote in his diary: "the Garden Seed Shop was broken open by a band of Robers, and property taken to the amount of $3,325. The amount was estimated by recounting the seeds all papered & then deducting 25 per cent." The value of the stolen goods, an enormous amount for the time, shows how lucrative the seed business was. A notice was posted offering the handsome sum of $400 for the recovery of the seeds and conviction of the thief.[18]

Eventually the facts emerged: the seeds were stolen by a former Shaker named Lewis Wheeler, who apparently intended to take them downriver and sell them in New York City. Fortune, however, was against him: not only had ice closed the Hudson River, but his wagon broke down about nine miles west of Hancock, in Canaan Corners, New York. Wheeler and two sidekicks managed to push the wagon to the home of Dr. Lorenzo Giles, arriving just after dawn, and asked if they could store the packages there until the river opened. Two days later Dr. Giles heard about the robbery and reported Wheeler to the Shakers; on March 14 the seeds were recovered and safely stored in the seed shop again. Wheeler was arrested and incarcerated in the Lenox jail until June, when his case was laid before the grand jury and he was indicted for grand larceny. The trial was delayed a few days, however, to give Wheeler a fair chance to make his defense. When the case was finally called, both Wheeler and his attorney had disappeared.[19]

The Shakers were among the first to market herbs on a large scale, beginning around 1800. Like many country people they may have been reluctant to use world's doctors, prompting them to explore and experiment with the various medicinal properties of herbs. Their diaries and journals are full of homemade "receipts" for cures for cholera, typhus fever, and other of the deadly diseases of the time. By 1820, however, the Shakers had become the chief suppliers of herbs to the burgeoning national pharmaceutical industry. Acres of land were devoted to medicinal herbs such as henbane, belladonna, taraxacum (dandelion), aconite, poppy, dock, burdock, valerian, horehound, and dozens more.[20]

Garden flowers were grown for their usefulness—nasturtium (whose berries were pickled to make capers), larkspur, foxglove, hollyhock, lobelia, marigold, and verbena. The sisters would go out to the poppy beds before dawn to slit open the pods that had just dropped their scarlet petals. In the evening they would return to scrape off and collect the raw opium, a particularly valuable product.

The Shaker herbalists also knew and used native herbs. On a fine summer's day an elder might drive a wagonload of children to the surrounding fields to gather wild plants. In order not to mix the precious oils, the children would fill tow sheets with only one type of herb each day, carrying home fragrant bundles of lobelia, pennyroyal, spearmint, peppermint, catnip, wintergreen, sarsaparilla, or dandelion. Out of these the Shaker herbalists would produce powders, oils, extracts, and ointments. Elderberries and dandelions were made into wine until 1828, when the Ministry forbade consumption of any intoxicating beverage except for medicinal purposes.

Fragrant waters, especially rosewater, were a popular item at Shaker stores. One sister remembers being instructed that the magnificent crimson roses climbing along the roadside fence were not to be admired for their fragrance and beauty; their purpose was functional, not ornamental. "It was not intended to please us by its color or its odor, its mission was to be made into rose-water and if we thought of it in any other way we were making an idol of it and thereby imperiling our souls. In order that we might not be tempted to fasten a rose upon our dress or to put it into water to keep, the rule was that the flower should be plucked with no stem at all." Rosewater was used to soothe the heads of invalids as well as to flavor the celebrated Shaker apple pies.[21]

Shaker candies were another fast-selling commodity, particularly wintergreen lozenges and sugared flagroot, lovage, and horehound. Vegetable dyes were concocted from sumac, goldenrod, madder and from barks like butternut, oak, swamp maple, hemlock, chestnut, and witch hazel. Culinary herbs such as summer savory and marjoram were prominent as well. In addition, the Hancock and Tyringham gardeners had several acres of sage—popular with sausage manufacturers—in cultivation every year.

Sophisticated machinery streamlined the processing of herbs. Benson J. Lossing, a noted nineteenth-century artist, depicted the vacuum pan, the hydraulic press, the crushing mill, the powdering mill, and the laboratory in engravings illustrating an 1857 article on the Shakers in *Harper's Monthly*.

Internationally famed for their quality, Shaker herbs were shipped across the country to such distant ports as San Francisco and Victoria, British Columbia. From London's Covent Garden Market came an inquiry regarding prices of henbane, hemlock, belladonna, dandelion, basil, and mayapple.[22]

It seems remarkable that items such as herbs, seeds, and broom corn actually reached their destinations in that era of uncertain routes and shipping lines. Sometimes bundles of seeds were broken and the seeds mixed up; other times the seeds arrived too wet to use. Occasionally, shipments were simply delayed by poor weather. A letter from Earl Jepherson, seedsman to the Enfield North Family, to Brother Nathan in Alfred, Maine, on November 15, 1826, listed fifty-six bundles of broom corn to be carried by one D. Johnson from Hartford to Boston and there re-shipped for Kennebunk, Maine, and finally Alfred. He charged $2 for handling ("trouble of bringing from Hadley sorting and carrying to Hartford"). Two months later, another letter explained why the broom corn never arrived: since no vessel was going to Kennebunk, the entire shipment was stored for the winter at Central Wharf in Boston. Nevertheless, Jepherson asked, in a postscript, for payment: "You may forward the money by mail if you please."[23]

The Western Railroad from Hudson to Pittsfield, completed in May 1841, passed over Hancock Shaker lands and must initially have been a great convenience in shipping out seeds and other goods, as well as enabling the Ministry elders to make their visits around the bishopric on "the cars" with great efficiency. A train station was built in the early 1840s near the East Family and in 1844 doubled as the West Pittsfield post office.[24]

But the whistle of that first train passing over Shaker fields signaled a new era—and the beginning of the end of the Shaker seed business. Railroads not only shipped out Shaker goods; soon they would also bring in competitors' seeds and products, often cheaper for being grown in kinder climates or richer soils. Throughout New England, other farm industries—sheep and hog raising, wheat growing, and cattle fattening—would similarly be undermined by the new link to the West. The agricultural base of the regional—and the Shaker—economy was beginning to erode. In contrast, the railroad was a boon to the local manufacturers whose millwheels turned by every mountain stream, producing cotton and wool cloth, paper, metal goods, leather, and lumber.[25]

By midcentury the Enfield community was at its height in productivity and assets. In its 1843 inventory of property the Church Family listed 6 oxen, 19 milch cows, 29 young cows, 7 calves, 4 beef cattle, 1 bull, 122 sheep, 6 horses, 6 swine, and 61 hens—certainly a very large farm for the time. The North Family, always extremely wealthy too and perhaps slightly competitive, boasted more oxen and swine and comparable numbers of other livestock.[26]

The cash reserves of these two families were even more impressive, based largely on the thriving seed businesses. The Church Family held cash that same year in the amount of $21,481.10; the North Family, $16,358, plus nearly $11,000 of "Notes with Mortgages." Each year's inventory was accompanied by long lists of shopkeepers who owed money for seeds. Jefferson White and Earl Jepherson were known throughout the Northeast and deep into the South for their fine seeds and fair prices. Much of their business took place in the South, perhaps following the routes set up by Enfield plow makers decades earlier.

Yet clouds were massing on the southern horizon. A letter to seedsman Jefferson Shannon from salesman Urban Johns in January 1840 told of a terrible depression in Mississippi. Vicksburg, "formerly the great seed market, is quite a poor place for us to sell seed this season, we have done in a manner nothing here. . . . We thought that 1837 was a hard year to get along with money matters, but it was nothing compared to this. It is impossible for us to describe the condition of Mississippi in relation to currency. Confidence is lost in each other and more especially, in the banks. . . . The fact is the whole state may be said to be broke."27

The Shakers' great success at industries such as growing and selling seeds meant that the communities now had to face the temptations of an increasingly materialistic, individualistic world. As the world began to pay attention to the Society, inevitably its values were penetrating the minds of the younger Believers.

By the time the United Society had survived for a generation, the Shakers had experienced apostasies, conflicts, discipline problems, and such other challenges as those presented by Valentine and Reuben Rathbun. In addition, they were now accepting new members who had not known Mother Ann and the charismatic early leaders. Many of the newcomers had never experienced a religious conversion; they may have joined because of the financial security the now-prosperous Society offered. Without an inward inspiration to guide them in the "straight and narrow" path, some of these newcomers exhibited lax, casual behavior that raised the elders' eyebrows. Perhaps in response to this challenge, in 1821, six months after Mother Lucy Wright died, the slow formalization of Shaker laws and worship finally became codified in a document titled *The Millennial Laws,* mostly governing temporal life.

Early leaders, including Mother Lucy, had shunned the idea of issuing a doctrinal statement. They felt that such an instrument would interfere with the immediacy of the Shaker religious experience; of primary importance was the individual's own relation to the spiritual world. Perhaps Mother Ann's illiteracy helped steer the Society in this direction. However, the Shaker community at Turtle Creek, Ohio, which would become Union Village, had, in 1806, created a thirteen-page treatise titled "A Candid Statement of Our Principles," primarily to present their beliefs to outsiders.28

The official justification for *The Millennial Laws* was that the "one general law, which is the law of Christ," must be divided into "a variety of statutes and ordinances which will apply to all general cases, and teach us our duty in the various situations, circumstances and relations to which we may be called." The laws certainly cover a variety of situations; different editions deal with everything from Sabbath day conduct to fire safety, from how to relate to the opposite sex to how to fold one's hands, from the proper shape of a garden to the proper method of eating cucumbers. The early elders' fears may have been well founded; except for the exuberant period in the 1830s called Mother Ann's Work, the Shaker religion would now focus more on correct behavior, less on the individual's private communion with God.[29]

Chapter 1 dealt with confession of sin. Believers could not hide any sin for any reason whatsoever. Not only were they forbidden to tell "filthy stories," irritate or wound a brother or sister, or drink "so as to be disguised thereby," but they were required to report to the elders anyone else who did such things; if the elders themselves transgressed, the matter was to be disclosed to the Ministry.

Chapter 2 governed the worship of God and customs for the Sabbath. No one could be absent from the meeting except with the permission of the elders. All Believers were to retire to their rooms in silence and labor for half an hour before the meeting, and after evening meeting there was to be no unnecessary conversation and none at all in bed. Rules for the Sabbath day were very strict: every Saturday evening the shops and work rooms were to be swept and put in order; no one was to "walk out for recreation" on the Sabbath; no reading of newspapers was allowed, nor any books except the Bible and books published by Shakers. Brethren and sisters were not to drink cider and distilled spirits on the Sabbath "except on important occasions, such as Brethren's fatiguing chores at the barns, & Sisters work in the kitchen which may require it; and in such cases they can be justified in using such drinks in the morning."

Chapter 3 further developed rules concerning relations between the sexes. A brother and sister must not be alone together except to do some short and necessary errand, and they could not touch each other unnecessarily. They must not work together, make presents to each other, or even pass each other on the stairs. They must not go to each other's apartments without a good reason, particularly after evening meeting, and brethren were to leave their rooms when the sisters came in to clean unless they were ill.

Chapter 4 established the rules regarding the order of deacons, "the place appointed for buying & selling and transacting business with the world." All financial documents (account books, deeds, notes, bonds, etc.) were to be kept at the office, and no buying or selling was allowed elsewhere in the community. "No private interest or property is, nor can be allowed of in the Church, exclusive of wearing apparel & working tools of which each member must have the particular care and charge of his own."

Chapter 5 contained "rules to be observed in going abroad & in our intercourse with the world of mankind." Brethren and sisters, excepting deacons, required permission from an elder to leave the farm.

Chapter 6 covered fire safety, a crucially important subject to the Shakers, who lost many buildings to fires throughout the nineteenth and well into the twentieth century. Lighted lamps and candles had to be carried always in lanterns, smoking was not permitted during work or in the kitchen, and spit boxes containing sawdust were never to be under stove hearths. Also, the last person to leave a room was supposed to shut the stove doors and make sure the room was secure from fire.

Chapter 7 set out the rules of neatness, prudence, and good economy that would so characterize the Shakers. Neglect of the physical setting was not to be allowed: buildings that became run-down, whether through age and decay or any other reason, were to be repaired soon or taken away, a rule strictly followed in all of the Shaker villages; and broken windows were to be mended before the following Sabbath.

Chapter 8 dealt with table manners; for example, all members were to kneel before and after eating, whether at home or away. Chapter 9 was concerned with care of animals, and later chapters addressed other miscellaneous duties.

Another publication of the 1820s, authorized and supported by Mother Lucy Wright before her death, was titled *Testimonies Concerning the Character and Ministry of Mother Ann Lee*. Like the 1816 *Testimonies* printed at Hancock, this was a collection of testimonies by many of the aging Shakers—including Daniel Goodrich, Jr., Samuel and Elizabeth Johnson, and Hannah Goodrich—who had known Mother Ann Lee and the first elders. The intention of this commercially printed volume was to redeem the reputation of Mother Ann and the elders, which had been tarnished by the anti-Shaker tracts that had been persistently appearing in print. Most recently, Mary Marshall Dyer's *Portraiture of Shakerism*, a rambling 450-page diatribe, had accused the early leaders of drunken and lewd behavior. The narrators of the *Testimonies* attempted to counter these charges by offering their own portraits of the elders as sober and inspired.[30]

In the first half of the nineteenth century the Shakers remained alert to ripples of revivalism, often sending out a corps of their most persuasive speakers in the hope of snagging potential Believers—"good Gospel fish," as one Believer called them. Revivalistic communities were still a rich source of converts. For example, between 1820 and 1830 the Enfield community prospered and showed its greatest demographic strength with, for the last time, a majority of its inhabitants between the ages of thirty and sixty.[31]

Those numbers were bolstered in 1826 by the simultaneous conversion of ten families from an area on the Rhode Island–Connecticut border. The Enfield elders and the Ministry had been courting this revivalist group, as indicated by a letter of the previous year: "As to the awakening at Rhode Island, there is a prospect that there will be a number gathered to the gospel, who are people of considerable ability, but how much time will determine. The elders at Enfield have made them a visit . . . and feel more encouraged about them than ever they have."[32]

Finally, in April, "there was a general move for the kingdom," wrote diarist Carsondana Benson. "Ten families set sail for Enfield Ct. six from Foster R.I. and four from Sterling Ct. a town joining."[33]

This very significant conversion would have a positive effect not only on the Enfield Shakers but on the entire bishopric. Among the new converts were several who would quickly take leadership roles at Enfield, including Philip Burlingame, Arthur Damon, and John Foster. Their children would in turn become the pillars of the Society a generation later.

Burlingame came from Sterling, Connecticut, with his wife, Polly; his parents, Richard and Sarah; two siblings; and two children and was the first signer of the new covenant of the West Family in 1829, witnessed by Foster and Damon.[34]

The covenant manifested the group's "desire to unite together in the order and form of a family and religious fraternity in gospel relation, according to the light and revelation of God, made known to us in the gospel . . . inasmuch as it enables us to be more useful to ourselves and each other in all things pertaining to our travail in the gospel." The signers could reserve for their heirs a part of their temporal interest when they joined. This money could be used by the Society, but when the heirs came of age, it was to be paid to them by the trustee.

Burlingame's wife signed in the space under his name, but instead of giving over all of her property to the Shakers, she exercised her right to leave a reserve for her six-year-old daughter Sarah Dana, a reserve that greatly resembled a potential dowry: "2 trunks 4.00—one Rocking chair 1.25—two chairs 1.50—one bid 12 one coverlett 300—two blankets 2.50—one large blanket 150 five cotton sheets 300—4 pillow cases 48 cts—one bedstead and cord 250—one table cloth 200 one towel 50 cts or the amount of same in money to be Delivered to her when she arrives at Lawfull age." Others made similar provisions for the possibility that their children would want to lead separate lives: Waty Foster reserved for her granddaughter Waty Ann Foster a bedstead, a bed quilt, a pair of sheets, a pair of pillowcases and one coverlet, one set of drawers, and one black silk cloak. And Betsey and Caleb Blanchard left detailed instructions for the exact amount to be given to each of their six children.

The 1826 gathering was lucrative in other ways than just new members. Richard and Waty Frey, for example, donated $3,900 to the Society—although ten years later they and all of their children separated themselves and returned to Rhode Island.

Of all of the new converts of those fruitful years, however, it was the second generation—the children entering with their parents, as Nathaniel Deming and Cassandana Goodrich had entered with theirs a generation earlier—who would become most prominent among the Shakers. George Wilcox, for example, born in 1820 and entering the community with his family that same decade, was from 1844 until his death in 1910, a powerful elder in the Church Family at Enfield.

Among the local people attracted to the Enfield society for its security and stability was a thirty-seven-year-old widower named Seth Pease. When his wife died, possibly while giving birth to their sixth child, Omar, in October 1815, he turned to the Enfield Shakers for help. Like many other widowed parents, he knew his children would be well cared for and educated there. They joined the Society in 1816. Seth's stay may have been short—he was buried next to his wife in the town cemetery in 1850—and three of his four sons left when they came of age. His daughter Clarissa, however, served as eldress in the North Family, the Church Family, and the Ministry, and her sister Martha became South Family trustee. The baby Omar grew up to become a dedicated elder and talented trustee of the North Family.[35]

In 1826 the Tyringham society welcomed John and Eunice Storer and their five children, from Winsted, Connecticut. John left after five years, soon followed by his daughter Eliza, but the others remained for their entire lives and took on important positions. Wealthy Storer (born in 1820), seven years old when her family joined, rose through the ranks of leadership until, in 1846, she was sent to Hancock to serve in the Ministry with ailing Dana Goodrich. Harriet Storer, her elder sister (born in 1817), became a trustee and then eldress at the Church Family in Tyringham and later in Enfield. Hasting, their younger brother (born in 1822), served as a key Tyringham Church Family trustee, overseeing the seed and herb industry, from 1850 until his death in 1873. The oldest son, Addison (born in 1811), was reported in the 1860 census to be illiterate, perhaps because of a learning disability. He worked his entire life as a farmer and died in Enfield in 1878.[36]

Several generations of the Van Valen family joined the Hancock society in the 1830s. Martha Van Valen arrived in 1833 at the age of twenty-nine, followed in a few years by her parents, Moses and Elizabeth, from Homer,

New York, and her brother John with his two small children and ten-month-old baby, Eliza. Martha would become one of Hancock's leading spiritual "instruments," or mediums, of whom it was said "to know her was to love her."[37]

But of all of the young people who entered with their parents during that period, the one whose name became most familiar to the entire Society was Thomas Damon. Damon was born December 26, 1819, in Johnston, Rhode Island. His parents were Arthur and Olive Damon, ministers of the Christian Church in Coventry, Rhode Island, which had arisen in a major revival in 1812. The enthusiasm subsided, and in 1827 the family moved to Enfield, "not being satisfied with the light they had received," in Thomas's words. During his childhood the boy learned woodworking; he signed the Sacred Roll in 1843. While still in his twenties, he was asked to assist Grove Wright in the Ministry, and he served as a beloved elder for thirty-four years.[38]

Damon was the only one of his siblings, however, to achieve such a notable rank. He was the third child in his family; the others were Susan (born in 1815), John (born in 1818), and Nathan (born in 1820 or 1821). Susan died relatively young, at age 38; John suffered from mental problems that sent him to a Springfield asylum for a while; and Nathan served briefly as elder and then abruptly left to marry a Shaker sister.

The mass conversions of the 1820s were a great boost for the entire bishopric, and the last big gathering of intact families. Thereafter, the families that joined would generally be headed by a widow, drawn to the Society out of need as much as devotion. To accommodate the new members, and perhaps also to express the community's optimism, the Enfield Church Family raised a new meetinghouse in May 1827, with the Ministry present. And at the end of this most prosperous decade, a letter from the Ministry had this to say about the present and future of the community at Enfield: "As to the Young Believers in this place we can truly say we feel greatly satisfied with them and think they are striving according to their best understanding to keep the way of God. There is a gradual increase in numbers about as fast as we are prepared to receive them, as their is some that the scails are so thick and tough that it is no small job to dress them."[39]

One increase in numbers at Hancock during the 1820s consisted not of new converts but of young brethren seeking sanctuary. On May 8, 1823, twenty-three brethren of the New Lebanon society announced in *The Pittsfield Sun* that they had moved to Hancock "for the express purpose of enjoying our civil and religious rights; and for the purpose of freeing the society in New Lebanon and Canaan from any burthen on our account." Eligible for conscription in New York State, they moved over the border to Massachusetts, where the right of conscientious objection had been established many years earlier—"where, to the honor of its government, the liberty of conscience is considered as the free and natural right of every man, and where those whose consciences direct them to *follow peace with all men*, are not required by law to bow down or sacrifice to the lofty image of military despotism." A year later twenty-seven more Shaker men moved from New Lebanon to Hancock.[40]

During the War of 1812 the Shakers and other religious groups, most prominently the Quakers, had asserted their pacifist principles by refusing to serve in the army or even, in the western communities, to care for the sick and wounded. The War of 1812 and the Mexican War were not widely popular in New York and New England; in 1814, Daniel Webster eloquently defended to Congress the right not to serve. Many Shakers had instead paid "muster fines" of about $4 a year; others had hired substitutes to serve in their place.[41]

In February 1815, however, the New Lebanon brethren faced the fact that these activities indirectly supported the war, and they published a declaration setting forth the reasons they would no longer participate in the military in any way. Three months later the Enfield brethren submitted a similar declaration to the Connecticut civil and military authorities. They argued that the law guaranteed them liberty of conscience, which included the right to abstain from the politics of the world. The Shakers believed that they could not assist one nation in destroying another.[42]

Although this petition was successful in temporarily exempting the Shakers from the annual fines, the New York law seesawed for many years on the issue. A new militia law of 1824 required that the fines be paid and stated that each society was liable for the brethren residing there. This precipitated the move to Massachusetts. The practice of moving across the border became so common that by 1828 the Hancock Shakers had a printed form available for the brethren's use in establishing proof of residence.[43]

Perhaps because of the influx of young men into Hancock during the 1820s, that society reached its peak in membership in 1830 with 149 brethren and 189 sisters, totaling 338 members. That spring the Church Family began construction of its substantial and quite magnificent brick dwelling, both masonry and joinery work being directed by Elder William Deming.[44]

Deming described the nineteen-month construction of the building in a letter to Elder Benjamin Youngs of the South Union, Kentucky, Ministry:

We began laying the foundation on the 15th of April 1830. . . . [W]e commenced our building and in ten (10) weeks from the placing of the first stone in the cellar, the house was neatly laid up and the roof put on. . . . The work is all well done. There is none to excel it in this country. And the same can be said of the joiner work—the stuff is very clear; scarcely a knot can be seen in all the work, except for the floors and they are yellow pine and very good. There are 100 large doors including outside and closet doors; 245 Cupboard doors—369 drawers—These we placed in the corners of the rooms and by the sides of the chimneys. The drawers are faced with butternut and handsomely stained—they take up but little room, and are not to be cleaned under.

Among the remarkable features of the dwelling is the meeting room at the north end of the main floor, with two partitions that slide smoothly down into the floor and up into the ceiling to allow unobstructed worship. There are two dining rooms, the main one, at the south end of the same floor, accommodating eighty persons at one time, and a smaller one adjoining for the Ministry's private meals. The sisters brought up the food from the kitchen below on two dumbwaiters. The kitchen, or "cook room," wrote Deming, "is very convenient; we have excellent water from a never failing spring that is conveyed into the cook room in three different places and two places in the second loft. There is two excellent ovens made on an improved plan which will bake four different settings at one heating. Also the arch kettles are on a new plan of my own invention, and which proves to be the best ever seen about here." Beyond the kitchens were dairy and storage rooms. On the first floor, in addition to the meeting room and the dining rooms, were various small retiring rooms for the elders and eldresses and rooms in which members could wait and meditate before meals or meetings. Upstairs were the members' sleeping rooms, sisters' on the west side of the long polished corridor and brethren's on the east. In order that brethren and sisters should never have to pass too intimately on a narrow stairway, men and women had separate staircases and doors to the outside.

The Shakers loved bright colors in their buildings, and the dwelling was stained inside a bright orange, with the doors to the outside painted green. The exterior received four coats of red paint, and the plaster was pure white. The cost of the building, Deming estimated, was about $8,000, even though the brethren took most of the materials—sand, blue limestone, white stone, timber—from their own land.[45]

The brethren and sisters held their first meeting in the brick dwelling on November 20, 1831. Within the next three days, forty-seven brethren and about fifty-four sisters moved into their new quarters.

On a tour of the United States during the 1830s the English writer Harriet Martineau, fascinated by economic experiments, visited the Hancock and New Lebanon Shaker communities. Martineau, like many observers, had difficulty reconciling the Believers' inner and outer worlds. To her the material world of the Believers seemed admirable, but their spiritual life was baffling and, in her words, "disgusting." She warmly praised the "flourishing" farm and spacious houses, and declared that every physical detail from floor to roof, from gate spring to spitting-box, showed "a nicety which is rare in America." This quality, however, she attributed to the Shakers' great wealth and subsequent leisure, which in turn was afforded by their communal life. And she suggested that a community could be just as successful without being ruled by "ignorance and superstition."

She harshly criticized the Shaker dance, the sisters' "frightful" and "drab" costume, and the worship service. "Their spiritual pride, their insane vanity, their intellectual torpor, their mental grossness," she wrote, "are melancholy to witness. Reading is discouraged among them. Their thoughts are full of the one subject of celibacy: with what effect, may be easily imagined. Their religious exercises are disgustingly full of it."

She cast a sympathetic eye on the children she thought might someday leave the community: "I saw many a bright face within the prim cap-border, which bore a prophecy of a return to the world; and two of the boys stamped so vigorously in the dance, that it was impossible to imagine their feelings to be very devotional."[46]

Curious about this religious and social movement that had sprung from their own country, a number of English travelers visited the Shaker communities in the nineteenth century. Many of these, like Martineau and Charles Dickens, found the Society grim and unappealing; others less celebrated took up the Shaker way of life. The Enfield community, in particular, had numerous lifelong members of English birth.

By now the hostility toward the Believers in the early years of the Society had given way, for the most part, to a more peaceable relationship between the Shakers and their neighbors. Now the conflict with the world took a different form, often involving the courts: members who had left in anger, parents who wished to renege on contracts indenturing their children, and incidents of vandalism. The same year that the gathering to Enfield from Foster and Sterling occurred, Elder Amaziah Clark of the North Family discovered a serious case of vandalism. In his words:

> Found the pump, south of the kitchen, did not afford so clear water as common, consequently, before we made use of it for cooking there was a number of pails full thrown away, but continuing not to look right they went to the spring; after bringing a number from there the pails did not appear to be rinsed from what came out of the pump. Daniel Pease fell to puking after taking a long draught. Examined bottom of pails considerable white substance found to be arsenic—near an ounce in the bottom of the pail, plus considerable more on the pump boxes and sides of the pump. Half a pound total. The lives of 50 or 60 at stake in one day, plus 50 people who called at the house for refreshment (returning from a camp meeting).[47]

Local legend holds that this hostile act was in retribution for the North Family's practice of lending money to area farmers using their land as collateral, but whether this is indeed true is impossible to say. Certainly the North Family did hold mortgages by midcentury.[48]

But even peaceful interaction with the world had a dangerous edge as the Society grew more prosperous and the world grew more materialistic. With worldly values of materialism and individualism infiltrating the villages, a spiritual cleansing was in order.

CHAPTER SIX

"Their Precious Mother's Word"

*"Thus have her younger children, who never saw her face,
While she was in the body and moving in this place,
Receiv'd her pure instructions, monitions, and have heard,
As did her elder children, their precious Mother's word."*[1]

On a summer day in 1837 three young girls, aged ten to fourteen, suddenly began to shake and twirl in the middle of a class at the Girls' Order in the Watervliet Shaker community. Murmuring to each other about a heavenly journey they were taking, they remained remote, rapt, absorbed, for the rest of that day and night. By the next morning they had recovered, but similar experiences of visions, speaking in tongues, and clairvoyance began to befall older children and then adults. Rapidly, such "gifts" and manifestations spread to the other communities, becoming a riot of expression. It was called Mother Ann's Work or the Era of Manifestations and continued in different forms for the next eleven years.

During the previous decades of prosperity and worldly success, the Society had been experiencing a severe internal crisis. Many of those who had been adults in Mother Ann's time had died. Even those who had known her as children, such as Elizabeth Wood of Enfield, were in their sixties by the 1830s. The initial fire of Shakerism seemed to be flickering, and the Believers seemed increasingly to be worshiping by rote, even less devout and obedient than they were before the publication of the regulatory *Millennial Laws*. Meetings were no longer the high point of the week—a diarist's entry for the Sabbath might now be simply "Meeting as usual." And new converts seemed to be more interested in the plentiful "loaves and fishes" of the Shaker dinner table than in the strict and narrow stairway to heaven.

Yet this certainly reflected a general trend in America during the second quarter of the nineteenth century. As Robert Meader has written,

> The early nineteenth century was an age of increasing urbanization and industrial proliferation, both basically inimical to a vital interest in religion, especially of the celibate, monastic type. . . . Further, the great days of burning religious fervor, which induced farmers to interrupt their plowing to argue religion over the stone

wall, and women to collapse screaming at church for fear of incipient hellfire, had evaporated under the siren calls of . . . the new textile and paper mills, the shipyards, and the lure of overseas trade in exotic ports of the Orient.[2]

The country was delirious with expansion. Railroad tracks unrolled in every direction—the twenty-three miles of track that existed in 1830 had become more than two thousand by 1840. Immigrants flooded into America, filling factory jobs or forging on westward to farm the fertile plains. The teeming, seductive cities had become worlds of their own, places of opportunity, intrigue—and corruption. For an enterprising and talented young man, the world must have seemed tempting and glamorous, with Fortune right at his fingertips.[3]

In addition to the pulls from outside, the demographic trends evident in Shaker communities in the early decades of the 1800s were now causing internal strain. Fewer members were in the right age group (twenty to sixty) to be tapped for eldership positions. Growing numbers of incoming children needed teachers and role models. Although some children did devote their lives to the Society and became important leaders, most drifted away. One way the leaders confronted this problem was through increasingly strict regulation, as with the frequently revised *Millennial Laws,* although they conceded that rules and regulations often had a stifling, depressing effect. A new spark was needed to rekindle the excitement and restore the momentum of a generation ago, to give the children and young adults of the 1830s a direct experience of faith, rather than one channeled through laws and traditions. That spark was provided by the spiritual firestorm unleashed in 1837 in the Watervliet schoolroom.

The manifestations had a wonderful, invigorating effect for a time, as Mother Ann and the other elders seemed to be present in the Society once again through spiritual instruments who interpreted their messages. The fervor was reminiscent of the early days of Shakerism. Not only did members just coming of age, such as Enfield's George Wilcox and Thomas Damon, become fired with enthusiasm, but the world's people were also attracted, and many joined. Elders themselves felt recharged. Grove Wright, who at forty-eight had spent his entire life in the Society, was thrilled by the spiritual contagion: "In the late manifestations of the marvellous outpouring of the mighty power of God, displayed in diverse ways by means of God's own choosing, and extending thru out Zion on earth for some years past, I can truly say I am a full believer. I have been an eye, ear and heart feeling witness of the same in very many instances, and can truly bear witness that it can be no other than the mighty power of God, sent forth in mercy for the further increase of His Zion on earth."[4]

Julia Johnson of Tyringham remembered this as a radiant time, when "the spirit of Shakerism was deep, and strong, and intense, rising at times and in particular individuals to ecstasy and periods of rapture." After sun-down on Saturday, she remembered, the elders and eldresses "walked on tiptoe," and a feeling of awe and solemnity passed through the entire com-munity. The Sabbath had begun, a day devoted only to spiritual pursuits.[5]

Several Tyringham Believers were spiritual instruments, seeing visions and speaking in unknown tongues, including Julia Johnson's two natural sisters, Betsey, later a Ministry eldress, and Almira. Almira became sick at school one day in 1844 when she was eleven. In the ten days of illness that led to her death, her sickroom seemed crowded with spirits with whom she rapturously conversed. She reported that angels escorted her through beautiful mansions and assured her she would soon be with their residents.[6]

Sister Julia remembered another young woman, seventeen-year-old Eliza Chapin, who entered trances that sometimes lasted several hours. Upon her "return" she would recount what she had seen—temples, mansions, gar-dens, and landscapes, all more beautiful than anything on earth. As a child of eight, Julia Johnson slept with Sister Eliza and listened with awe as the older girl described angels hovering in the room.[7]

The excitement grew. Meetings became so exuberant that for a while they were closed to the public. In Enfield, in early February 1838, Believers claimed to have seen strange lights and spirits and heard the sound of angels' wings. From Hancock, Grove Wright wrote in 1839 that "the blessed work of God is increasing among the Believers here, attended with most won-derful manifestations of the divine spirit," and later, "the same blessed work is going on with an increase many are the gifts and divine manifestations from the spirit world. Wonderful visions, Gifts of Inspiration, Heavenly Songs—Messages and Solemn Warnings, all tending to encourage the faith-ful to perserverance."[8]

The tide of revivalism was so powerful that the elders may have felt com-pelled to channel it into useful directions, at least after the spontaneity and tumult of the first months of manifestations. Such efforts, beginning in early 1838, no longer served merely to increase religious fervor; now they also attempted to steer behavior into correct paths. Through inspired in-struments—increasingly, adults instead of children—Mother Ann, Jesus, and the early elders paid spiritual visits to the communities, sometimes ac-companied by such personages as King David and George Washington. These heavenly visitors were invariably shocked and disappointed at the casual behavior of Believers, said to be so far from the perfect order estab-lished by Mother Ann.

Mother Lucy's spirit appeared frequently to visionaries and left many specific observations, as recorded by instruments: "I have seen some of these daughters standing a long time before their looking-glasses prinking their caps and their handkerchiefs with lust in their hearts saying such a one or such a one will notice me and think I look very handsome, I am sure some body will notice that my cap or some of my clothes look better than the rest of the sisters do. And with this sense they have come into meeting to undertake to worship God all plastered over with lust and pride."[9]

The instruments that conveyed such messages seemed to have the light of God shining upon them, to have been divinely chosen from among the Believers. One Hancock brother remarked, "I have oft times felt as if I could crawl upon my hands and knees and lick the dust off the feet of those who had the power of God, if I could receive enough to move one finger."[10]

New dances enlivened the meetings, with such evocative names as the winding march, lively line, moving square, mother's star, and cross and diamond.[11] Other new gifts took different forms, ranging from the "sweeping gift" (a spiritual cleansing) and the "laughing gift" (one member started giggling, another picked it up, and soon the room was rocking with laughter) to dietary restrictions such as abolition of coffee, tea, tobacco, and pork. These restrictions were greeted with annoyance and exasperation by members.

Children, who had initiated the era of Mother's Work, played a vital role in the community; they were coming or being brought in large numbers at the same time that the entire Society was beginning to lack a demographic core of young and middle-aged adults. Because the Shakers were hard-pressed to supply competent adults to teach and care for the children, many of the latter, though well loved and carefully trained in trades or domestic arts, did not receive the spiritual direction that would have kept them in the Society. Even so, most of the elders and leaders in the Hancock Bishopric—Cassandana and Daniel Goodrich, Jr., Nathaniel Deming, Grove Wright, Thomas Damon, George Wilcox, Omar and Clarissa Pease, Betsey Johnson, Cassandana Brewster, and the Lyman sisters, just to name a few—had entered the Society as children, indicating that Shaker education was far from ineffective at producing faithful Believers. Jane Osborne, for example, who studied arithmetic and music at the Hancock school in 1833 and wove flannel and worsted in the weaving loft in 1844, was teaching school herself by 1851 and, after taking "Lucy" as her first name in honor of Lucy Wright, served as second eldress in the Church Family in 1856.

Thomas Damon was another who was educated by the Shakers and remained to become a leader. He recollected his youthful perceptions of the Shakers as follows:

At that time I was between seven and eight years old, and was, consequently, too young to appreciate [his parents' reasons for joining the Society] . . . ; nevertheless my mind received many serious impressions; and when attending the meetings of the Believers, was frequently led to reflect on the purity of that life which God requires and which shone so conspicuously in the devotion of the worshipers. As I increased in years and understanding, I became able to comprehend, in a greater degree, the nature and design of the gospel, with its requirements. That, although it is merciful in its offers, yet it is humiliating in its means, which by it purposes to bring low the lofty books of man, and reinstate him in union and favor with his Maker. I perceived also that I possessed a corrupt nature, which filled my mind with pride, selfishness, and impure desires; that I retained passions which remained unsubdued; and that my thoughts inclined, more naturally, to things of time and sense, than to those of eternal duration. [12]

Like worldly parents in the pre-Victorian era, the Shakers were said to be rather strict with children, although this probably varied from family to family. Almira Johnson, who died at age eleven conversing with spirits in the Tyringham Church Family, had been so rebellious a child that the sisters once confined her in the cellar until she repented. An 1840 "Book of Orders Given by Mother Lucy" includes strict orders curbing the natural exuberance of children. "If any one sees a child leaning out of the windows running into the halls, out of the door, into the rooms they do not work in, singing and talking in a loud boisterous sense, they may know that they are not my children and that it is very displeasing to me." [13] And a communication from Mother Ann asked:

Dear children, for what reason do you wish to appear popular and grand, in the eyes of the filthy unclean children of this world? Do ye seek the honor and glory of men, rather than the blessings of God, and that peace and comfort which the pure gospel brings to every faithful obedient soul? No doubt your answer would be *nay*. Then why will ye not separate yourselves from these things, and follow the example of your heavenly Parents, while upon earth, and those faithful children that embraced the gospel in that day? [14]

In examining "testimonies" written by various Shakers who, as children without their parents, voluntarily entered the Society during this period, one finds certain patterns of experience preceding their arrival at the Society. Many, such as Olive Stebbins, Margaret Hopkins, Carsondana Benton, and Hannah Quance, were born into poor families and were "put out" to other homes while very young. Others were orphans who were fortunate enough to find their way into the Society instead of the nightmare of a poorhouse or a state orphanage. As they grew, these parentless children often became very religious, aware of the basic tenets of the doctrine of election and fearful of hellfire and damnation. As Stebbins, who became Elder Sister in the Enfield Church Family, recollected, "Fearing that I was not one of the elect, I expected to be eternally miserable after death." The security, community, and spiritual certainty of the Shakers must have warmly beckoned children such as these. [15]

Others were brought to the Shakers by their parents at a very young age, and the children, girls in particular, who grew up to become lifelong Shakers and elders tended to be among this group. At the Enfield community six-year-old Sarah Dana Burlingame entered in 1826 with her parents. Anna Erving, later a Ministry eldress, was placed in the United Society by her seafaring father when she was five years old, and Ministry Eldress Clarissa Pease arrived with her father and five siblings in 1816 when she was four. All three signed the covenant soon after their twenty-first birthdays and remained for their entire lives.

Julia, Almira, and Betsey Johnson were great-granddaughters of Samuel Johnson, the Presbyterian minister who was an early convert to Shakerism. Their grandmother still lived at Hancock, where both their father and mother had grown up. Their mother left the community when she was twenty and moved to Utica, New York, but in 1837 she sent the three girls, ages four, eight, and ten, back to be raised by the Hancock Shakers. Since there were too many children there, they were sent to Tyringham. Of the three girls, Betsey became a Ministry eldress, Almira died as a child, and Julia became Church Family eldress, left at age forty-nine to reside in the world for a period, and returned to live her last years in the Hancock community. The lifelong devotion to Shakerism is evidence of their effective education among the Tyringham Believers.[16]

Through the early 1840s the communities continued to be swept by the bracing winds of revivalism. The members received a new gift or spiritual direction every week, it seemed, climaxing in 1842. That year some particularly notable gifts were introduced by the Ministry: the establishment at each Shaker community of a "holy hill," or sacred ground, where the families held outdoor worship services; the assignment of spiritual names to each of the communities (Hancock became the City of Peace, Enfield the City of Union, and Tyringham the City of Love); and the appearance of new spirits, "unbelievers" and heathens—particularly Native Americans and Africans—who became converted and redeemed through the medium of younger members. "The elders have a hard time of it in this hurrycane of gifts," remarked Barnabus Sprague, second elder of Hancock's East Family, "to know what is revelation and what is not." But always, the elders were the judges.[17]

During 1842 and 1843 each community carefully marked out its sacred feast ground, usually on the highest hill, making a great deal of effort to clear and level what was generally primitive forest. The establishment of the feast grounds was a development of great creativity, even romanticism. For the first and only time the Shakers were transforming their landscape into a spiritually symbolic one, wedding their inner and outer worlds, fulfilling their promise of heaven on earth. In Hancock the chosen ground was a wooded mountaintop a few miles to the north, which the members called Mount Sinai or sometimes Mount Zion. It was said to be close enough to New Lebanon's Holy Mount for Believers at both places to exchange shouts. They cleared a third of an acre, leveled off the hillside, filled in the western edge, and built a rectangular shelter. Then they laid out a plot for the sacred fountain, with a conical altar at the north end and in the center a bowl-shaped depression paved with shale. Here they may have placed the marble Fountain Stone itself the following year. On this marble tablet an inscription read "Written and Placed Here By the command of our Lord and Saviour Jesus Christ THE LORD'S STONE Erected on this Mt. Sinai, May 4th, 1843, Engraved at Hancock." The Ministry directed the placement of the stone and may have dictated its inscription, judging from the fact that on April 10, 1843, Thomas Damon came up from Enfield to learn to letter the stone that was to be placed at the fountain on that society's consecrated ground.[18]

Finding the right place for the holy ground was a special ritual of its own, and the Believers searched out the appropriate spots in Hancock, Tyringham, and Enfield during the summer of 1842 with the assistance of the Ministry elders. When the Tyringham Shakers climbed their mountain on a July day to find their holy spot, christened Mount Horeb, the party included Ministry elders Grove Wright and Cassandana Brewster; the prominent leaders at Tyringham, including Desire Holt, Fanny Jonson, Betsey Gardner, Harriet Storer, Wealthy Storer, Eliza Chapin, Calvin Parker, Willard Jonson, Albert Battles, Hasting Storer, and Michael McCue; and three instruments from Hancock, Joseph Wicker, Martha Van Valen, and Judith Collins.[19]

A month later the Ministry, including Nathaniel Deming, an aging Cassandana Goodrich, and Cassandana Brewster, joined fourteen brethren and sixteen sisters in searching for a feast ground suitable for Enfield, to be called the Mount of Olives. They ascended Tiffany Hill, halting under a huge oak to sing a hymn to summon the spirits' help, and chose an appropriate site. Two days later about 130 brethren and sisters met to prepare the holy ground. The work filled the members with eager purpose: "We went to work with zeal and animation all appeared to feel interested in the good cause." Full of joy, they cleared, leveled, and seeded the area, and the following year they erected a Lord's Stone.[20] According to an 1854 account, "There is one of the finest views to be taken off this Hill that you would wish to see; You can see the 4 families of believers and all their lands which is about 2,000 acres."[21]

Twice a year, in May and September, the Shakers held an outdoor meeting or "holy feast" at their feast ground, a precious chance to get away from the bustle of everyday life and enjoy a spiritual cleansing and purification.

Sometimes they would ritually "dress" beforehand in magnificent spiritual garments that contrasted splendidly with the Shakers' sober everyday smocks and aprons—for brethren a coat of twelve colors, a sky blue jacket with gold buttons, white trousers spangled with stars, white shoes, and a silver fur hat; for sisters a gown of twelve colors, silver shoes and bonnet, and blue silk gloves. The Hancock ministry brought home an invisible chest of such raiment, received by inspired instruments at Enfield.

A typical outdoor meeting occurred in Hancock on September 14, 1842. The carefully organized description might indicate that this account was to serve as a model for similar meetings. A "shining company"—probably several hundred Believers—left the City of Peace at eight A.M. and marched in an orderly fashion until they reached the walnut grove, a stand of trees about a mile along the route. There the group halted and formed a circle to hear, through instruments, spirit messages. Jesus Christ spoke through Joseph Wicker, and Father Calvin Harlow spoke through Martha Van Valen, asking the Believers to express themselves by giving four bows and four claps. Next a band of angels appeared to guide them on their journey. Mother Sarah Harrison spoke next and gave the members spiritual spectacles, the better to see spiritual things. They resumed marching, two abreast, until they drew near the edge of the holy ground, where they gave a great shout toward the City of Peace. Then the sisters and brethren slowly marched together, four abreast, to the fountain itself.[22]

At the holy fountain the group bowed low three times, poured spiritual incense on each head, and donned mantles of strength. They began to sing, bowing low to "gather up the love." Then came a lively dance; according to one participant, the members were instructed to

go forth with as much energy as though we were going into the hayfield. The brethren strip off their coats and go to work. . . . Some were reeling and stagering; some leaping and skiping, some rooling upon the ground, and some acknowledging the mighty power of God. And so strong was this mighty powerful wind pressing through the crowd that if there was an unbeliever among us they must have had cause to lay their hand upon their mouth, or have cried out in confirmation of the mighty power of God, which was surely displayed beyond all natural caviling.

After a short rest and a speech by Eldress Catharine Williams, the group launched into another quick dance—clapping, shouting, bowing, turning—"It was self-evident stuborn feelings had no room to act."

One instrument informed the group that Jesus Christ had poured anointing oil on the heads of the people and had placed a flaming trumpet on their shoulders. Another announced that spiritual tubs had been placed next to the fountain, which was filled with holy water, and next to them were sponges to scrub one another clean—brethren assisting brethren and sisters assisting sisters. They were told to give each other a good scrubbing and were given spiritual water pots for rinsing. Other gifts appeared: the spiritual staff of Elder Nathaniel, a loaf of living bread from Father William, a loaf of white bread from Mother Ann on a silver platter, a dove with a roll in its mouth, a cross. Mother Ann then gave them comfort to carry home, and Mother Lucy gave a golden sack to put it in.

Then the company marched home. The band of angels, which had escorted them the entire time, sang a farewell hymn through Joseph Wicker at the walnut grove and then parted with the Believers. They arrived home, physically exhausted and spiritually refreshed, at 2:30 P.M.

The following year the marble slabs, or Fountain Stones, were inscribed with "the words of the Lord," warning non-Believers about the power of the spot. Enfield's stone, 4½ feet high and 2½ feet wide, standing at the head of the 6-foot-square Spiritual Pool in a neat, fence-enclosed lot, contained the following message:

The word of the Lord. On this consecrated ground I have placed a living fountain, and here shall my laws be proclaimed, and my name be revered; and I command all people who shall come to this place, not to step within this enclosure, nor place their hands up on this stone when they are polluted with sin; neither harm ye aught in this place. Bow before me the Lord Jehovah and fear to violate my laws, for I will surely punish the wilful violator of my commands, and those who injure my sacred things.

I am a God of justice and am abundant in mercy, calling upon all to honor me, in the purity of their lives Yet will I chasten with Judgements those who defy my power, and set at naught my commands.

My word is truth. Amen.

Similar words appeared on the Tyringham stone:

The word of the Lord. Here is my spiritual fountain which I have placed here for the healing of the Nations. And I command all people who shall come to this Fountain not to step within this enclosure nor place their hands upon this stone while they are polluted with sin. I am God the Almighty in whose hands your breath is and I will cause my judgments to fall upon the wilful violater of my commands in my own time and according to wisdom and truth whether in this world or eternity. For I have created all souls and to me are they accountable. Fear ye the Lord of Heaven and earth and bow before him.

Written and placed here by the command of our Lord and Savior Jesus Christ. The Lord's stone erected on this Mount Horeb Nov 7th 1843.[23]

Another gift occurring in 1842 was the appearance at meetings of heathen spirits through the instruments of younger members and children; after a great spiritual struggle they were converted. Pocahontas was a favorite, but there were many others. Julia Johnson described one young man who took on a Native American identity for hours on end; while working he would demonstrate surprising skills and entertain his comrades with his "memories" of Indian life. "Many other people," she went on, "were often controlled by 'native spirits,' as well as those of foreign nationalities, speaking in different tongues, and manifesting by some peculiar trait belonging to each. Those from the frozen lands would start on a run, and then slide back and forth the whole length of the floor, as if on skates. The clairvoyants could see these different peoples, and describe their costumes. The Indians brought blankets, beads, 'wampum,' and wine."[24] This gift continued for a few years but may have been the beginning of the end of Mother's Work because many older Believers were offended and troubled by the wild demonstrations.

The following year was filled with work on the Sacred Roll, whose contents Philemon Stewart of New Lebanon said had been dictated to him in a vision. Its purpose was to promote the cause of peace by enlightening the world on the principles and hopes of Shakerism, and to this end the leaders decided to try to furnish a copy to the government of every state and every country in the world. Grove Wright became an enthusiastic participant in this project, traveling to Tyringham with Giles B. Avery to read the book to the members there and making several trips to Boston with Stewart and Avery. When the Sacred Roll was signed by dozens of members, printed, and bound, it was taken by the elders to various state governors and foreign consuls.[25]

Gift, or spirit, drawings, which appeared between 1841 and 1859, may have been the final outpouring of the revival. Like the other spiritual gifts, these were messages received by selected individuals, in this case at least ten women and one man in New Lebanon and Hancock. The drawings were unique, however, in that they were such exuberant graphic expressions of the Shaker experience. No longer was color subdued or form simplified to its essence, as in every other area of Shaker creativity. Using symbols from the natural world—trees, fruit, birds, gardens, stars—the Shaker spirit artists depicted the spiritual landscape of the Believers. Accompanying texts, sometimes entwined right into the drawings, explained the symbols, making this art much more than purely decorative and thus acceptable to the Shakers.[26]

Hannah Cohoon and Polly Collins were two of these artists who lived at Hancock and may have stimulated each other's work and even collaborated at times. Hannah Cohoon, perhaps the most celebrated of all of the spirit artists, was born in Williamstown, Massachusetts, on February 1, 1788, the youngest child of Noah B. Harrison, a revolutionary war veteran, and his wife, the former Huldah Bacon, both members of prominent local families. Hannah married and then, in 1817, was admitted to the Hancock society with her children, five-year-old Harrison and three-year-old Mariah L. Although her children eventually left the community (Mariah returned much later), Hannah signed the covenant in 1823 and stayed for her entire life, dying at Hancock in 1864.[27]

Hannah was painting by 1845, at the age of fifty-seven, and left four extant works that are unique among known Shaker spirit art. First, as June Sprigg has pointed out, she signed these paintings, which is unusual for a Shaker (though not untypical of world's craftspeople at the time).[28] The bold style of her work is singular as well: unlike other Shaker spirit artists, who produced diverse, sampler-like montages of Shaker emblems, messages, and ornamentation, Cohoon focused in each of her known paintings on an individual element—always a tree or apples—simply and graphically presented and accompanied by a written explanation. This explanation adds a religious dimension to a painting that could otherwise stand alone as a graceful, balanced—but secular—work of art. For example, in the text accompanying "The Tree of Life," she wrote:

City of Peace Monday July, 3, 1854. I received a draft of a beautiful Tree pencil'd on a large sheet of white paper bearing ripe fruit. I saw it plainly; it looked very singular and curious to me. I have since learned that this tree grows in the Spirit Land. Afterwards the spirit shew'd me plainly the branches, leaves and fruit, painted or drawn upon paper. The leaves were check'd or cross'd and the same colors you see here. I entreated Mother Ann to tell me the name of this tree: which she did Oct. 1st 4th hour P.M. by moving the hand of a medium to write twice over Your Tree is the Tree of Life. Seen and painted by, Hannah Cohoon.[29]

The dreamlike detail of her observation—the description of the checked and crossed leaves, for example—are typical of Cohoon's explanations. Folk art historian Ruth Wolfe has pointed out that this painting in particular seems to reveal the artist's familiarity with the techniques of appliqué— indeed, the leaves and apples seem not to be painted but to be carefully cut from gingham and calico.[30]

If Cohoon's paintings seem to indicate a knowledge of appliqué, then the work attributed to Polly Collins displays the exquisite detail of an expert embroiderer. The earliest extant painting signed by Polly Collins appeared in 1841, when she was thirty-three years old. According to Daniel W. Patterson, she was born in Cambridge, New York, on April 7, 1808, and came to live at the Hancock North Family at the age of twelve. Eventually, she moved to the Church Family and served as caretaker to the girls at the West Family from 1857 to 1867. Between 1841 and 1859 she produced at least fifteen watercolor paintings.

Hancock second Elder Joseph Wicker produced one painting in 1844. No works by any of these artists have been found for the years 1845 to 1852, perhaps because they have been lost or destroyed—which might have been the case if the drawings were particularly expressive during the height of the manifestations.[31] On the other hand, the community may have suppressed the spirit drawings for a time, particularly when the fervor of the early 1840s had passed—such vivid, colorful objects looked suspiciously like worldly ornament or, worse, like Catholic iconography. *The Millennial Laws* of 1845, after all, included strict prohibitions against decoration—"No maps, Charts, and no pictures or paintings, shall ever be hung up in your dwelling-rooms, shops, or Office"—and instructed that curtains and spreads should be of "some very modest color, and not red, checked, striped or flowered."[32]

Later, in the 1850s, however, when every other manifestation of Mother Ann's Work had subsided, the two Hancock sisters and the other spirit artists produced the majority of their known works. In this quieter time the drawings, with their luminous portrayal of Shaker ideals, were probably loved and cherished even if secreted in drawers and trunks. For nearly a hundred years the drawings were in fact kept hidden from public view.

Both Cohoon and Collins utilized the image of the tree to represent the Shaker church. Interestingly, Cohoon's *The Tree of Light or Blazing Tree* may be a rendering of Father James Whittaker's vision, while in England, of the Shaker church taking root and thriving in America. As Jane Crosthwaite has written, "What Father James saw in a time of persecution, Sister Hannah painted as an image of fulfillment. Her trees are alive, full of fruit, her basket brings fresh apples. Hannah Cohoon's gift to the community is an affirmation of its own promise."[33]

The world beyond the Shaker communities was suffering from the same stresses of growth and prosperity that were affecting the Society, and a revivalistic outburst there paralleled the course of Mother Ann's Work. The Adventists, or Millerites, believed that the end of the world was imminent, basing their conviction on research by a farmer named William Miller in upstate New York. Miller had studied the Bible and concluded that Jesus Christ would return and that the world would end sometime in 1843. In the 1830s and early 1840s he toured the Northeast, preaching to frenzied camp meetings and winning tens of thousands of followers from Philadelphia to Montreal and west to Cleveland. Many did not bother to plant crops; some even gave away their property. The excitement reached its height during the designated year, when people could not see the sky stained red at sunset without fearing that the end had come.[34]

When 1843 came and went, Miller recalculated and set a new date for the beginning of the millennium, October 22, 1844. Vigils were held in churches and parlors, awaiting the coming of Christ. The day passed, leaving the expectant Adventists unspeakably disappointed and desolate.

The Shakers, always alert to revivalism, had closely followed the Adventist movement and now welcomed a number of the disappointed members into the Society, particularly in the western and New Hampshire communities. The Adventists continued to believe in the imminent appearance of Christ—one group, the Seventh Day Adventists, survives to this day—and remained on excellent terms with the Shakers. In 1846 an Adventist camp meeting was held in Enfield and was attended by many Shakers, including brothers Frederick Evans and Harvey Lyman and Hancock Second Family elders William P. Williams and Barnabas Sprague. The group erected a tent, where they preached and sang and soon were surrounded by women, men, and children anxious to hear their message. Brother Frederick spoke to the newcomers, who "seemed hungry for something which they had not yet found." Afterward, the Enfield sisters served baked beans to one thousand—nourishing their bodies along with their souls.[35]

A letter from Tyringham the following year, however, said that though they expected some families to join in the spring, so far the Adventist ranks had yielded only some children. "Some [of the prospective members] were well off in property, but the most of them are no more than even with the world, and a part are considerably downhill. Their embracing Shakerism makes something of a stir in the neighborhood where they live."[36]

Inside the Society the more violent spirit demonstrations had ended by 1845, around the same time as did the Millerite excitement, although for several more decades the Shakers continued to commune with departed spirits. As Stephen J. Stein has pointed out, the preponderance of aged members made death a familiar preoccupation, and thus the communication with spirits became especially comforting. Nevertheless, the heights of ecstasy reached in the early 1840s would never again be approached, as the Believers withdrew into a more contained and private style of worship. The holy grounds were neglected after about ten years of use and eventually dismantled. And undoubtedly as a reaction to the delirium of the previous eight years, the Millennial Laws were revised in 1845 to set forth the strictest and most detailed rules of behavior in Shaker history.[37]

In 1847, Grove Wright reported: "As to the . . . young believers, there are a goodly number of them who appear to be doing well and increasing in faith and good works, but there are some who seem to me like to prove *bad fish* caught in the Gospel net and have to be separated and cast away."[38]

Heady as the Era of Manifestations may have been, the departure rate from the Society was at its highest during the 1840s and early 1850s. Many members were simply alienated by the extreme displays; others found their faith in the elders strained to the breaking point. One apostate told of a deaf old Hancock brother who was unable to understand the message an instrument was relaying to him and asked, "Who can believe that the Lord would come down from heaven and incarnate himself in a human being, make a formal address to an old man and not make him hear it! . . . It was not the Lord who spoke to us, but Jo Wicker."³⁹

The author of those words was David R. Lamson, a spiritual seeker like Joseph Meacham and Samuel Johnson. A former pastor, he had grown disillusioned by what he saw as the established church's support of the world's great evils: slavery, war, intemperance, and licentiousness. His outspokenness cost him his job, and he subsequently joined the utopian community at Hopedale, Massachusetts. That experiment also disappointed him, when the community seemed to abandon its original socialist principles, and he sought "a society or denomination which practiced in a tolerable degree the spirit and principles of Christianity."⁴⁰

In early 1843, the year of the great Millerite excitement, he and his wife, Mary, and two young children came to the Hancock Shaker community to reside at the South House, the gathering order. The Shakers treated him and his family with "great kindness," he reported, and his initial impressions were extremely favorable:

Here I found everything to all human appearance, neat, plentiful, orderly, peaceful, devout and beautiful. As a people they appeared to be temperate, frugal, industrious, honest and simple hearted. And the great majority of them (to say the least) *are* all this. They acknowledge no allegiance to human government, and have no connection with slavery or war. And as to the licentiousness of the flesh, . . . of this they seemed wholly pure.⁴¹

Before long, however, he grew unhappy with the Shakers. He was revolted by such displays as the "hugging gift," in which an individual "felt a gift" to be hugged and was soon the center of a group embrace—segregated, of course, by sex. He also faulted second elder Joseph Wicker for using his role as instrument to "entertain" the members during a mountain meeting with reports of extravagant visions, like some kind of spiritual mountebank. Wicker's personality dominated the meeting: "Grove Wright being a diffident man," he wrote, "the management of the meeting fell upon Joseph Wicker."⁴²

Significantly, Shaker sisters were primary instruments of Mother Ann's Work; young girls were the first affected by the spiritual manifestations, and women were the primary recipients of gift drawings and songs. The outpouring of emotion and creativity during the 1840s was reminiscent of the time of Mother Ann; it also occurred when women were beginning to dominate, in terms of population, in the Shaker community.⁴³

The era of Mother Ann's Work also reflected some of the disturbing changes and trends occurring in the larger world. There, the beginnings of industrial expansion were making material wealth a more common goal than spiritual fulfillment. In the Shaker society a new individualism was evident as ambitious individuals achieved power and authority through their roles as instruments. Conflict between instruments—touched as they apparently were by divine light—and the elders' temporal authority could therefore be devastating for the Society. At least one Hancock instrument clashed with the elders and consequently left the community.[44]

Also characteristic of the period was a desire for instant gratification, not waiting patiently for a remote future reward; this era was bursting with wild, exuberant displays of fulfillment in the here and now. Materialism also reared its head—the very things that were denied the Believers, such as gold and silver, fancy garments, jewels, and wine, were received and enjoyed in spiritual form. Although the period was exhilarating, and seemed to evoke the early days of the Society, it marked the end of the Shakers' forward momentum, perhaps partly because of this flirtation with worldly values. As if all its fireworks had been set off at once, the Society expended great spiritual energy and had little left afterward. From this point on its challenge would be not only to attract new members but also to hold onto those it had.

CHAPTER SEVEN

"This Hundred Fold Blessing"

While I am possessing this hundred fold blessing
The choicest of treasures that God can bestow
My life I'll be giving his cause be sustaining
And pray heaven help me their value to know.
—Enfield, 1886

Despite the tumult of Mother Ann's Work, the records and diaries of the 1830s and 1840s portray a serene agricultural community, the whiff of new-mown hay practically emanating from their pages. Problems may have lurked, but they did not yet ruffle the surface. The diarists recorded the Shaker year, from cracking butternuts and plucking turkeys in January, through planting potatoes and onions and plowing for oats in the spring, to blackberrying in August and making applesauce in the fall. The weather was a constant feature—droughts, with a diarist's mild "A little rain would be very acceptable," or the long, cold winters: "May 15, 1834. This morning the ground is covered about 4 inches deep. . . . The ground has been hard frozen for three nights past, leaves are killed on the trees, fear the fruit is lost though the trees are not full in blow."

Hancock in the 1840s was a "neat, orderly, and sober little village" of six families. In May 1846, Grove Wright noted, "The season uncommonly forward, appletrees look considerable green, and begin to show the red buds for blossoming; grass is up a pretty good bite." The budding fruit trees were a particular source of pride. Hancock was improving its orchard at the time; having procured from the Groveland, New York, Shakers the promising new variety of apple tree called Northern Spy, they set them out on the west side of the meetinghouse yard and planted thirty more apple trees from Enfield. Comments about daily work, visits, the farming schedule, the sleighing conditions, and changes in leadership were occasionally interspersed with homely sayings: "A man can show his religion as much in measuring onions as he can in singing Glory Hallelujah."[1]

Much of Elder Grove's time was spent on the road, traveling between the three communities under his ministerial care. In a given two-month period he and the other elders would spend two or three weeks in Enfield and a week in Tyringham, during which time they would appoint or release elders and trustees or help raise buildings. In the early years they traveled by carriage or sleigh—snow conditions were a great preoccupation of the elders' diaries—and in 1850 a barn was built just for the Ministry's hard-working horses. Later, the train would make travel between Hancock and Enfield easy and efficient. According to Thomas Damon, who became a ministry elder in 1846, one could leave Enfield by the morning train from Springfield and arrive at Hancock by eleven A.M. Damon became particularly adept at getting around on "the cars," sometimes traveling to Albany, New York City, Enfield, and back to Hancock in just two days.[2]

Julia Johnson of Tyringham described life in that society's North Family during the 1830s and 1840s. There were thirty members then, eight sisters sleeping to a room in the gambrel-roofed dwelling house, except for the two eldresses, who roomed together. Two long tables in the dining room seated the men and women separately. The dairy house was a general sisters' shop with a weave room and a cheese room downstairs. Upstairs, the north chamber was the spinning room; the south chamber, a sewing room.[3]

The brethren, meanwhile, slept in the upper story of "the red shop," situated across the road on the stream. In addition to farming, doctoring, carpentering, and wagon making, the brethren manufactured ox yokes, ax helves, and rakes.

Johnson said the North Family women would rise in pitch dark at 4:00 A.M. on a winter's morning and wade through the snow drifts to reach the dairy, where the spinning room was a snug center for sisters of all ages. "I have seen a ninety-year-old woman sit in a rocking chair spinning," she recalled, "with a tiny six-year-old tot on the platform beside her, also spinning. Eight to ten would spin at a time. The stints were two 'runs' a day for wool and one 'run' for tow."

The Tyringham Shakers raised their own flax, spun their linens and wool, and wove a range of products, including flannel and linen for the Society's clothing, herb and seed bags, and chair tapes. Rushes were woven on cotton warp to make carpets. When the weather was simply too severe, the women would remain at home and dip tallow candles, producing a year's supply of a hundred dozen in two or three days. "We were always busy," wrote Lucinda Day (who lived at the Church Family from 1843, when she was thirteen, until 1861 or 1862), "cooking, washing, ironing, milking, making butter, cheese, doing all the sewing, besides the knitting of our stockings and sox."

The Church Family had between seventy-five and one hundred members in the 1840s, according to Day. "The sisters did all kinds of house work," she remembered later, "made most of their wearing apparel, spinning the flax for the linen cloth and the wool for winter wear. They made many kinds of fancy work, like mats and cushions, for sale." The brethren, meanwhile, "carried on all kinds of mechanical business, worked the big farms, did cooper work of all kinds and carried on the broom trade." She said the Tyringham Shakers had a lucrative business in raising and drying sweet corn, with both brothers and sisters involved in that industry.[4]

The sisters were divided into two groups, one for cooking and the other for chamber work and washing. Two women and a little girl formed the regular kitchen force, the children changing every four weeks. The community was eating well by now—on the shelves in the little cheese house might be fifty or sixty cheeses curing for two or three years, and in the cellar were apples, root vegetables, and cider. The sisters on washing duty did their chores in the morning, Johnson said, and then were free for the rest of the day. She remembered berry picking, picnicking, and riding up to Hancock on horseback with fifteen or sixteen sisters to attend Sunday service.

One fine portrait of Tyringham during this period was left by Brother Daniel Myrick, visiting from the Harvard Society of Believers in 1846. The brethren's industry particularly caught his eye, as he noted the sawmill near the South House processing "not small" logs of ash, oak, rock maple, and walnut. Like every visitor to Tyringham, he commented on the "great primitive" maple trees—"stately towering and majestic trees . . . by far the largest I ever saw . . . entirely clear of underbrush"—and the sugar houses and furnaces. The North Family was building a new stone dam on the west, or upper, side of the road, just opposite the brethren's shop.[5]

With a party of brethren and sisters Myrick ascended Mount Horeb to see the holy ground, located not on the exact top of the mountain but on its western slope. "The mountain and the scenery around it has more of that wild grandeur which in my [mind] I have ascribed to Horeb in the east." From the mountaintop, Myrick claimed, one could see in the distance Hancock's Mount Sinai and New Lebanon's Holy Mount.

Myrick inspected the Shaker school, located between the Church Family and the South House. "Here is the most pains taken to attract children to their lessons of any similar place I have yet seen," the writer observed, "and gives demonstration of an admirable and devoted teacher." He was probably describing Sister Desire Holt, the teacher of the girls. David Lamson visited Tyringham around the same time and complained that the boys' teacher was "poor"; he had broken his leg, according to Lamson, and he was teaching only because he could do no other work.[6]

Holt had been in ill health and originally came from Connecticut to be nursed by Christiana Herrick, who had studied medicine with her father, Dr. Henry Herrick, possibly in order to treat the Shaker sisters. Sister Desire had a tumor of some sort, which was successfully treated in 1847 by an electromagnetic machine. Judging by initials stenciled over hooks in an upstairs closet in the Church Family dwelling, she may have lived at mid-century with three other sisters, possibly including Lucinda Day and Harriet Storer, in a women's dormitory.[7]

The main goal of the Shaker school was to produce faithful Believers to strengthen the community. The Tyringham society, however, may have been better at producing strong leaders than faithful followers. For such a small community they were rich in leaders; Grove Wright was only the most prominent example. Others were Eldresses Lucinda Stanley and Mollie Herrick, both daughters of original Shakers; Eldresses Wealthy and Harriet Storer; and Elders Daniel Fay of the Church Family and Calvin Parker of the North Family. Hasting Storer was second elder and head farmer for the Church Family and an able businessman. Michael McCue (or McKeough), born in Canada and indentured as a boy, was an especially successful salesman for Shaker products.

Another outstanding leader was Albert Justus Battles (or Battle), born in Tyringham in 1809, the illegitimate son of the widow Katharine Johnson and perhaps one Lieutenant Justus Battle. He may have worked as a patternmaker at the Richmond Iron Works; he was also known as a furniture maker. Battles was Elder Brother at the Tyringham Church Family for thirty-one years, from 1844 to 1875. He saw the Family through the disruption of 1858; he saw Tyringham close. He succeeded Thomas Damon as Ministry elder, holding that position until 1893, when the Hancock Bishopric was abolished.[8]

Richard Van Deusen was yet another example. Born in Tyringham in 1829, he had lived with the Shakers from the age of seven. David Lamson met Brother Richard when the boy was about sixteen, and sarcastically called him a "good believer"—because due to inadequate education he was "prejudiced against knowledge" and "obedient to his lead."[9] Van Deusen served as caretaker of the boys until 1851, when he became second elder at the North Family, assisting Calvin Parker. Seven years later he became first elder; but when the North and Church families were consolidated in 1862, he was appointed trustee. When Tyringham's North Family was sold in 1867, he went to the Enfield Church Family and eventually became deacon at the North Family.

Brother Daniel Myrick visited Enfield as well as Tyringham and again left a fine description of that community at midcentury. He described going from the Church Family to the North and East families, passing the holy ground, the Mount of Olives. On the way he stopped at the cider mill— "a grate mill driven by an endless chain 2 horse power. The pomace drops directly into the rack and is pressed by 2 iron screwes." He noted the large orchard and fine vineyards and cornfields. Arriving at the North Family, he observed that "the Church and this family appears more like the palaces of princes than the habitations of the humble children of hated and abused but blessed Mother Ann." And he said the buildings of the entire community were "beautiful, substantial and commodious supplied with every convenience that could be desired to soften the toil and lessen the trials of terestial life." He was impressed by the stone walks, some of which contained individual stones 9 feet by 3½ feet, and by the aqueducts "holding out water at every corner for the laborer's hands and his mouth."

The East Family, across the fields from the Mount of Olives, was, Myrick declared, "situated on the best land I have seen they keep two large yoke of working cattle and said they cut 15 tons of rowen and had one barn completely filled with grain." He passed the graveyard, which he described as "small and nearly filled" already.

The traveler visited the carding mill and gristmill. Brother George Wilcox—then second elder in the Church Family, assisting aged Elder Asa Tiffany—accompanied Myrick to the West Family, a branch of the gathering order. Harvey Lyman was the deacon there and Philip Burlingame and Hawley Kellogg the elders. Myrick viewed the carding mill and the sawmill, which he called "well contrived," embracing "most of the improvements of the best mills." At one point on the tour Brother George stopped to pull a tooth.

Myrick approvingly noted a barn full of unthreshed rye, which he estimated would yield four hundred bushels of grain. A new seed house and a boys' dwelling were under construction, both with brick-paved basements. He also commented on an apple slicer, "a curious laborsaving machine—it would slice apples enough for a pie as quick as one can be done by hand." In the dairy, he said, "they have finer cheese than I ever saw in any market city or country. Saw the little girls in their apartments knitting in hand which they laid by and repeated some pretty pieces which they had committed." As the group departed, Myrick noted that the land in the area was rich and easy to work and yielded abundant crops.

In an increasingly alien world Myrick, like other traveling Shakers, recognized kindred souls and found comfort in the familiar customs and routines. "All these gifts and operations were so similar to what I have so often seen in our little vineyard," he remarked, "that they no longer seemed like strangers."

Carsondana Benton's diary also records—from the inside—the peace and productivity at Enfield at the time. Life at that community was particularly comfortable; the village was prospering on its broad, fertile plain. Sister Carsondana described "new potatoes, beets and squash for dinner"; other entries mention meals featuring strawberries (strawberry shortcake for breakfast in June), black cherries, green peas, quahogs, shadberries, new potatoes, pigeons, chestnuts, and whortleberries. Throughout her teens she worked at various activities, putting up seeds in the new seed house after 1847, spinning wool, picking quinces for sauce, picking up wood chips.[10]

Like other diarists, Carsondana faithfully recorded the comings and goings, changes of leadership, and deaths in the order. She often noted the rising number of world's people attending meeting: "90 in the Church. Encouraging," she commented in September 1848. Sister Dana Brewster, who was soon to become first eldress in the Ministry, visited now and then, "assembled the young sisters in the chamber and puzzled their brains most wonderfully."

Yet her diary also reveals a change in mood. Few comments of a spiritual nature are made, compared with the earlier writings of Daniel Goodrich, Sr., and Calvin Ely. By 1848, Carsondana Benton's religious fervor seemed to be on the wane; the exclamation points in her diary are reserved for such entries as "Extraordinary season for whirtleberries!!!" or "Elder Elisha built a new cheese tub!!!" or a particularly lovely sunset. In her lively way she describes a scene where the young sisters "took a circuit round the square without a man and boy to drive they were in high glee." By the 1840s diarists often looked outside the community and mused on the events of the world, particularly catastrophes such as a fire in Pittsfield or the earthquake of 1843 in Guadeloupe. Sister Carsondana commented on the "Fammine in Ireland. Complete starvation" and on the twenty beggars at the Church on Christmas Day.[11]

In addition, relations between the sexes seemed to have softened, judging by the numerous relationships that developed between the 1830s and the 1850s. Tyringham sister Julia Johnson had a love affair with a young Shaker brother named Michael, according to Tyringham historian John Scott. The elders sent Julia to Hancock for a "love cure," and while she was there, Michael died. Lucinda Day left the society after eighteen or nineteen years to marry William T. Hall, who had lived with the Shakers from age eight to eighteen.[12]

When young people came of age and chose to depart from the Society, some took with them a highly developed moral sense in addition to the values of community and hard work. Hannah Pease and Jedediah Dudley apparently developed a warm relationship in the Enfield community before they separately left. After he went west to Durham, New York, where he worked as a patternmaker at an ironworks, Jedediah wrote Hannah, praising her "purity of mind" and "sincerity of soul," qualities he seemed to value more as he became acquainted with the world. Hannah, meanwhile, wrote back loving, lighthearted letters, continuing to wait for him despite several other offers of marriage. Hannah and Jedediah did eventually marry, moved to Greene County, New York, and had one daughter before Hannah died in 1851.[13]

The newspapers took particular pleasure in romances among the Shakers, judging by an interchange in *The Pittsfield Sun* in 1837. First a notice announced the marriage of Justus Brewer to Permelia Fuller, "both of the Pittsfield and Hancock Shaker Society . . . [where] Mr. B. was a Trustee." The correspondent then gloated, "So we sometimes see that even the callous and frigid heart of the Shaker is not always impervious to the keen darts of Cupid. May all the rest of our Shaker friends, who remain in a 'single state of blessedness,' take a salutary hint from the above, and pay their homage to the altar of Hymen; and learn the important truth before it is too late, that eternal celibacy was never intended by the Creator, for a world constituted like ours; for 'male and female created he them.'"[14]

This poke earned an angry retort from the Shakers two weeks later. They denied that anyone, particularly the correspondent, could know what the Creator intended; hence, the Shakers used Christ as a model. Furthermore, Brewer had never been a trustee, the letter stated, because the Shakers "never reposed confidence enough in him to put him in such an office." Justus Brewer may have been Justus Brewster, Jr., brother of Cassandana Brewster and son of Justus Brewster of Pittsford, Vermont. That name appears on a *Catalogue of Garden Seeds, Raised and Sold by the United Society, Pittsfield, Berkshire County, Mass.* in 1836, indicating that Brewster had been a traveling seedsman.[15]

The Shaker letter in turn generated a sarcastic response from the correspondent, revealing a lingering hostility to Shaker celibacy and dance. Linked to this comment was a notice announcing the marriage of two more members of the Pittsfield/Hancock Shaker Society: Asa Patten to Almira Fuller, probably Permelia's sister. "Cupid, it seems," wrote the correspondent, "has again been playing his pranks among the Shakers and meets with very flattering encouragement. The good work goes successfully on, and will, the doctrines of Ann Lee to the contrary not withstanding." The Shakers answered one more time, and this time included a history of celibacy. That was the end of the altercation, although two weeks later the *Sun* published Catherine Sedgwick's "A Shaker Bridal" without further comment.

Despite Shaker defensiveness, every departure left a touch of melancholy. Thomas Damon wrote, in April 1848, that "on going into the washroom a few days ago one of the sisters who was to work there alone, mentioned to me what a lonesome feeling she had come across her that afternoon, and remarked that if all the folks were only here that had gone away in all these years it no need to be so, as she could then have help and company enough."[16]

At Enfield the three families had become five, and the community now reached its peak in population. According to census figures gathered by Priscilla J. Brewer, Enfield went from 79 males and 96 females in 1840 to 104 males and 106 females in 1850. The vigorous growth, however, is deceptive, as Brewer has pointed out: twenty-seven of those males in 1850 were children under the age of sixteen, and twenty-six more were over sixty, jeopardizing the future strength of the community. Those twenty-six aging brethren bore the names of the original families who had joined en masse—Terry, Tiffany, Wood, Slate, and Allen. Twenty-two of the males were between sixteen and twenty-nine years old and particularly vulnerable to the temptations of the world: by 1860 the population of men would be more than cut in half.[17]

Nevertheless, new members continued to arrive. In October 1840 the remarkable Lyman family, several generations of whom would play parts in Shaker history, came to the Enfield Society from South Hadley, Massachusetts. The patriarch, Israel Lyman, was a farmer; born in 1776, he was the son of the ferry keeper on the Connecticut River between Springfield and Hockanum, near South Hadley. At age twenty-five he married Sarah (Sally) Moody, with whom he had eleven children, two of whom died in infancy.[18]

In 1818, Lyman built a big brick house on his hundred-acre farm near Rock Ferry. The couple's six sons and three daughters grew up in this house, which was always full of friends and sometimes, since Lyman was clearly a spiritual seeker, missionaries. He was said to have entertained the Mormons there during the early 1830s, but a description of the group sounds more like the Shakers, who were proselytizing in South Hadley at the time:

> The large room, on week days a kitchen, was now arranged with rows of chairs on three sides, leaving a large space vacant in the center. . . . There was the brooding stillness of a Quaker meeting. At last [a] woman arose, stepped into the vacant space and began a solemn march. Others joined in the silent promenade around the floor until all who felt moved to take part had done so. Then the men and women formed lines facing one another, and in Shaker style began a shuffling dance toward each other, singing, under lead of the large woman's clear and powerful voice, strange psalms to stirring tunes. Gradually the dance grew faster, forward and then back again, and the singing louder, until those who came to look on were drawn by the exciting scenes to join this strange people, and dance and sing."[19]

Israel and Sally Lyman converted to Shakerism in 1835, and the following year Israel died. Her daughters and three older sons having married, Sally Lyman joined the Enfield Shakers in April 1837 with her three younger sons, Harvey, age twenty-two; Elijah, fourteen; and Edward Mason, eleven; along with ten-year-old Hannah Quance, who lived with them (see Lyman family tree in Appendix III). Later Sally would have her husband's body removed from the burial ground in South Hadley and reinterred in the Enfield Shaker cemetery.

In 1840, Sally's third son, Almon, and his wife, the former Clarissa Burnett, moved to the Enfield West Family with their three children, Sarah Maria, nine; Alden Burnett, five; and Clarissa Kezia, three. Sally Lyman's eldest son, Alonzo, died in September of that year, and two years later, his widow placed four of their children with the Shakers: Eli Dyer, thirteen; Harriet Amelia, eleven; Seth Alonzo, eight; and Edward Israel, three and a half, placing them in the guardianship of their uncle Harvey.[20]

Almon, Clarissa, Harvey, and Edward Mason Lyman all affixed their names to the Sacred Roll in 1843. Five members of the third generation—Amelia, Seth, Maria, Edward Israel, and Kezia—signed the covenant between 1852 and 1860 after their twenty-first birthdays.

Many members of the Lyman family would play important roles in the history of the Enfield Shakers. Clarissa was eldress in the South Family from 1874 till her death in 1897. Maria, Clarissa's eldest daughter, was a trustee of the North Family and also ran its productive cheese house. She left an indelible mark on Shaker history through her tart, succinct diaries and was among the Shakers still living in 1917 when the community closed. Amelia, Maria's cousin, was deaconess and office sister. Seth Lyman worked as a printer at the Church Family until he died of consumption at a young age. Alden B. Lyman, Clarissa's son, though very lame from scarlet fever suffered at the age of two, was a beloved, productive member of the community until its declining years.

Yet the family also included some notable apostates. The three brothers, Harvey, Elijah, and Edward Mason, the first to come with their mother to Enfield, all left in disgrace. Harvey was not only the children's guardian; he was also a trustee and then first elder at the South Family until his abrupt and sensational departure in 1854. Elijah and Edward Mason had already left the Shakers and in 1855 were arrested for forgery and theft of garden seeds from the Enfield Church Family. Edward M. Lyman had become a seedsman in Springfield by the 1860s and by 1873 had at least one employee.[21]

Kezia Lyman (born in 1837), Clarissa's youngest daughter, came to Enfield at the age of three. She grew up surrounded by her siblings and cousins in the serene environment of the Shaker Church Family, gathering gooseberries and chestnuts with the other young sisters, attending an occasional "improving" lecture in Springfield or Hartford, taking her turn in the kitchen with her cousin Amelia, weaving rugs, dressing turkeys for the market, making currant wine with her sister Maria. At eighteen she slept in the chamber of the dwelling house with Lydia McIntyre and one other sister. By the time she was twenty she was in charge of the school, which, for the girls, operated from May to September. At twenty-two she signed the covenant.[22]

In June 1857, Kezia awakened to discover the empty bed of her roommate, Sister Lydia. At one thirty that morning Lydia and Carsondana Benton had slipped out of the community and fled to Hartford. It must have been a searing experience for the young woman, left to ponder the reasons prompting her friends' flight and possibly torn in her own mind between the spiritual commitment of her mother, sister, and cousins and the urge for freedom expressed by so many of her male relatives.

Nine years later, at the age of twenty-nine, Kezia herself left the community under much more difficult circumstances. She was seven months pregnant with the child of twenty-five-year-old John William Richmond Copley, who had also grown up in the community and who had departed the previous day. The couple went to Springfield, probably to Kezia's uncle, Harvey Lyman, by then a prospering grocer. A week after their departure from the Shakers, on November 8, 1866, they married. It is impossible to know what Kezia Lyman's feelings were during that week, whether she was terrified and anguished or happy and excited to be with the man she loved. The couple went to Long Island, New York, where they had the first of their five children the following January. The family's life would continue to be interwoven with that of the Shakers at Enfield.[23]

In September 1845, Grove Wright noted in his diary that the Ministry "moved our lodgings out to the shop, in order to take care of Elder Nathaniel, in his last sickness." Elder Nathaniel died of cancer on November 10, ending a remarkable tenure that had spanned nearly fifty years. Old enough to remember Mother Ann, he had steered the Hancock Bishopric from the lean early days to a time of great prosperity. Grove Wright was named his successor.

Within weeks after Deming's death the Ministry, consisting of Elder Grove, Eldress Cassandana Goodrich, Sister Cassandana Brewster, and Sister Clarissa Hawkins, went to Enfield with the express purpose of choosing a certain young brother to become a Ministry elder. On Christmas Day, after a vigorous meeting, twenty-six-year-old Thomas Damon was asked to move to Hancock and live with Elder Grove in the Ministry, the change to take effect on the first of January following. After he agreed, the Ministry announced the appointment to the family, and in January 1846, Thomas Damon moved to Hancock. One of his first acts was to record in his journal the names of the elders and the number of members in each of the three societies. In 1846, Hancock had 217 members in six families; Enfield had 206 members in five families; and Tyringham had 97 members in two families.[24]

During the 1840s, Damon engaged in a lively correspondence with George Wilcox. The two had arrived at Enfield as young boys, had grown up together in the Church Family, learned their excellent woodworking skills at the knee of the same master carpenter (probably Abner Allen), signed the covenant on the same day, and had been tapped for important leadership positions while still in their twenties (Wilcox became an elder in the Enfield Church Family). Brother Thomas's letters to Brother George scarcely a year after his appointment to the Ministry reveal much about his personality—his deep devotion to the Shaker philosophy; his playful wit, which found expression in communication with his old friend; and his early attempts at preaching, practiced in the safety of letters before being aired in public. One letter commiserates with Wilcox for an unusual burden of work, adding a typical note regarding the short time left in this world:

> The feeble health of your and my beloved Elder Brother [Enfield's Asa Tiffany] is grievous, and I desire with all my heart that he may recover his usual health. His inability throws an additional burthen upon your shoulders, which where already bowed with care and watching. But let us be encouraged, Time passes swiftly away, and in a few more days if we continue faithful we shall be called from our toil and labor to an inheritance with all them who are sanctified. The aged Father and Mother are going on before us. What a solemn thought, but how blessed. Their carriage is ready first, but we shall soon follow.[25]

Sometimes the two would exchange woodworking plans; more often the correspondence revolved around religion and philosophy. One letter preached on the theme of self-denial:

> When we rise in the morning it must be with the words "self-denial" upon our lips, and it must be our labor through the day to deny self. Remember we are but learners in the school of Christ; and that the first condition of discipleship is to "deny self." When this principle is placed as a check upon all the desires of the mind, and applied to all the windings of the human heart, then every thought is brought into subjec-tion to the monitor enthroned in every breast; then, and not till then, shall we behold life and animation where apathy and indifference now reign.[26]

Unlike Reuben Rathbun fifty years earlier, Damon could accept Shakerism not as a state of perfection, but as a condition of constant struggle and aspiration. The way to God was not easy among the Believers, he seemed to realize, merely easier.

Thomas Damon was well loved till the end of his life. He and Elder Grove Wright, whom he assisted in the Ministry, worked together on proj-ects ranging from whitewashing the meetinghouse to building a handsome bureau for their dwelling. He may have had a sweet tooth (one entry in his diary notes a year-long abstention from pies and cakes), and he was not immune to the charms of the opposite sex (one entry, in shorthand, described a visitor as "a very pretty woman.")[27]

Observant, curious, and creative, fascinated by the innovations of the industrial revolution, Damon was credited with the following inventions: "a lathe for turning iron, a device for planing and edging table swift slats, a machine for matching floor boards, as well as apparatus for washing seeds, and another for counting seed papers as they are printed." One traveler visited his shop in 1869 and left the following description:

> We found Elder Thomas Damon to be a universal genious and Mechanic his shop bore marks of this unmistakeable character throughout. He has built an ingenious turning lathe for turning Iron, which is a most complete specimen of workmanship, and has constructed machinery for cutting out and dressing up the various parts of the kind of swifts that are screwed to a table for use, which does the business most completely. He is the inventor of these swifts and manufactures them by the wholesale at 50 cts per pair, and was at this time filling an order for 20,000 pair at that rate. Several of the Sisters were aiding in this Job, at such parts as they could perform, which were not a few.[28]

Despite the serendipitous choice of Damon as Ministry elder, the Society of Believers was perceptibly changing in the period following Mother Ann's Work. Although Shaker industries were at their peak of creativity, and all of the communities were thriving in a monetary sense, certain ominous, undeniable problems had surfaced, perhaps as a sign of the Society's middle age. In 1849 the Hancock South Family closed, lacking sufficient members to continue. The surging excitement, fervor, and optimism of the early 1840s was yielding, in all three communities of the Hancock Bishopric, to a quieter, more introspective, perhaps more fatalistic attitude about the future. A more intellectual approach to religion developed, exemplified most prominently by Elder Frederick Evans of New Lebanon but also by Thomas Damon.

It may have been that the Era of Manifestations went too far, turning the heart of the Society inside out. The 1840s were a watershed in regard to retention of male members. Perhaps the gifts so prevalent in the previous decade, while delighting the more naive members, had strained the credulity and faith of some of the very Shakers who were most needed—potential leaders. Certainly, the world had changed, as had the people growing up in it, and presented a more seductive invitation than ever before. At any rate, true to the warnings of the census reports of the 1830s, it was becoming difficult to find elders.

Elders—strong, charismatic leaders who could inspire and serve as role models for wavering members—were the single most important element in the Shaker Society, more important than numbers of converts or amount of income. This was never truer than at this time, when the Society was still reverberating from the upheavals of Mother Ann's Work and the second generation of American leaders was passing on. Changes in the eldership began to come more quickly now. And when elders departed to marry one another, it was no wonder that the community began to drift.

The Ministry attempted to patch things together, placing the most talented and trusted members in the eldership at the expense of the trusteeship. After releasing elderly William Deming from his position as Elder Brother in the Hancock Church Family, for example, Grove Wright appointed Joseph Wicker to succeed him, with Isaac Augur as helper. It was hard to spare Isaac at the office, Wright commented, where he had exhibited great skill and judgment, "but we thought it was of the first importance to have the Eldership well supplied with suitable members, and then supply other lots as well as can be made out." Joseph Patten and William Augur, Isaac's older brother, remained at the office. Ultimately, the weakness of the trusteeship would cause new problems.[29]

Nathaniel and William Deming were not the only venerable leaders who retired or passed away in the 1840s. Their contemporary, Ministry eldress Cassandana (Dana) Goodrich, also of the second generation of Shakers who had met Mother Ann in their teens, died in 1848 after decades of ill health. Thomas Damon's first trip to Tyringham as Ministry elder, in February 1846, was also Eldress Dana's last. She was exhausted by the journey, Damon reported, and could not speak for some time after she arrived in her room in the meetinghouse. Because of her condition the elders appointed Sister Wealthy Storer of Tyringham to the Ministry, with Clarissa Hawkins, so that two eldresses would be actively serving. By May, Eldress Dana was "blind and feeble" but retained sharp memory and sound judgment, and unlike most Ministry elders, she never requested to be released from her lot. By 1848, however, Grove Wright recorded, "Mother appears to be rather more feable and she thinks herself that she is failing, & shall not live long, which is verry unusual for her. And we think it doubtful wheather she continues thru the month of May."[30]

Like most Shaker leaders, Eldress Dana was enveloped in love in her last days, with sisters tending her at all times, visitors coming to pay their last respects, elders consulting with her about the future, and according to instruments, the spirits of departed elders hovering over her and protecting her. She stubbornly held on for months but finally died on June 1, 1848; according to an inspired sister who witnessed her death, Mother Ann "took her into her arms and wafted her spirit to a Mansion of rest." Sister Cassandana Brewster, who had named herself after Eldress Dana, succeeded her as first in the Ministry, and the elders and eldresses moved back to the meetinghouse after a three-year absence.[31]

"Labor to be peacemakers," Eldress Dana Goodrich once said,

strive to make each other happy, and not do or say anything but what is true. And don't tell everything you hear. You may not always hear the truth. And more than this, it may hurt the feelings of some needlessly. If you see anything wrong go to your Elders, and tell them the truth, and let it rest there don't be talking it around in the family, and from house to house.

. . . You all ought to bear in mind that your calling is holy, and you are called to keep your union pure and holy between brothers and sisters; at no time say or do anything to cause or excite any wrong feelings or sensations on either side. It is not one without the other that will mar this pure and heavenly union.[32]

Sally Lyman, matriarch of the Lyman clan, also died that spring, at age sixty-two of typhus fever, probably caught from a prospective member she was nursing at Enfield's South Family. Grove Wright called the news of her death "heavy tiding, verry heavy indeed." "She was a verry worthy woman," he wrote, "& one in which was placed the fullest confidence, and one who possessed excelent qualifications, & was able to fill almost any station."[33]

For most Believers, life in the various communities settled into quiet patterns of work and worship in the late 1840s. Individual Shakers were still unaware of the steady loss of members, noticing instead the positive developments such as new buildings going up and some key converts coming into the Society. The signs of decline would have been subtle—workshops vacant, beds empty, chairs and then entire tables unused at meals, farther fields growing up to brush. The villages were probably quieter as well, with fewer sisters and brethren bustling around on chores or errands, less uproar of industry, fewer shipments and deliveries. Yet there remained plenty of children and visitors.

The new buildings at Tyringham and Enfield were, for the most part, utilitarian. The Tyringham Church Family put up its last major building, its imposing seed house, in 1854; it towered, five stories high above a full stone basement, over the other buildings of the village. In Enfield the Church Family erected a machine shop, a brick washhouse, a sawmill, a cow and ox barn with sheds, and a wood house; the North Family put up a brick office, a "large and commodious" horse barn, "both covered with slate—the rest of their buildings are mostly covered with Tin"—and a shed; and the South Family built a dwelling house, a wood house, a cow barn, a large washhouse, and miscellaneous sheds. In 1852 the North Family moved a blacksmith shop to build its office. These were obvious signs that a productive farm was bursting beyond its capacity. Only one of the fourteen buildings erected at Enfield during this decade was a dwelling house, the second dwelling of the South Family (1852); and two years later that family would need the extra accommodations when the West Family merged with it. The North Family, wrote one visitor in 1854, had about fifty members and "has appearance of wealth," feasting guests on "love, good dinner and Melons with sugar sprinkled on them."[34]

At Hancock, the brethren raised a horse barn on June 5, 1850, moving the old wagon house to the north side of the road next to it; later this barn would house the Ministry carriage horses. In May 1852 a crew of brethren took the chimneys off the old office in order to raise an addition, extending the building about thirty-five feet to the south, the first of several distinctive changes in that building. In 1854, Brother Thomas Damon wrote: "Our large stone barn 147 long and 50 wide is going up gradually, we expected to cover it with Warren and Company gravel and . . . cement. The Artesian well is also going on, they have just commenced on the 4 hundred feet." The following year Brother Thomas set a Shaker-developed muscadine grapevine at the south end of the Hancock wood house and set out four other grapevines in the horse yard north of the meetinghouse yard.[35]

Other changes were made for convenience. In the summer of 1852 Elders Grove and Thomas built a stone-posted horse fence fronting the meeting-house. In 1854 the remains of Father Calvin Harlow and Mother Sarah Harrison were taken from the old burying ground near the West Family and interred in the present ground. "After fifty-eight to sixty years," noted Thomas Damon, "the coffins were well preserved."[36]

Until about 1850 there had been two Ministry shops at Hancock, one for the elders and one for the eldresses, situated just east of the meetinghouse. After 1850 the elders' shop was used by both sexes, and the eldresses' shop was moved across the road to become a garden seed house for the ever-expanding seed industry. The Hancock Ministry used the elders' shop until the Ministry was dissolved on June 18, 1893, and thereafter it was used by the New Lebanon Ministry of Joseph Holden, Harriet Bullard, and Augusta Stone.[37]

Other modernizing went on at the end of the decade. The community still depended for its power on the stream turning the large overshot waterwheel located in the basement of the machine shop. This now met increasingly complex needs, not just the heavy mill work and laundry but the power needs of the stables and barns as well. In 1858, Thomas Damon wrote that he had "sent to J. R. Clarke of Cohoes for plans and drawings of this improved turbine to take the place of the 20 foot overshot wheel at the Church Hancock agreeing to give him $15.00 for the same." During the next two years the waterpower system was overhauled, with the addition of water turbines, new pipes, a shaft, and bearings.

Most Americans at midcentury were avid consumers of wood; consequently, the old-growth forest was gone by this time throughout Berkshire County, and the area was farmed to the mountaintops. Even when coal came into use, wood was still the first choice for heating, and fifteen cords were burned every year by an average household. Wood was also used for building, forging iron, making charcoal, tanning hides, powering locomotives, and many other purposes. The Shakers had particular needs, with their substantial, solidly constructed buildings, their thriving furniture and woodenware industry, and their use of quantities of stove wood in chambers, shops, and meeting rooms. Most commonly, local white pine and maple were used, but cherry, yellow birch, butternut, and walnut also were used for both construction and cabinet work by brethren of the Hancock Bishopric.[38]

Harvesting the woods was a major part of the brethren's wintertime chores, skidding logs from the swamps and woodlots for next winter's stove wood and for spring building projects. Sometimes they would construct chutes to slide great logs down mountainsides. According to Grove Wright, the Tyringham Shakers were already going far afield—to Great Barrington and New Marlborough—for wood by 1814. That February the brethren sent seven teams to a place called Muddy Brook to get white oak logs, possibly for use in constructing their horse barn later that spring.

An illustrious group of visitors to Hancock in August 1851 included Nathaniel Hawthorne, Herman Melville, and Evert Duyckinck, editor of the New York magazine *Literary World*. With his unflattering description of the community in *American Notebooks,* Hawthorne joins the company of writers (including Charles Dickens and E. M. Forster) who visited the Shakers and, based on a cursory impression, soundly criticized them. Hawthorne's description reveals his ambivalence about the Society; as a young man he had considered joining.

The group was shown by "an old man in a gown and a gray, broad-brimmed hat" into the brick dwelling:

It was a large brick edifice, with admirably convenient arrangements, and floors and walls of polished wood, and plaster as smooth as marble, and everything so neat that it was a pain and constraint to look at it; especially as it did not imply any real delicacy or moral purity in the occupants of the house. There were spit-boxes (bearing no appearance of ever being used, it is true) at equal distances up and down the long and broad entries. The sleeping apartments of the two sexes had an entry between them, on one side of which hung the hats of the men, on the other the bonnets of the women. In each chamber were two particularly narrow beds, hardly wide enough for one sleeper, but in each of which, the old elder told us, two people slept. There were no bathing or washing conveniences in the chambers; but in the entry there was a sink and wash-bowl, where all their attempts at purification were to be performed. The fact shows that all their miserable presence of cleanliness and neatness is the thinnest superficiality; and that the Shakers are and must needs be a filthy set. And then their utter and systematic lack of privacy; the close function of man with man, and supervision of one man over another—it is hateful and disgusting to think of; and the sooner the sect is extinct the better—a consummation which, I am happy to hear, is thought to be not a great many years distant.[39]

One can sense Hawthorne's intense emotional reaction to the Shakers underlying his criticism of them. The neatness was "a pain and constraint" to view; yet a few sentences later he claims their reputed cleanliness is merely superficial. Neat, indeed; lacking privacy, certainly; but one cannot conclude from the facts in this description that the Shakers "must needs be a filthy sect." The animosity in his account must have been aroused during earlier experiences, perhaps involving an internal struggle over whether or not to join, at other societies.

In contrast, Duyckinck's account of the same visit is much less emotionally charged:

We met them in their carefully groomed fields and at the Hancock settlement met again old Father Hilliard and trod the neat quiet avenues whose stillness might be felt. Here is the great circular barn where the winter cattle feed with their heads all to a huge hay mow in the centre. I . . . induced venerable Father H. to open to us the big house. Its oiled and polished pine floors were elegant in spite of Shakerdom. The glazed finish of the white walls were as pure as yesterday's work, though they have been there these twenty years. Among these marks of neatness was a small funnel and pipe to carry off the smoke of each lamp to the chimney. A tall old clock stood in the hall but some gay flowers on its face had been covered with white paint. You see no flowers in the sisters' rooms but a volume of unreadable theology (of its kind) with a pair of crossed spectacles by its side on a small table.[40]

The Shakers were people of their age, not only in their own ingenuity and inventiveness but also in their fascination with new machines and processes. They were always among the first to try new devices, often tinkering with them and perfecting them in their own workshops. Eldress Betsy Smith from South Union, Kentucky, was particularly impressed with the washhouse at Enfield's South Family in 1854:

They carry on their washing by steam.—Have their Tubs made something like a flaring trough 10 or 12 feet long by 20 inches deep with a partition lengthwise, and again subdivided into square boxes. It is all raised about 2½ feet from the floor. Here is also a wringing Machine that flirts the water out of the clothes, by running around at the velocity of 300 revolutions in a minute. They boil their clothes ring, and wash them all by steam engine of 5 horse power. Cost of which was for the Engine 130 dollars—for the Boiler 150. Total $280.[41]

In 1853, Thomas Damon manufactured 972 swifts, and the following year he "started a new machine for planing and edging swift slats—It worked charmingly and bid fair to be the 'Ne plus ultra' in that line." Damon was continually investigating the latest inventions; he may have procured the steam apparatus for the Enfield South Family after examining a similar one at the Deaf and Dumb Asylum in Hartford in 1853. He often went to the booming industrial towns of Holyoke, Chicopee, Springfield, and Brattle-boro to examine a new herb press or a matching machine and weigh whether it would serve the Believers' needs.[42]

In January 1854 a sewing machine arrived and proved so successful that Damon took a few courses in "sewing by machinery." His diary records his trip to buy three more machines, two for Hancock and one for Enfield. We can picture him in his broad-brimmed hat and frock coat, looking all around New York City for a certain company called Wheeler and Wilson. When he finally found it, he learned that the boss had left for Bridgeport, Connecticut, the previous day. The persistent Thomas went to Bridgeport and managed to purchase the machines. He then took the six-thirty train to Thompsonville and walked out to Enfield in the rain and mud with a borrowed lantern. He reached the shop around midnight and ransacked the orchard for apples to eat. After creeping in a window he bedded down till morning, "being pretty well jagged with my week's perambulating" and undoubtedly rather pleased with himself. The machines arrived a week later, to the sisters' great delight.[43]

Though the farming life was no less arduous for the Shakers than for others in New England at the time, at least it wasn't lonely: there was plenty of companionship to enjoy while working. One record chronicles the daily life of a farmer at the Enfield community, a typical day consisting of the following activities: "May 3, 1852. Elijah, John, and I worked in the nursery. Seth and Alfred plowed the potato ground. Henry and Andrew finished plowing the corn stalk ground in the forenoon. Marcus dragged the early potato ground. In the afternoon a strong company took hold and planted the early potatoes."[44]

In the 1850s the Enfield Church Family owned ten oxen, twenty milk cows, 21 young cows, 95 sheep, six horses, and 150 hens. The oxen were employed year round for clearing and plowing fields; dragging timber, fire-wood, hay, and dung; and drawing heavy loads needed by the family for any purpose.[45]

As seen through this diarist's eyes, the farmers' duties were still as nu-merous and varied as in Calvin Ely's time and were shared and rotated among different work teams within the family. Spring and summer would be spent plowing; planting oats, corn, and potatoes; drawing loads of man-ure, stones, and hay; making gates; working in the nursery; building and repairing fences; building bridges and irrigation dams; hunting crows' nests; fallowing new fields; working on the roads; performing maintenance on barns and sheds; washing and shearing sheep; tending bees; picking strawberries; mowing; haying; weeding; hoeing potatoes and corn; and reaping, binding, and shocking rye. In winter, in addition to gathering the next year's supply of fuel, workers would be winnowing the usual large crop of rye. As soon as it was cold enough, sometimes on Christmas day, the brethren would turn out to fill the ice house, packing the great slabs with sawdust.

In addition there would be specific yearly or occasional jobs such as repairing the aqueduct, butchering, and digging graves when needed. Many of the men had their own special fields of expertise; this diarist often punctuated his careful record of the brethren's farm activities with the note "I worked in my nursery."

The families combined forces for major jobs. The Church Family brethren helped raise the North Family's cart shed on a day in May "cold as Norway." In July, "George and 15–20 others of us went over on the plain to help the North family reap their rye. We reapt 10 acres and bound it up and shocked it."

The productivity was impressive. The men of one family easily cradled twenty-six acres of hay in a day, brought in fifty-three loads of hay in a week of weather "superlative for haying," and winnowed hundreds of bushels of rye over a winter. Separate orchards were maintained for apples, peaches, and cherries. In 1856 the Enfield Shakers sent out fourteen thousand pounds of herbs—powdered, papered, and labeled—particularly extracts of dandelion, thoroughwort, and butternut.[46]

It was an arduous life, relieved by the camaraderie of working with others, the sense of common beliefs and goals binding all, and the knowledge that everyone would share equally in the bountiful harvests. The prosaic farmer's record would occasionally be interrupted by an observation such as "Horse team plowed in the little orchard. Cherry trees on the blow." Or even a spontaneous ode to May:

> The spring unfolds its green beauties
> To cheer the toilsom way.[47]

The only rest would come on the Sabbath—"In the forenoon read Church orders. In the afternoon had a Shaker dance."

In its parallel course, the life of a Shaker sister, such as Maria Lyman in Enfield, continued in its relatively peaceful way. She would move into the kitchen to "take the cooking" or "take the bread" for four to six weeks at a time. At other times she would spin, cut paper or cloth seed bags, or create elaborate fans of peacock and turkey feathers. In the company of a large group of sisters she might make currant and blackberry wine in July, pick cranberries in September, gather chestnuts in November, kill and pluck geese in January, make molasses candy in February, and make dandelion extract in May. Frequently, a group of sisters, demure in their starched caps and plain gowns, would go into Springfield to attend lectures or to Hartford to spend the day. And sometimes the Society hosted distinguished visitors: in April 1855, Maria Lyman reported, they "had a preach from a Negro slave called her name Sojourney Truth."[48]

In 1856 her cousin Amelia was allowed the privilege of traveling with five other Shakers to the four communities just west of Enfield—New Lebanon, Watervliet, Hancock, and Tyringham. Her companions on the journey were Elder Philip Burlingame, Robert Aitken, Lucy Walton, Carsondana Benton, and Margaret Hopkins. The young sisters prepared for the journey for months, sewing new clothes for the occasion.[49]

On their departure day Amelia rose at 3:30 A.M., and the group was on the road by 5:30. They traveled forty-seven miles by team and wagon in one windy, rainy day, stopping in Cummington, Massachusetts, when darkness fell at 9:00 P.M. The next day they continued through Savoy, North Adams, and Williamstown, and into Pownal, Vermont, there cutting westward through the mountain pass. The group first visited Watervliet and then Mount Lebanon.

On June 28 the travelers arrived in Hancock. Amelia described going to see the steam-powered woolen factory at the North Family, where Richard Wilcox was the engineer. The group visited the Ministry and was greeted by Elder Thomas, Eldress Dana Brewster, and Sister Sarah Harrison. They saw the round barn, the hen roost, and horse barn. "Around we went," wrote Amelia, "accompanied by a number of young sisters which made our travel very agreeable, being strangers in a strange place."[50]

By midcentury the Shakers also took regular trips to the seaside—often to Coney Island, New York, or New London, Connecticut—for health and recreation, revealing that they did not deny themselves all of the pleasures of the world. The summer following Amelia Lyman's visit to the other Shaker communities, she took a seaside holiday at Wickford, Rhode Island, with Elder Brother George Wilcox, Elder Philip Burlingame and his daughter Sarah, and Elder Sister Jennett Augur from the Hancock community. That these two young sisters, Sarah and Amelia, were invited to share the rest and recreation of elders indicates how highly they were regarded and trusted.

Notes from Amelia's diary show the pleasant and free ambience of such an outing:

We arose with the sun had our breakfast about 7. Elder Philip then went with the sisters down to the shore to see the packet start for Newport. Elder Brother and Euclid tried their luck at fishing. Got one or two flatfish which were not worth much. We tarried till eleven when we thought we would try and see how the water felt, so we rigged up and jumped in. It being quite warm we lingered over an hour got a little behind about our dinner it being one o'clock when we returned. In the afternoon between four and five we took another ducking which was a little too much. . . . Sailed out on bay saw Porpoise and whitefish. . . . Gathered shells. Rode over the waves, spread wet clothes on the rocks to dry. Fished. Saw a live lobster. Homesick. . . . In the forenoon in a bathing. Afternoon up to the knees in mud seaweed and water after Quags. . . . At Westquague beach again; rode the waves, made a "bedroom" in a niche in the rock to change in. To Newport on packets. Supper—boiled corn, sweet cake, pie, bread and butter. Traveled home September 1 and 2—through towns and past farms—rested on rocks in an orchard, ate lunch. Met a shower, took shelter in a barn."[51]

The trip wasn't entirely devoted to play, however; the party also visited a Baptist, an Episcopal, and a Methodist church while at the seaside.

A Harvard sister recalled in her later life the duties of Shaker children in the 1860s, which may have been similar to their activities at Hancock, Enfield, and Tyringham. At age four, she said, both boys and girls learned to knit, and when their hands weren't otherwise busy, they were expected to knit a certain number of rows per day.

Even as young children the boys and girls had different jobs. The sorting of broom corn was a little boy's job—and an unpleasant one because the dust from the corn would irritate his skin. The young sisters, meanwhile, would be learning to wash, iron, cook, clean, and mend for the family. The sisters also operated the dairy, each adult milking three cows apiece morning and evening, as well as making butter and cheese.

In the fall, Marcia Bullard remembered, all of the younger Shakers would participate in apple-paring bees several times a week. These were, she wrote, "far from amusing":

In the first place we were all tired after a hard day's work. In the second, the brethren sat on one side of the washhouse, the sisters on the other, and general conversation was absolutely forbidden. A whispered remark to one's next-door neighbor was all that was countenanced and a particularly stern eldress was chosen to patrol the ranks of the younger sisters, that no tender glances might be exchanged across the chasm. The brethren ran the noisy paring machines, an occupation not conducive to sentiment, and we sisters trimmed and cored, while the children emptied pails of apples or refuse. The work went on until everyone was nearly asleep—for, remember, we all rose at five in the morning—and until 50 or 60 bushels of apples had been prepared."[52]

The apples were then dried in the drying house, which the Shakers felt kept them whiter and more flavorful than if they were sun-dried. The soft or bruised apples became cider. Some barrels of cider were left to turn to vinegar, and the others went into the famous Shaker cider applesauce.

Marcia Bullard also remembered sugaring expeditions, which must have been similar to those in Tyringham, when the Shakers turned out to tap the massive sugar maples near the Church Family. In early spring the sisters went out first to scrub all of the buckets before they were hung on the trees. The brethren boiled down the sap in enormous iron kettles at camp and then transported it on ox sleds to the "sugar shop," where the sisters took over, clarifying the syrup by adding milk (one quart to twelve gallons of syrup) at just the right moment. The sisters then bottled the syrup in two-gallon jugs, sealed with resin. Every Sunday morning a jug was opened for breakfast. The syrup itself was just for use in the families, but the sisters made little scalloped maple sugar cakes for sale.

CHAPTER EIGHT

Challenges from Within

O Lord I will praise thee
Whatever ills surround me
Yea I will trust Thee
When dark the billows roll.
Then why should I falter
To walk upon the water
Since by thy whisper
Thou canst the waves controll.
    —Enfield, April 4, 1886

Like other families who joined the Shakers during the first half of the century, the Kellogg family consisted of a widowed mother and a number of children. Ruth and Elijah Kellogg may have been converted in the intensive missionary effort the Enfield Shakers pursued in South Hadley, Massachusetts, in 1835. Elijah died in June 1836 at the early age of forty-six, and that month Ruth took four of her nine sons—Harvey, twenty, Hawley, fourteen, Elijah, Jr., nine, and William, seven—to live with the Enfield Shakers. Three younger boys, four-year-old Otis, three-year-old Charles, and two-year-old Andrew, came later.[1]

After twenty-five years the sole member of the original family remaining in the Enfield Society was Harvey Stoughton Kellogg, who served as second elder in the South Family for many years and died at the age of sixty-six. Consumption ravaged the family: Ruth Kellogg died of it in 1840 after five years at the South Family; Charles, in 1856 at the age of twenty-three; and Elijah, Jr., in 1862 at thirty-six.

Four of the other sons, Hawley, William, Otis, and Andrew, all apostatized as young men, several taking Shaker sisters with them. Hawley, who had been an elder at the West Family, left in 1851, marrying Sister Susan Maria Holman and becoming a grocer and city politician in Hartford. William, after serving as second elder in the Church Family for five years, left in 1861 with Sister Maria Blackman, with whom he eventually went out west, to Illinois, and had seven children. Otis also married a Shaker sister, Susan Griffiths, originally of Foster, Rhode Island (Thomas Damon's home town), in 1856; and the couple went to Springfield, where Otis, a machinist, was employed in the United States Armory during the Civil War. The youngest son, Andrew, left in 1861 to marry Maria Jane Shumway, and they returned to the family farm in South Hadley. Several of the Kellogg boys continued to visit the Shaker community.

Clearly, the 1850s must have been a turbulent decade for the Shakers, with many disturbing changes and losses of members to the world. In addition to the general decay in the quality of leadership, this decade would see the first obvious imbalance of the sexes. According to census figures gathered by Priscilla Brewer, in 1850 the five Enfield families collectively claimed 104 males and 106 females; in 1860 the total was 49 males and 97 females. The number of women stayed almost the same while the number of men declined by more than half. According to Thomas Damon's figures, the 217 members (88 brethren and 129 sisters) at Hancock in 1846 had dropped to 193 (58 brethren and 135 sisters) by 1852—a severe loss of male members in only six years.[2]

The simple fact was that young men usually left the community, and young women were more likely to stay—unless they left with a young man. Economic realities, not different attitudes toward celibacy, probably caused this split. The nineteenth-century world was full of opportunities for a young man on his own. For a single woman, on the other hand, or a widow with children, it would have been hard to surpass the advantages of the Shaker society, with its security, serenity, network of friends, and unique chance to achieve a leadership position.

Along with the Kelloggs, another family may serve to illustrate what happened to membership between 1830 and 1860. In 1850 thirty-two-year-old David Richmond was working as a wool carder in the Enfield South Family; according to Thomas Damon, he had arrived four years earlier.[3] That same year his twenty-seven-year-old cousin, Thomas Richmond, from Yorkshire, England, signed the Enfield Church Family covenant, and the following spring he was dutifully plowing with the other brethren on the Shaker farm. A year later, on May 4, 1852, their extended family joined them. The Richmond-Copley family made a significant impact on the Enfield community, and it is worth looking at its members closely. Though their experiences are in some ways unique and even extreme, they can nevertheless illuminate the experiences of other families.

David Richmond, who was evidently a lifelong spiritual searcher, had been the first of the family to discover the Society. During the 1840s he had, in his words, "traveled through all the phases of gross unbelief" until he heard of the Shakers. "We concluded there must be some *uniting principle* in the faith of Believers," he later wrote, "which cements its adherents in Love, and enables them to withstand all opposition, and to prosper; which was not possessed by us and our friends (at least in the same degree)—for we failed in our every attempt to reduce our principles to *practice.*" He and his friend William White left their wives and families in England and paid a visit to Enfield in 1846, where, he later wrote,

> . . . we began to examine, in our way, for Love, Truth, and Goodness; calmly viewing the fruits of *Shakerism* in words, actions, and external arrangements; and endeavoring to look deeply into their souls for error, hidden craft, and hypocrisy; but we found, to our great joy and gladness, that they had found and obtained the "pearl of great price" and that this, firmly rooted and blossoming in their hearts is the source of their beautiful and simple harmony and love, and constituted the difference betwixt us and them, and the secret of their success. Seeing then the value of this "pearl," we resolved to purchase it, let the price be what it might. Feeling the presence of God and the truth of the Everlasting Gospel, we repented of and confessed our sins, and were received with heart-felt joy by our new brethren and sisters, into relationship with them."[4]

Such letters home to England reached Thomas's sister Elizabeth Richmond Copley, who, with her sixth child on the way, was wearying of the "toil and trial incumbent upon the marriage relationship," according to a later Shaker historian. Elizabeth, later praised for her "executive ability, religious sentiment, and strong character," was probably the driving force that brought the extended family across the ocean.[5]

The family members who arrived in 1852 were (in addition to Elizabeth) her mother, Hannah Teasdel Richmond (born 1796); her two brothers, one also named David (born 1832) and one named Harry (born 1838); her sister, also named Hannah (born 1834); and her five children, aged four to eleven (see family tree in Appendix III). Twenty-year-old David was ill with consumption when the family arrived; he died at the Church Family office six days later. The six children—Elizabeth's five and fourteen-year-old Harry— were taken into the Church Family; Elizabeth herself went to the South Family.

The Hancock Ministry commented, "Elizabeth is a very understanding, intelligent woman, her children are very pretty active children"; and later, "How many of the number will make believers we cannot tell. But one thing we do know. It makes labour four us. But as it is only the beginning of the answer to our prayers, we have no wish to complain, but rather rejoice, and pray Lord send from every quarter of the globe, all that seemeth good in thine eyes."[6]

Elizabeth's husband, John William Copley, visited that summer; but although Elizabeth decided to remain with the Shakers, Copley went back to England, still a relatively young man of thirty-one. According to Ricardo Belden, one of the last Shakers at Enfield, the father was relatively well-to-do for the times and never really understood "how or why the Shakers could agree to raise a whole family without asking any financial aid from him."

As a gift to the Shakers he presented the bell that was placed in the big brick house at the South family.[7]

Several months later John Copley came for another visit, arriving at the Church Family on January 4, 1853. Perhaps because his presence was feared to be somewhat disruptive, the Copley children were taken to stay with their mother at the South Family for entire days during his visit.

But the greatest effect of Copley's visit was not on his children but on other adult males, particularly his wife's cousin, David Richmond, and her brother Thomas. The three men took frequent trips together into Springfield. Thomas Richmond, now twenty-nine years old, was evidently thrown into confusion by the temptation of returning to the world. The elders were even more concerned about David Richmond, who was considered an unstable, volatile personality and whose plan to become a Shaker missionary in England was seen as grandiose and erratic.[8]

Evidently, the elders decided that if they were going to hold onto Thomas he would be better off at Hancock than at Enfield, so near his relatives. When he visited Hancock on January 31 with John Copley and William White, Elder George Wilcox followed ten days later with his clothes—a Shaker method of telling a person he was not welcome back. Wilcox brought the other two back to Enfield the next day, leaving Thomas Richmond to make a new home at Hancock "and get weaned from David R." Meanwhile, Elder Thomas Damon's concern about David Richmond prompted him to visit the New Lebanon elders ten days later to discuss excommunicating him. "Views favorable to the expulsion," he noted.[9]

The excommunication of David Richmond, on February 24, 1853, and the events that followed provide a fascinating example of how the Shaker leaders would combine forces to "cleanse" the community of a difficult problem. The cause of the excommunication is impossible to determine. In this case it was unlikely to have been sexual misconduct, since no woman was incriminated along with Richmond. He may have been preaching unacceptable ideas; he may have been overly ambitious or unbalanced. Or it may have been a matter of personal style; Richmond comes across in his writings as an excitable, somewhat egotistical personality, far from the mild and modest Shaker ideal.

Different diarists recorded the excommunication in their different styles: Thomas Damon in guarded detail, Maria Lyman in terse summaries. Present were Ministry elder Thomas Damon, Elder Brother George Wilcox of the Enfield Church Family, Elder Nathan Damon of the Enfield North Family, Elder Harvey Lyman of the Enfield South Family, and three trustees, Arthur Damon, Erastus Webster, and Edward Lyman. David Richmond was formally "excommunicated from all privileges of membership in the South family, Enfield, Ct." David said good-bye to Elizabeth and Harry at the Church Family and then went to Hancock, ostensibly for a last interview with Thomas Richmond.[10]

At this point, however, the formal process broke down, as Richmond stopped cooperating. He sneaked into the Hancock village at 11:00 P.M., climbed into bed with a hired man, and talked to Thomas first thing the next morning. At 6:00 A.M. they were on the early cars for Springfield. The pair arrived at the Enfield South Family around 11:00 P.M. February 28, and were taken into the sisters' shop by Hannah Richmond and Elizabeth Copley.

Elders Grove Wright, Thomas Damon, and Frederick Evans, summoned from Hancock and New Lebanon, confronted the pair in the morning and told them they would not receive another meal or spend another night in the community; they then offered the two men passage to England. A wagon appeared, and the elders loaded in the Richmonds' gear. ("All hands on deck, Richmonds in the street," wrote Maria Lyman.) The two men were urged to get in but refused. Finally, after many hours of threats and persuasion, they left, riding the train toward Hancock under Thomas Damon's watchful eye and then heading for New York.

On March 7, just four days after this incident, John Copley—who could be considered the catalyst of the above events—bound his five children to the Shakers and departed for England. A month later, Maria Lyman wrote, "The mother of the Richmonds [Hannah] left, took her son [Harry, age fifteen]."

The story did not end there, however, for in October 1854, Thomas Richmond, the prodigal son, returned to Enfield from England and asked to become a member. He was received into full union and remained a faithful, productive Shaker until his death in 1894 at the age of seventy-two. His sister married and became Hannah Tate. Later she left two sons and a daughter at the Enfield Church Family.

David Richmond, meanwhile, continued to search for spiritual enlightenment; by 1857 he had set himself up with a printing press in Warehouse Point, Connecticut, near Enfield, where he produced religious pamphlets. He appeared again in the 1870s near Durham in the north of England, where in 1879 he published a pamphlet titled *An Explanatory Address and Testimony of Light and Truth to the United Society of Believers or Shakers, in the United States of America, and to whom it may concern.*[11]

The four Copley daughters all remained Shakers for their entire lives and in fact became pillars of the Church and North families. Sophia Copley (1846–1898) was eldress at the Church Family from 1874 until her death in 1898, and Emily (1843–1911) was a trustee at the North Family.[12]

The two Copley sons, however, did not remain Shakers. The younger son, Matthew, went out to Minnesota and died there at the age of twenty-

two. And the eldest child, John William Richmond Copley, worked in-
dustriously on the farm until he abruptly left Enfield in 1866 to marry Kezia
Lyman, who was pregnant with their child.[13]

A continually destabilizing influence on accessible communities like
Hancock, Tyringham, and Enfield was the increasing contact with the
world. The village of Tyringham was becoming a popular vacation spot,
and the Shakers, their reputation spread far and wide by their excellent
goods and their singular worship, had become an object of fashionable curiosity. During the 1850s, according to Julia Johnson, as many as three hundred world's people at one time would come from Lenox and Lee to the
Shaker meetinghouse to observe the services. The spectators were capti-
vated by the gray-clad brethren hanging their wide-brimmed hats on pegs
on the meetinghouse wall and by the sisters with their white caps, straight
brown dresses, and muslin capes pinned in front. One observer described
a typical meeting: "When assembling, they all marched in at once and were
seated in silence until such time as the spirit moved, when they would rise
and march around the room, singing, in a sort of trotting jog. At intervals
they would turn and face each other and take a double shuffle which they
had been trained to do in perfect harmony."[14]

This situation must have been psychologically damaging for the Believers, disallowing the separation desired from the world and turning them
into overly self-conscious performers. Sister Elizabeth Thornber, who was
indentured to the Tyringham Shakers in 1847 as a ten-year-old orphan, had
as one of her jobs the task of serving dinner to the world's people who
visited. She served as many as forty customers in one day and saw people
coming by the hundreds in their carriages to buy baskets, fancy articles,
jellies, essences, catsup, and so on. Among the purchasers, she recalled, were
the well-known Beecher family.

But it was not just the sturdy products that attracted customers to the
Believers' doorsteps. The worldly, sophisticated upper and middle classes,
jaded by accelerating city life, must have found the Shakers' quaint purity
and Arcadian surroundings a source of refreshment and fascination. As the
industrial revolution radically transformed the world, many people viewed
the Believers with romantic nostalgia, as vestiges of an innocent, primitive
life-style. And the Shakers, ogled by these visitors, undoubtedly found
themselves trading some of their precious purity for cynicism.

As Shaker membership declined, small or outlying families were closed
or combined. In 1849 the Hancock South Family, originally established to
accommodate the overflow from the Novitiate, or East Family, was dissolved—there were not enough new members in the East Family to justify
a second family. Other families also shrank and then vanished; by the turn

of the twentieth century Hancock had three and Enfield only two small families left.

In 1848 David Lamson observed that the Hancock society contained around 150 members, exclusive of about 30 children recently indentured by parents and guardians. A very large percentage of the members, he said, were aged, and "the efficient laborers in the society are few." He estimated that the Hancock society possessed five thousand to six thousand acres in the 1840s. "The mountainous parts are well wooded," he wrote, "with beach [sic], maple, and hickory. The lower lands consist of those beautiful swells or undulations which are always productive, including a considerable extent of bottom land, which make very valuable natural mowing."[15]

He went on to say: "Although everything is plain, there is about the whole village an air of plenty, neatness, and comfort which gives it the appearance of a little paradise as it were. And then the singular dress, the mysterious and exclusive manners of the people give them at first sight almost the appearance of a different order of beings."[16]

This description was actually part of a denunciation of the Shakers that Lamson published at his own expense in 1848 after living for two years in the Hancock East Family. Disillusioned, in particular, with the gifts of Mother Ann's Work, he charged, among other things, that the elders were cohabiting in their quarters above the meetinghouse; that the community was held together by means of spying, deceit, and psychological cruelty; and that many of the infants left on Society doorsteps were, in fact, the illegitimate children of Shaker brethren. The elders comprised a separate class, he implied, with separate shops, living quarters, dining rooms, and, at Hancock, the Ministry carriage barn. Common members could call on them only when invited, and even elders could visit the Ministry only at their shops, not at their dwellings.[17]

As in any close-knit community, favoritism and jealousies were undoubtedly present in the Shaker societies. And considering the age of Elder Nathaniel Deming and Eldress Dana Goodrich, it is likely that the Ministry and elders were offered special treatment, treatment Mother Ann Lee would have shunned. It is difficult to imagine Grove Wright, however, with his humble, positive attitude toward life and Shakerism, cultivating such an attitude among members.

Lamson's account of his experience dwells frequently on Church Family elder Joseph Wicker, whom he describes as very good-looking and extremely able, with an excellent education. Yet there is venom in his description of Wicker; the personalities of the two men may have conflicted. Lamson's denunciation of the Shakers may have been colored by frustration with his own inability to enter the leadership ranks; even so, his account is full of detailed observations and perceptive insights and is an important part of Shaker history.

The elders had encouraged him to speak out in meetings, at least initially, when he was excited and positive about the United Society. But when he voiced his growing exasperation and disgust with the extreme nature of the gifts, he sensed a sudden coldness: this was, he wrote, "the death blow to my union."[18]

The government of the Society, he claimed, was "a perfect despotism" and "a most crafty game played by the few at the expense of the many. The ministry, elders, and some of the more intelligent and favored of the members, understand well their part. The remainder are kept as ignorant as possible; and by means of the grossest superstition are made to render the most implicit and servile obedience 'to their leader.' They are most thoroughly enslaved."[19]

He objected vehemently to what he saw as a double standard for behavior—the strict rules for members did not apply to elders. Even worse, he charged that elders and eldresses told each other the substance of the confessions they had received. He even described peepholes, on the stairwell ceilings, through which ministry elders and eldresses spied on meetings.

He charged that the elders continually violated the strict rules of behavior set up for the rank and file. Intoxicating beverages, for example, were prohibited except for individuals who were "past the meridian of life"; these could have cider, the amount to be determined by the elders. Yet the ministry and the elders, Lamson maintained, were "abundantly provided by the sisters of the church with wines, cordials, etc." Elder Brother William Deming, for example, who was by nature "well endowed with alimentiveness and mirthfulness," Lamson wrote, "loves a joke, a witty remark, and a glass of wine. He keeps his brandy and other stimulants without reserve or concealment."[20]

According to Lamson another elder, probably William Williams of the East Family, was more discreet: every day he had a private little glass of cider-brandy, which was left for him in a certain cupboard by Nancy Riley, second eldress and family nurse.[21]

Great reverence was paid to—and demanded by—the ministry. The main rule was simple, childlike obedience, followed by industry, economy, and neatness. Questioning was not encouraged—Lamson's request to examine the "Holy Books" was denied—and the elders believed "too much learning [was] a dangerous and hurtful thing." Solomon Wollison, for example, described by the author as his "intimate friend," had "outgrown his slavery" and was considered by the elders to be a "ruined man," Lamson wrote, because he was in the habit of "secreting books and stealing opportunities to read them."[22]

Greatly concerned by the impending publication of Lamson's book, the Hancock Ministry planned to neutralize its effect by circulating a fervent testimony Lamson had written while a believer. Grove Wright revealed the plan to the Harvard Ministry:

> Enclosed a copy of David Lamson's testimony, which he wrote while he lived at the gathering order and was in tolerable good union, and according to his testimony, was a full believer in Shakerism. The testimony written at a time when there was a general gift for all under a certain age to write their faith, their experiences & travel &c. We think the testimony will be of great use, & may be the means of doing much good, after his Book comes out. We have concluded here to keep it a profound secret untill after his book is printed & by no means to let it get out so that David shall get the knowlege of it, lest he should put a clause into his Book, either denying it, as being his testimony, or try to make out, that he was compeled to write as he did. Yea or try to take some way to evade, or hurt the force of it. Most likely, he has forgoten that he ever wrote such a testimony, or is in hopes that we have forgotten it.[23]

The strategy had backfired by the following month because "that wicked Solomon Wollison" overheard the plan. The schoolroom, where Lamson's testimony was being copied, was entered one night, a desk was broken open, and both the original and the transcription were stolen. The Shakers assumed that Wollison either was responsible for the theft or had hired someone to execute it.

It was some comfort to the Shakers that at least one Pittsfield bookstore refused to purchase copies of Lamson's book. In the store, Lamson "was pretty severely reprimanded for his base conduct and was told that they were well acquainted with the Shakers."[24]

The following year the Ministry formally excommunicated Wollison after trying him before an assembly of elders and brethren. Three of Wollison's male relatives had preceded him out of the Society between 1846 and 1849. Wollison later took the Shakers to court, accusing them of withholding his clothes and $60. However, the judge, who had been counsel for Daniel Webster in Boston, decided there was no cause of action, and the jury agreed. The case was thrown out, and there was no cost for the defendant.[25]

Formal excommunications were obviously not uncommon in the Society at midcentury, but the Ministry always exhibited reluctance to carry out such extreme action, in the hope that the reprobates could be persuaded to leave voluntarily. Whether this was an exemplary tolerance on the Ministry's part or a simple inability to cope with dissenters is unclear. Although the Shakers developed an excellent relationship with the world, they never perfected or indeed came to terms with their attitude toward members of their ranks who defected. As the nineteenth century proceeded, individual diaries and record books bemoaned the loss of Believers. When the Society was challenged overtly, however, the response was primitive and clumsy, as demonstrated most clearly with the Hawkins/Canon case.

Hannah Canon was born around 1800 into a locally prominent family. She signed an agreement with the Tyringham Shakers on February 3, 1818, and signed the covenant in 1832. She lived in the Church Family, working as a weaver and dyer, and in October 1838 took a trip to Enfield with Desire Holt, Harriet Storer, and Wealthy Storer. By the 1840s she had become involved with Jeremiah Hawkins.[26]

Hawkins was born in 1799 in Sharon, Connecticut, the youngest of six children. He entered the Hancock society at age four with his father, Peter, who was possibly a widower, and five siblings. Like his contemporary Grove Wright, he was brought to Tyringham to be raised. Whether Hawkins ever held a leadership position is unclear, although he served for many years as the Shakers' representative to the Tyringham town school committee. His brother Reuben, ten years older than he, rose to become Elder Brother in the Hancock Church Family; and his sister Clarissa, six years his senior, became eldress of Hancock's Second Family and, briefly, second in the Hancock Ministry. Jeremiah's closest brother, Osee, however, was a carpenter at Hancock until he abruptly left to marry twenty-year-old Mary Starr Pomeroy, a weaver like Hannah Canon, in 1826. They had three children.[27]

In April 1849 a letter from Grove Wright to Grove Blanchard mentioned that the Ministry had had "some old rotenhearted hipocrits to purge out who had aught to have been gone twenty years ago, who have grown old & gray, in sin & abominations." He was referring to Hawkins and Canon, who by then had apparently been engaged in an open affair for some time. Wright probably knew both parties well, having grown up with them in the Tyringham society and being just a few years older. That March, Hawkins and Canon had finally left the Shakers, a week apart.[28]

"You probably know something about the circumstance of Jeremiah Hawkins, at Tyringham," he wrote,

who has carried on and supported a union contrary to the Gospel, for many years in open defiance of all that could be said or done to reform him. We were at Tyringham the fore part of March and found that matters in regard to him were still grown worse, & he had become so rebelious that it was concidered high time to have some thing done in good earnest, as it was generally felt that it could not be bourn any longer. So the work was undertaken, and he & his old wife Hannah Cannon were both purged out, & have gone to their own company, but not without a pretty severe contest and struggle as they were determined to not leave the ground, but to keep their foot hold, unless they could have a large sum of money, as they were not boath of them in their 50th year, and J. had been there from about 4 years old. But the fire became so hot, they could not endure it, & finally left the ground.

J. threatens [highly?] of having a law suit, but what he will finally do we can not tell.

Wright's letter ended with an innocent note: "P.S. We have not found out, neither do we suppose, that Jeremiah & Hannah, ever went so far, as to get into gross whoredom, notwithstanding their long connection & much lacivious & unseemly conduct."

Instead of making a life for themselves outside the Society, however, as Osee and Mary Hawkins had, after three years the couple moved into a Shaker-owned house near the South House and the sawmill, claiming that after many years of labor in the Society they were entitled to the property. "[N]ot being exactly needed in that location," wrote Thomas Damon in March 1852, "it was thought best to take measures to have him remove." Church Family Elder Albert Battles summoned Jeremiah's natural brother, Elder Reuben Hawkins, from Hancock, who tried unsuccessfully to persuade the couple to leave.[29]

One day the following month, when Hawkins was not at home, the brethren resorted to drastic measures, taking his goods and furniture from the house and depositing them in the road. They then dragged out a furious Hannah Canon. When Hawkins returned, he obtained a warrant for the arrest of Brother Willard Johnson and several others. "Between 11 and 12:00 at night," reported Thomas Damon, "the writ was put into the hands of Egbert E. Wilson, a young constable who summoning a lot of rowdies (15–20) proceeded to the house from whence the goods were removed to exhibit his prowess in capturing the delinquents. The house at this time contained nine or ten pretty smart chaps as its defenders." The brethren assumed it was a ruse and denied the constable entry, so the gang beat the door in with large stones. Hawkins bounded into the house but was met by five or six of the inmates, with sticks, who gave him a bruising. He rushed out again, and they shut the door. The constable left to round up a bigger posse.

A neighbor appeared, advising the brethren to surrender and informing them that it was no joke; this was a real constable with a genuine warrant. The brethren did give themselves up and spent the night "in keeping" at the constable's rake shop.

After a trial in Lee the case was finally dismissed on a motion of Hawkins's attorney, the brethren agreeing to give Hannah Canon Hawkins, in compensation, a good cow. Jeremiah died four years later, and he and Hannah are buried together in the Tyringham cemetery.[30]

In March 1852, Hancock eldress Cassandana Brewster wrote to another eldress about the general state of things, speaking of Tyringham in particular: "There has been a few added to their number the winter past. But O how few there are that are willing to bear the cross and come into the purifying work of the Gospel. Yet we have many words of promise from our heavenly parents that the time is near when souls will flock to Zion crying what shall I do to be saved." But then she expressed sorrow "lest we as a people are not prepared (Hope it is not so in other places). I fear we are not so faithful to pray and fervantly desire that Souls may be awakened and come to the Gospel."[31]

But amid the doubts and difficulties of the early 1850s a note from the irrepressible Grove Wright: "July 18, 1852: A remarkable outpouring of the spirit, and at evening had such a meeting as was never known in this place. Perhaps from 40 to 50, all under the opperation of the Power of God at once, mostly among the youth and children."[32]

Gregarious and keen-witted, Harvey Lyman seemed to Ministry elders and members alike to be a fine example of a Shaker brother. He had entered the Society in 1837, at age twenty-two, with his mother and younger brothers, and quickly rose through the Shaker ranks to become trustee. In May 1852 he was chosen to succeed eighty-year-old Elisha Allen as first elder of Enfield's South Family.

His sudden departure in May 1854 and subsequent marriage to South Family eldress Mary Ann White were thus particularly disturbing. In New Lebanon, Isaac N. Youngs lamented in his diary, "From South Enfield the doleful sound rings like a death knell! *Elder* Harvey Lyman gone to the Devil! O Shame! Distress!"[33]

On June 22, 1854, Lyman (aged thirty-nine) and Mary Ann White (aged twenty-nine) "were tied together," wrote Thomas Damon, "with the galling cords of wedlock." Although on the marriage license he listed his trade as that of joiner, Lyman became a prosperous grocer and later part owner of Lyman and Woods, a second-hand furniture and realty company in Springfield, and had several children. Perhaps when he returned to the world he missed the large, close-knit Shaker community, for he also became an energetic organizer of Lyman family reunions.[34]

Enfield sister Maria Lyman's day-to-day diary of the 1850s is full of descriptions of the loss of friends and companions. Soon after her uncle Elder Harvey's apostasy she noted the departure of Otis Kellogg, three years older than she, who had, incidentally, been the one to carry Lyman's belongings to him in Springfield. Sister Maria's good friend, Susan Griffiths, followed Otis out of the community the next day and eventually married him. In March of that year, Caroline Blodgett had left the South Family office, followed the next day by trustee Edward Lyman and then married. William White, David Richmond's erstwhile companion, left in June without his children; Hannah Richmond and Hannah and Nancy Blanchard departed the same month. Louisa Mumford, frequently mentioned in Maria's diary, left in September 1854, and in November "Pierce and his woman left." Eunice Day, another friend, left in early 1855, and fourteen-year-old James White, probably William White's son, "ran away" soon after. Roby Blanchard left in June.[35]

The exodus of members from the community, climaxed by Elder Harvey's departure, precipitated the merging of the South and West families in 1854. "After due consideration," North Family eldress Anna Granger wrote, "it was felt for the most safe protection of this branch, our little West family to become one united inheritance with the South family in all things both spiritual and temporal, this being the gift and requirement of the Ministry. It was opened to the members of both families, and all harmoniously united, feeling it would be for the mutual protection and invariable progression in the Gospel, and all commenced acting to bring it to effect."[36]

Alden B. Lyman, Elder Harvey's nephew, went to the North Family to live; Arthur Damon, Thomas Damon's father, went to the Church Family; and the rest of the West Family "inmates" went to the shattered South Family. John Wilcox was appointed first elder there to replace Harvey Lyman, but he would "fail" after five years and be replaced by Philip Burlingame, who had been first elder at the West Family since its founding in 1829.

Hancock experienced its share of apostasies during the 1850s, losing some of its leaders to the world. Sometimes it seemed that the Ministry closed its eyes to indiscretions in the hope of retaining valued elders. Barnabas Sprague, second elder at the Hancock East Family and leader of many missions, including the one among the Adventists in 1846, left in April 1854. "He had *long* supported a fleshly union with a femail by the name of Selia Demsy," wrote Grove Wright, "and they finally Rated out, completely, and fell thro', and sank to rise no more." Demsy, by this time about forty years old, had been taken in by the Shakers as a small child and lived in the East Family. In 1870 she returned, alone, under her married name.[37]

Wright's feelings about the turbulence of the period are revealed in a series of letters to his close friend, Grove Blanchard of the Harvard Ministry, showing his hopes and disappointments as the Ministry tried to place people in the best possible arrangements. First, in May and June 1852 he described appointing Harvey Lyman to be first elder at the Enfield South Family. Two years later, after the apostasies of Elder Harvey and Eldress Mary Ann White, John Wilcox and Anna Irving (or Erving) replaced them at the South Family, assisted by William White, who would soon also apostatize. "Perhaps you may think by this time, and justly too, that we are running somewhat wild," wrote Elder Grove. "If so, I hope you will come this way *soon* when we can talk over past matters."[38]

Then, a month later, he wrote: "What can be more grievous and heart rending than to have those whoom we have placed confidence in as helps, prove traitors, and further do all in their power to destroy others. The Whites have proved themselves rotten hearted, and have all gone except three of William's children. The Richmonds are all gone except two children. One thing is favorable. Barnabas is married and gone to Michigan."[39]

In June 1857, Maria Lyman reported from Enfield, "Night wakers, Cassandana and Lydia left us ½ past 1:00 last night. North family's young sisters to Hartford. . . . What do you think of the times? Doleful times and it's come out now."

Carsondana Benton, whose midnight departure was recorded by Lyman, Thomas Damon, and other diarists, was born in Ellington, Connecticut, in 1826. When she was thirteen months old, her mother left her in the care of a small family, where she lived till she was ten. She had "religious thoughts," she later wrote. In the winter of 1836, some Enfield Believers made visits to her foster family, and she felt clearly that these were the people of God. Very attracted to them, she left the family the following year and went to live in the Society. She wrote these words at the age of seventeen: "It is my prayer that I may be so faithful as never to lose the blessing I have gained in this heart-searching work of the Lord; But that I may ever be increasing in the same: that when I have done with the things of time, good Angels may guide me to a peaceful share of rest." At twenty-one, on February 4, 1848, she signed the Church Family covenant (a few lines below her friend Susan Griffiths, who left to marry Otis Kellogg six years later), and in 1856 she took a trip with Amelia Lyman, Elder Philip Burlingame, and several others to Hancock, Tyringham, Watervliet, and New Lebanon.[40]

Carsondana's fascinating two-volume diary reveals, in addition to daily events, her close friendship with Lydia McIntyre, her occasional moments of sadness ("O the dejection which over shadoes; will hope for the best; we'll not despair"), and the meticulous training she received in domestic work—baking, cleaning, and ironing, as well as the myriad of other tasks she would be called upon to do. It also records her departure from Enfield—she took her diary with her—and, remarkably, her life in the year following.[41]

On June 22, 1856, she noted in her diary, "I am preparing for a journey. Lydia and I melt over the beeswax for the last time!!! . . . this is my last day here." The two sisters had arranged for a team to meet them when they slipped out at one in the morning, and they drove to West Ashford, Connecticut, where Lydia's brother George lived. He and their mother had visited the Shakers in previous years, possibly to persuade Lydia to leave. Though George was away, not having expected them, his wife, Abba, received the young women warmly.

Old habits die hard, and Carsondana, continuing her careful Shaker ways, continued to write in her diary, giving us a rare chance to observe the life of an apostate. In the days after her arrival at the McIntyre home she wrote: "Abba combs our heads this morning and fixes us up in style, we strip off our Shaker garb and go a shopping we feel quere . . . We have some sport with hoop skirts. . . . [Sabbath] we dress up the morning in our own dress We begin to look quite fashionable. George say he is glad to see us look like *folks* we are congratulated on all hands. . . . We made over our Shaker dresses and many other odd jobs during the week."

Two Shaker brethren arrived and were apparently convinced that the young women were sure in their decision. Carsondana and Lydia traveled back with them to the Enfield community to pick up their belongings, Lydia suffering from a severe headache as if from the stress of seeing their old friends.

In the next week they were busy making themselves skirts and aprons, and then they secured jobs in the silk mill in Mansfield Hollow. "Lydia goes upstairs to clean colored silk while I remain in the lower on raw silk this is our first day in factory life." No more entries appear in the diary until Thanksgiving, four months later, when the factory closed to put down a new floor. The two young women dined with Lydia's family, and Carsondana, who evidently appreciated food, described the Thanksgiving dinner—"turkey weighing 16 pound chicken pie onions 2 kinds of plum puding 2 kinds of pie 2 kinds of cake etc. etc."—just as she had always described the Shaker strawberries and green peas.

The millworker's life was apparently not satisfactory: two months later both women had secured new jobs as housekeepers in different towns. Carsondana began keeping house for a farmer named Hamond Root and his invalid wife in North Coventry. (Coventry, curiously, had Shaker connections as the original home of the Allen brothers, first Believers in Tyringham.) Here her Shaker upbringing and domestic training—her skills in baking (daily production of apple pies, gingerbread, soda biscuits, and Indian, rye, or wheat bread), washing, ironing, cleaning, and mending, as well as her meticulous personal habits—proved invaluable.

Yet Carsondana now encountered a problem that had been unknown in Shaker life: loneliness. Although the household was full of people—the doctor visited daily and Mrs. Root's relatives often came to stay—she didn't really fraternize with her employer and had no other friends around. Depression loomed again: "I had a cry and couldn't be helped," she confided one Sabbath after Mrs. Root had taken a turn for the worse; and another time, "I feel like having a good crying spell." She precisely noted the anniversaries of her new life—"A year ago I attended the last Shaker meeting," and "It is a year to day since L. and I quit the Shakers." She had continual troubles with her back, for which she was told to bathe in alcohol and apply a plaster of mullein leaves. Once Lydia came to help out while she was laid up, but the two friends rarely met otherwise.

Whether Carsondana Benton ever regretted leaving the Shakers is impossible to determine. She had to cope on her own in a world very different from the one in which she had spent most of her life, and she suffered from occasional bouts of despair. She and Lydia visited the Enfield society in October 1858 with Otis and Susan Kellogg. Another former Shaker also may have helped fill the gap: the two called on fellow apostate Harvey Lyman in Springfield that same month. And by September 1863 a change had occurred in Lydia's life. Maria Lyman reported, "Cassandana and Lydia Aspinwall here with a babe."[42]

In August 1858, Isaac Youngs, writing from New Lebanon, summed up the feelings about this turbulent decade in the following passage:

> August, 1857. This is a year and time of much bearing and tribulation among Believers—at least in the Eastern Societies—a kind of bearing and sorrow that comes particularly hard on the Ministry: an account of much failure. At Alfred and Gloucester, the state of things is disturbing—but few able-bodied people—not enough that are fit and able to stand in care and bear burdens—scarce any of the young have been saved—as things appear now they must soon cease to exist as a society—the few that now are struggling to get along must soon be unable to support themselves. . . . Much apostacy has reduced the numbers lamentable in many families—at Watervliet Here at Lebanon—Hancock—Tyringham—and Enfield etc.—rarely any adults come in that abide or are worth much—and scarce any children can be saved any where. O my soul feels sorrowful—how are we coming out? Must believers really run out and become a reproach—and a bye word? We have to hire the world in among us, which is only making [it] worse.[43]

Youngs did not yet know, however, of the Hancock Bishopric's most shocking mass apostasy. The Tyringham society had reached its membership peak at the beginning of the decade. As late as September 1857 the New Lebanon ministry returned from a few days at Tyringham and noted in their records, "Good time."[44]

In 1858, however, twenty-three members of the Tyringham society are said to have departed on the same day, effectively taking the heart out of the community. Sister Elizabeth Thornber remembered fifty years later "the sadness of that day and how she weighed in her mind the question of going or staying, deciding never to break her Shaker faith."[45]

The reason for the mass exodus is undocumented, perhaps because Shaker hands destroyed records mentioning it. The Ministry journals at

New Lebanon recorded every case of measles, every visitor, every hat made but neglected to report this crisis. Even Isaac Youngs left it out of his personal diary, although he seems to have foreseen it in his above lament.

It is hard, in fact, to determine who actually left that day in 1858. A close examination of the Federal Census reports for 1850 and 1860 shows the loss of members was comparable to that in other communities over the same period. The prominent individuals in the Tyringham society in 1850 were still there in 1860. The one substantial loss was among the twenty-seven young people in the Church Family whose ages were between eleven and twenty in 1850: in ten years only one of the fourteen brethren remained, now in his twenties, and four of the thirteen sisters. Of the seven North Family brethren aged eleven to twenty in 1850, only one remained in 1860. There was more stability among the North Family sisters, however: the three North Family sisters who were in their teens in 1850, including future Ministry eldress Betsey Johnson, were still in the community ten years later. The Shakers may also have decided to take in fewer children. No other major loss is detectable in the Census reports.

Yet the loss of the new generation was a serious blow. These were the men and women who would carry on the Shaker tradition. And if indeed they all left simultaneously it must have been staggering to community morale.

Local tradition holds that the rule of celibacy was violated, and perhaps that was the case; or there may have been a conflict in leadership. Whatever specifically precipitated the departure, morale had been low in Tyringham for several years. The apostasies of leaders contributed to this, particularly the Jeremiah Hawkins affair, which had dragged on in court for years. One loss had been Desire Holt, who in November 1854 left the South House to live with her sister, perhaps because of ill health or perhaps because of disenchantment.[46]

Contact with the world, which had intensified during the 1850s as the Believers received hundreds of worldly spectators every week, also put pressure on the community. Of the three societies in the Hancock bishopric, Tyringham was closest geographically to a settlement of world's people. Although the town of Tyringham as a whole had steadily lost population in the 1800s, the little hamlet of Jerusalem, adjacent to the South House and half a mile south of the Church Family, was thriving at midcentury with two rake factories, one pitchfork factory, a carpenter's shop, and nine houses. Shakers and 'world's people probably mingled more freely there and at the Shaker sawmill and blacksmith's shop than at other communities, and worldly values may easily have rubbed off onto the Believers.

Furthermore, the community was located in a difficult site for agriculture, as the rest of the world became more competitive in supplying goods.

Dwelling house, Church Family, Tyringham, ca. 1920. (Collection of Eugenie Rudd Fawcett.)

Church Family, Enfield, view from southwest, undated. (Hancock Shaker Village, Pittsfield, Mass.)

Second meeting house and dwelling, ca. 1877, Church Family, Enfield. This meeting house, built in 1791 by Moses Johnson, was subsequently moved. (Hancock Shaker Village, Pittsfield, Mass.)

Church Family sisters, Enfield, 1886. Front row, second from left, Amelia Lyman; second row, second from right, Sophia Copley; second row, far right, Caroline Tate. (The Shaker Museum, Old Chatham, N.Y.; identified by Magda Gabor-Hotchkiss.)

Elder George Wilcox, Church Family, Enfield.
(Hancock Shaker Village, Pittsfield, Mass.)

Elder Walter Shepherd, Church Family, Enfield.
(Williams College Archives and Special Collections.)

Eldress Caroline Tate, Church and North
families, Enfield. (Williams College Archives and
Special Collections.)

View from east, North Family, Enfield, undated. The building on the left is the trustees' office, the large white building at center in the rear is the sisters' shop, the small building in front is a workshop, and the white building on the right is a dwelling. (Hancock Shaker Village, Pittsfield, Mass.)

North Family, Enfield, early twentieth century. The bearded man on the left is Elder George Clarke; the second man from the right is Gilbert Avery. (Hancock Shaker Village, Pittsfield, Mass.)

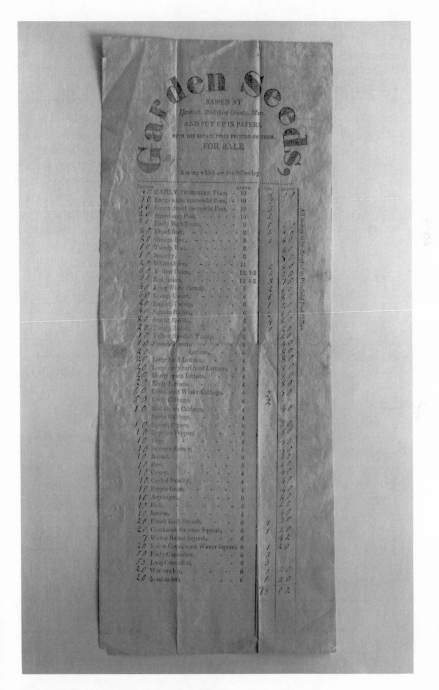

Seed order form, Hancock, 1820s. (Hancock Shaker Village, Pittsfield, Mass.)

Ricardo Belden, 1951. (Photo by
Bartlett Hendricks.)

Eldress Fannie Estabrook, 1951. (Photo by
Bartlett Hendricks.)

Perched on an east-facing mountainside, the Tyringham Shakers could see their fields and gardens in shadow in midafternoon, when the farms across the valley were still bathed in sunlight. "Those hills were steep and rocky, farming was back-breaking, discouraging over there on that hillside. Other communities had better and more profitable land," one Shaker sister recalled.[47]

Certainly, though, it was not a poor community. In 1861, down to a combined total of thirty-six members twenty-one and over, the North Family and the Church Family merged. An inventory taken in the spring of 1862 shows how wealthy this small society had become.

The Church Family owned 285 tons of hay, 938 pounds of broom corn, 200 pounds of pork, 6,500 pounds of beef, 500 pounds of codfish, 530 pounds of butter, 3,100 pounds of cheese, 700 pounds of tallow candles, 760 pounds of sugar, 1,050 bushels of potatoes, 40 cows, 24 oxen, 16 young cattle, 30 yearlings, 26 calves, 11 colts, 9 horses, 247 sheep, 6 fat cattle, and 150 fowls. That March a "wonderful" bull named Comet was moved from Tyringham to the Enfield society. They also possessed $3,000 worth of garden seeds, as well as herbs, tea, sweet corn, pickles, vinegar, applesauce, rice, Indian meal, soap, cider, apples, potatoes, oats, carrots, turnips, barley, buckwheat, salt, cabbages, linseed oil, lamp oil, molasses, 86½ brooms, tubs, pails, cheese hoops, and paint.[48]

Despite its prosperity the Tyringham society was stunned by the loss of members and the blow to morale. With just a handful of members—fifteen brethren and twenty-one sisters in 1860, most either young or old—the community struggled on, but its serene, productive days were over.

To cope with the problem of decreasing membership the Shakers took on more young people as apprentices—a common practice in the world as well—promising to house, feed, and usefully train boys and girls in exchange for their labor. Nathan Bradburn of Great Barrington, for example, was indentured to the Tyringham Church Family by his father at the age of five on December 28, 1843, probably along with his elder sisters Elvira and Samantha. Upon his release at age twenty-one, the agreement stated, Nathan was to be given "2 suits of wearing apparel, one suitable for Lord's Day and the other for working days."[49]

Some of these agreements collapsed, and there were numerous episodes of parents attempting to extricate their children from the Shaker communities. One case involved a boy named William Pillow, Jr., who had been indentured by his father, along with his two younger brothers, at the New Lebanon community in 1846. A few months later the senior Pillow turned up again, attempting to break his agreement and seize his sons. Unsuccessful, he obtained a writ of habeas corpus. The Enfield Shakers tried to conceal the boys, but their father, assisted by none other than apostates Jeremiah Hawkins and George and Solomon Wollison, found them there. Although young William reportedly wanted to stay with the Believers, a Hartford judge decided in his father's favor, and he had to depart.[50]

The father in this case may have indentured the boys because he was in desperate financial circumstances. Perhaps he then had second thoughts or found a way to keep them and tried to withdraw them. If the boys had been indentured to an ordinary farmer, this would have been just a legal matter. The Shakers, however, saw the father's change of heart as a challenge; in their eyes he was trying to drag three potential Shakers back to the temptations of the world, and they fought for every child.

In 1851 the Hancock Shakers faced a particularly heart-rending episode. John Irving of New Haven, Connecticut, had joined the community with his family in 1847 and then departed, leaving five of his children behind. In 1849 his wife tried to bring the remaining three children to the Shakers, but they would not admit them without John's consent. The two youngest girls, Jestina and Elizabeth, later became the objects of a tug-of-war between their father and the Believers. Grove Wright described an "interruption of sobs and groans at dinner":[51]

> A man named John Irvin came with the Sheriff and one of John's daughters for their "pilot" rushed into the dining room and seized two of our dear children (John's daughters). And such a time was never witnessed by any of us. The girls resisted, screached, beged and cried with all their might. At the same time clinging to the sisters with deth like grasps, crying do, O! do so help me. I cannot go I had rather die. O Father, my father how can you cause your children to feel such trouble; you brought us here, and you bound us here and promised you would never take us away. All the other children were weeping, too. The girls were finally taken, screaching and screaming through the village, the whole scene lasting ¾ of an hour. The girls were good girls and much beloved by all. . . . The Sheriff surprised to hear them talk, and to see their love for their home and their friends here.

After the sheriff arrived in Pittsfield with the children, he declared that he would not go through another such scene for fifty dollars. Elder Brother Joseph Wicker and Brother Joseph Patten followed the group to Pittsfield and took out a writ, placing it in the hands of the same Pittsfield sheriff. At 7:00 P.M. he arrived at the Shaker village with the two girls and was met at the carriage by a great crowd of sisters and brethren. The girls stepped out of the carriage, the eldest clutching her Shaker cap, which her father had attempted to tear off her head and burn. The sheriff, apparently relieved to have "now done his duty," was quite moved by her concern for her cap.

In October the two girls were taken by Ministry eldress Dana Brewster, her assistant Anna Irving, and Brother Isaac Augur to Enfield to stay. (Sister Anna's involvement suggests that the Irving girls were related to her; she also hailed from Connecticut.) The case dawdled on for years, and the girls finally ended up with their father, whom the Shakers paid $225 in 1855. The next year Grove Wright wrote sadly that the eldest girl, Jestina, "lay at the point of death with quick consumption," and she died soon after.[52]

Some of the attempts to withdraw children were less successful than others. In 1856, Deacon Joseph Fairbanks of the Enfield Church Family went to Boston after young Emily Curtis, who "was captured by her Mother and Brother and carried to Lowel." He brought the girl back a week later, and Emily Curtis grew up to become an eldress in the North Family.[53]

The spiritual nicknames given the communities probably seemed like a cruel irony to Thomas Damon in the spring of 1852: the "cities of peace, love, and union" were neither peaceful, loving, nor unified. That was a difficult time for the Shakers, and for Damon in particular, who traveled back and forth between the Hawkins/Canon situation in Tyringham, the "Richmond English question" at Enfield, and the Irving case being heard in Lenox.

As if things were not discouraging enough, Elder Grove Wright's health was failing. In 1852 he wrote the Harvard Ministry that he had erysipelas fever, a skin disease that frequently plagued the brethren. "My hands have pealed nearly all over, the insides several thicknesses have pealed off, so that they are now quite tender. But when I come to get to work pretty steady I think they will get tuff again. I have already made some beginning to do a little work, but I find that I am not as strong, as I used to be."[54]

The other Shakers, valuing Wright's leadership and dreading his loss, sent him to the seaside and to various spas, hoping to obtain a cure, but their valiant attempts were unsuccessful. His health continued to deteriorate, with head and neck pains, weakness, fever, and "a roaring in his head, as if under a tin roof in a gale of wind when it thundered, rained and hailed." Nevertheless, according to Thomas Damon, Elder Grove continued to do considerable work. Even in February 1854, though he was still suffering, he managed to make 116 pails in a month or two, sending some to other communities "filled to the brim and pressed down, with our choicest and best love." That year, however, he made his first request to retire from the eldership.

After years of enduring what he called "the old scratcher," Wright found his condition growing worse in the summer of 1860. That October he asked again to be released from his position in the Ministry, where he had served for forty-two years, and this time his request was granted. He was obviously relieved to be "at liberty," and a reluctant Thomas Damon was appointed to the first position in the Ministry, with seedsman and Church Family second elder Phidelio Collins second. "It was a most *extreem* cross to Elder Thomas to take the first lot in the Ministry, but as the Ministry could not consent to anything else he took hold in obedience to the Gift they felt."[55]

Wright himself wrote of "a most blessed releasment in the change." He died of pleurisy in April 1861, described by a later Shaker as "said to be an almost perfect man." Maria Lyman nursed him at Enfield in the second meetinghouse, turned into an excellent infirmary, in his final illness.

His funeral drew dozens of mourners from the world. In a letter from Tyringham that autumn the Ministry wrote sadly, "Every heart was over-flowing at the unexpected departure of our elder brother Grove . . . . Having been actively engaged in the counsels of the Minnistry for nearly half a century, combining in a desirable degree a copious and retentive memory, his advice was frequently sought with the same faith and confidence that attaches to an oracle." A mournful passage in the same letter said, "It is evident that the world moves, and we will not question but that it moves forward. But where are we to look for all of our friends, if this state of things is to proceed much farther—shall we be able to keep track of their whereabouts."[56]

Wright's epitaph might best be the following statement: "I have never seen a moment that I felt willing to exchange my privilege among Beleivers for all the riches, honor, pleasures & vanity which is to be found in the world."[57]

CHAPTER NINE

"Roll Swiftly On, Remaining Years"

Roll swiftly on, remaining years,
Though robed with joy, or washed with tears,
We ask not further stay;
To earth, and all her shifting scenes
We bid adieu for holier themes—
Allied to endless day.[1]

Early on a frosty December morning in 1864 two boys were feeding livestock in the Hancock Shakers' round barn when they noticed, above the odors of cows and hay, the sharp smell of smoke. Their lantern might have tipped over, or perhaps it was arson or spontaneous combustion; at any rate, the enormous hay-mow was on fire. One lad tore off to ring the bronze bell atop the brick dwelling to summon the community from breakfast while the other hurried to release the cows and other livestock from their stalls, already thick with smoke. Blazing brands were blowing onto the roof of the nearby cider mill by the time a fire engine from the hamlet of Barkersville arrived and helped prevent a major conflagration. Although the animals were saved, the fire consumed seven wagons and one hundred tons of hay (worth about $3,000), along with two small sheds. The barn itself, the pride of the community, was reduced to blackened walls, and trustees Isaac Augur and Ira Lawson estimated the total damage to be nearly $10,000.[2]

Ira Lawson, only thirty-one and recently made a trustee, took charge of the barn's prompt reconstruction, engaging a Pittsfield crew to cut and saw lumber on a Shaker-owned timber tract on Washington Mountain (twelve miles east of the village). By spring the barn was framed and by July it was ready to store hay. Yet one brother wrote, "We soon found by getting in hay that we had mad a great mistak in not raising the central part over the hay in order to give more room for hay and to avoid thumping our heads against the rafters." The brethren took advantage of the calamity to improve the barn's convenience and safety. Using levers to raise the roof over the hay, they replaced the conical roof with a twelve-sided, many-windowed monitor, thereby increasing light and ventilation. Increased light would mean less need for lanterns. They also dug a cellar for manure under the stabling, which required that they build two new circular walls. Finally, they built a root cellar under the hay wagon entrance, not finishing the project until 1883.

Fires, always a threat, particularly plagued the Hancock Shakers during the 1860s, and one can trace some of the changes occurring in the Society by reflecting on what and how the Believers rebuilt. In 1865 a fire destroyed the profitable carding and fulling mill, the center of the community at the North Family. In April 1867, two years later, the wind carried sparks from a burning brush heap to ignite two Church Family buildings, the hospital and the tailor's shop, both situated just west of the brick dwelling. The brick dwelling itself was in danger of catching fire, and the barn and the large wood house were already ablaze when the Barkersville fire engine arrived to help. The loss was estimated at $7,000.[3]

With the loss of its mainstay, the carding and fulling mill, the Hancock North Family closed in the winter of 1867, and the dwelling house was hauled downstream to the Church Family and placed at the site of the burned hospital. Installed just west of the brick dwelling, this building became the central sisters' shop, where they made and later sold baskets, candy, and sewing boxes until the building was finally demolished in 1958. The loss of a manufacturing industry and the simultaneous expansion of handicrafts epitomized a pattern that was occurring throughout the Society.[4]

After the death of Elder David Terry the West Family also closed, on November 25, 1867. A journal kept at New Lebanon explained that family's location: "on a mountain side much like the Tyringham community, is a very unprofitable and hard place to support a family, the soil is very cold and wet. The buildings, that is, their foundations, difficult to keep in repair, and they have not able abilities to manage a family there." In the same way, poorer farms were being abandoned all over New England. Now the Hancock community became concentrated at the Church, Second, and East families, and by the end of the decade membership totaled 125.[5]

The closing of families was just one sign of the strain the Shakers were under in the 1860s. The Civil War meant the suspension of practically all of the military service exemption laws for which the Believers had struggled for more than sixty years. If the Shakers had had a difficult time asserting their pacifist beliefs in peacetime, the war made it nearly impossible. Brethren from all societies had to appear before draft boards to be classified for military duty.

New Lebanon's Elder Frederick Evans and Benjamin Gates appealed personally to President Abraham Lincoln and War Secretary Edwin M. Stanton with an ingenious solution. Because many of the brethren had served in the military before they joined the Society, the federal government owed them more than half a million dollars for their services. Yet, consistent with Shaker principles, the Ministry forbade the brethren to collect their back wages. The total of muster fines owed by the Shakers ($28,000) amounted to far less than the amount owed to the Shakers by the government (more than $600,000), and Evans proposed that if the brethren were exempted from military duty, the Society would forgive the federal debt. The result was that the brethren did not have to serve, although President Lincoln was apparently so impressed by the two Shakers standing before him that he remarked, "We need regiments of just such men as you."[6]

Spiritually and economically, the Civil War was a watershed for the United Society of Believers, just as it was for the entire nation, and marked the end of the Society's growth and forward momentum. Many Shakers followed the war closely: diarist Anna Granger of Enfield's North Family commented on the soldiers stopping by for meals in 1863 and later on the Northern victory, followed hard by Lincoln's assassination. Like all Americans, the Shakers were stunned by the horror and atrocity of civil war and newly sobered regarding human nature. Perhaps partly because of their disillusionment, many Shakers in the second half of the century grew less preoccupied with heaven and hell and more interested in improving earthly life—how humans could live together in peace and harmony. And American priorities had changed: whether because of the new cynicism, postwar prosperity, or both, the midcentury marked a subduing of the urge toward spiritual fulfillment that was so common in the first half of the century.

The wholesome pastoral life that had so suited the Shakers was receding into the past. While the rural South, ravaged by opposing armies, lay in physical and economic ruins, the victorious North was vigorously expanding. Mechanization was transforming every industry, particularly between 1860 and 1870. Telegraph lines linked cities and crossed the Atlantic Ocean. Immigrants poured into Northeastern cities to take jobs in factories. Out west, meanwhile, good cheap land would be available for another generation or so, and the Homestead Law allowed anyone to own 160 acres of public land after working it for five years.

Farming-related industries were working at top production to accommodate western farms. Factories began producing plows, McCormick harvesters, mowers, and, by the 1870s, barbed wire fencing. Railroads whisked farm products to flour mills, breweries, boot and shoe factories, and meatpacking plants in cities like Chicago and Cincinnati. Those entrepreneurs involved in mechanization, the opening up of the West, or both, could make fortunes.

Although many new businesses were booming in the 1860s, the Shaker seed industry, for a number of reasons, abruptly declined. Confederate money was now worthless, and the long-term accounts the Shaker seedsmen held with southern dealers were erased. On September 25, 1861, Elder Thomas Damon told the New Lebanon Ministry that "the society at Enfield, Ct. are sustaining a loss of about $25,000.00 by the Southern rebellion movement, it is in Garden seeds mostly." By 1863, Jefferson White's entry in Enfield's annual report to the Ministry listed "large sums due from the South, and parties at the North, a part of which is good—a large amount of seeds on hand perhaps $20,000 worth." That same year Earl Jepherson held notes payable totaling almost $73,000. Hancock's earnings had plunged by $4,000 since 1850, to $2,922,54.[7]

But the South's defeat was far from the only reason the Shaker seed industry never recovered after the Civil War. The Hancock seedsmen's western route, for example, stayed mighty until the 1870s. But other entrepreneurs had seen the Shakers earning $1,000 from an acre's worth of seeds, and when the transcontinental railroad connected the east and west coasts on May 10, 1869, the opening of the West brought into the seed business new companies that could produce seeds cheaply: rolling midwestern farms, their rich black soil said to be five feet deep. By the 1870s they were competing with the Believers for customers, producing lavish color catalogs that playfully exaggerated the virtues of their seeds, such as the illustration in *Maule's 1887 Annual Catalogue* of an enormous cauliflower barely fitting in a chair. The Shakers were unwilling to engage in this type of false advertising, although they did eventually print seed catalogs and envelopes in color.

In addition, rail transportation had created a market for seeds and produce that now spanned the entire nation. The Shaker seed peddler and one-horse wagon, ambling over the circuitous country routes, had clearly become an anachronism. Like New England farms generally, the Shaker farm was of a size and capacity to serve itself and the area around it. The larger, nationwide market, served by a vast transportation network, meant seed production had to expand beyond the capacity of the Shaker communities.

In 1872 the Hancock society's Pittsfield and New York seed routes were abandoned, and the most lucrative western route brought in only $1,900 in 1874, compared to $6,154 in 1865. With manpower shrinking, acre after acre was planted in grain or left to grow up to brush.[8]

Although it was not immediately evident, other Shaker farm-related industries were entering a similar decline. Big companies were beginning to dominate the American marketplace. Medicinal herbs, for example, for decades grown and prepared by the Shakers, were now the product of pharmaceutical companies. The 1835 Hancock tannery, though still an important business in 1860—annually producing 600 sides of leather, 200 calfskins, 400 kips, and 510 sheep skins—closed when the Tillotson Tanning Mill expanded in Pittsfield; after 1865 it was converted to a forge and woodworking shop. Its ingenious windlass, designed to hoist heavy loads of hides from the basement to the attic, now carried lumber and blacksmith's supplies.[9]

The Shakers were not alone in watching their farm profits shrink; they were witnessing the great movement of agriculture westward. The sheep industry, once centered in New England, moved west to the Rocky Mountain states; the beef cattle and wheat industries also found greener pastures in the Midwest and West. And despite the decline of northeastern agriculture, the U.S. production of corn, wheat, oats, and barley more than doubled in the two decades after Lincoln's election, as did the number of cattle, sheep, and swine as new lands came under cultivation.

In some ways the Shakers were fortunate to become less dependent on farming as a source of income. The farmer's life was radically changing as machinery costs skyrocketed and farms became heavily mortgaged. Simultaneously, the value of many farm products plummeted: in 1881 a bushel of corn sold for 63 cents; in 1890, for 28 cents. Shaker farming had been labor intensive, but the new style of farming required expensive equipment, fewer hands.[10]

Even though it was less lucrative, farming was still a vital part of Shaker life. In 1861, as mentioned, the Tyringham society owned an impressive amount of livestock: 112 dairy cows, 24 oxen, 6 fat cattle, 20 horses and colts, 247 sheep, and 150 fowls. The Hancock society possessed 22 horses, 154 cattle, 28 oxen, and 206 sheep in 1860.[11] In Enfield, meanwhile, in 1863 the Church Family alone owned 4 yokes of oxen, 20 steers, 60 cows, 125 sheep, 7 horses, 100 hens, as well as pigs and ducks. They were improving their dairy herd with the help of two thoroughbred Durham bulls and one Alderney bull, and by 1880 it doubled in size, along with the number of horses.[12] In 1873 the Enfield society still owned fifteen or twenty work horses, one of which was valued at the hefty sum of $400, and several yokes of oxen; the following year Hancock's Second and East families each possessed four oxen.[13]

By the late 1860s nearly a thousand acres were still under cultivation at Hancock, but instead of seed crops these fields grew mostly grains, with hay, Indian corn, oats, barley, and rye as major crops, plus potatoes (New England's most important export vegetable) and orchard fruit and products. The dairy and poultry industries were still flourishing in all of the societies, though, as elsewhere in the region, they were not big money-

makers. And onion seeds were still a lucrative industry for the Enfield North
Family in 1882, when head gardener Richard Van Deusen showed a *Farm
and Home* reporter the onion field and said, "That's what brings in the
money"—$2,200 from two acres the previous year. All three Hancock fam-
ilies dried green sweet corn and sold it in "tin-lidded, bent wood contain-
ers" until 1920.[14]

The surviving Shaker industries had become more sophisticated. Where
two dozen well-made brooms in a day had once been an accomplishment,
six to eight dozen a day were commonly produced in the late 1870s. In 1877
one man with a horse and a double planting machine could plant ten to
twelve acres per day. In four months one man could raise and harvest six
acres or more, producing six hundred pounds of broom corn from an acre.
There were also improved methods of removing the seed from the brush.
In the hayfields the brethren now used a horse-powered mowing machine
instead of a hand scythe, so that just one man and a team could mow what
had required twelve to twenty men fifty years earlier. The horse also pulled
a rake with long iron or hickory fingers, replacing the hand rakes of previous
years. A reaper took over from a cradle, a cultivator and side-plow were
used for potatoes and corn instead of a hoe and plow, and underground
drains had replaced slough-holes. Improvements also had reduced the sisters' labor: steam laundries were in place, along with ranges for cooking
and soapstone ovens for baking.[15]

Mechanization was accompanied by the decreasing involvement of
Shaker men. Even though new machinery allowed one man to do the work
of two, often that one man had to be hired. As early as 1865 the Enfield
North Family paid $1,378 for farm work. The seed and tanning industries
had been skilled and demanding work for the brethren, employing numerous men and boys. Their loss meant a loss of focus and achievement
for young men. In 1850, 85 men and 123 women lived at Hancock; by 1900
there were two men, both older than fifty, and 41 women.

In Enfield, during the same fifty years, the male population dropped
from 104 to 28, the female numbers, from 106 to 57.[16] By 1870, the numbers
of men were sharply reduced: there were six men apiece in the Church,
South, and North families. Of the three brethren in the East Family, one
was blind and one unstable, and that family closed during the 1870s.

To cope with shrinking manpower and declining industries the Shakers
had to find new sources of income. Increasingly, they relied on the sisters'
labor. This shift in Shaker economy was epitomized by the loss of the Hancock North Family's textile mill in 1867 and the transformation of that family's dwelling into the Church Family sisters' shop. Much of what Americans
wore was now made by big companies; even the Believers no longer spun
and wove the material for their own clothing but bought alpaca and linen

for summer and woolens for winter. However, Shaker sisters still dyed, spun, and wove counterpanes, braided palm-leaf hats, and hooked rugs and sold these products, along with refreshments, applesauce, preserves, and brushes, to visitors at the office. Anna Granger, a diarist, seamstress, office sister, and later eldress, created wooden-handled fans of peacock and turkey feathers. Unlike most Shaker products these were not simple and modest, but they were snapped up by the public at one dollar each.[17]

The dairy was traditionally the sisters' domain. At Enfield it was in the house, and sisters at the East Family alone made 1,500 pounds of cheese in 1860. Later in the century the dairy was moved to a separate building and became a brethren's industry. Sisters also did much of the work in the poultry industry, although men like Hancock's Louis Basting were usually in charge.[18]

More important than handicrafts in their overall economic picture, however, was the Shakers' acceptance of nationwide changes and their financial support of the country's vigorous new industries. Partly because the seedsmen were alert to market trends, many of the Shaker villages successfully transformed their economies in the decades after the Civil War. This was a profound change: from primary producers the Believers soon became investors in the new America. Quickly, the Enfield seed merchants' lists of accounts due were replaced by equally long lists of lucrative holdings in companies such as Steamboat Stock Co., Western Bonds, Hartford Life & Annuity, Stockbridge and Pittsfield Railroad (143 shares), and Boston and Albany Railroad. In 1885 the list included shares in Wells & Fargo Express, Manhattan Railroad, and Western Union. In the same few decades this community's seed industry dwindled to a fraction of its former strength: whereas in 1861, $70,000 had been due the North Family on account for seeds; in 1890, just $4,275 was due.[19]

The Enfield North Family invested in other capitalist ventures as well. During the 1860s it collected rent from a Holyoke, Massachusetts, tenement, a store, a farm, and the "land on which Gowdy's Still stands" and owned "considerable property in Berkshire County." In 1866, North Family trustee Omar Pease reported holding "cash notes against over 90 persons, mostly secured by mortgage amounting to $71,071.00."

That the societies flourished despite shrinking membership was largely thanks to canny business managers such as Pease. Certain trustees, in fact, were more effective at retaining the communities' wealth than the elders were in retaining their members. Many trustees were in fact more powerful than the elders. Some, like Pease, were educated within the Society; others brought skills sharpened in the world.

Clearly, the skills required by trustees were changing as they learned to speculate with the communities' money. Their farming activities had changed as well: now the Shakers were raising purebred stock and improving their fruit and ornamentals, activities more typical of wealthy gentleman farmers than of the average sustenance farmer.

Pease, who had lived in the Enfield society from the age of two, was praised by Canterbury brother Henry Blinn, passing through in 1873: "He is considered to be an excellent 'Provider' for the family & a very industrious and faithful man." He involved himself in big projects and through them left his mark. He loved forestry and sowed 150 acres of pine forest acclaimed throughout Connecticut (and mostly lost during the hurricane of 1938). He supervised the construction of several magnificent buildings at the Enfield society, including a stock barn that was considered a model of convenience. He had his own method of keeping bees: "At the NF Omar has his bee house in the garret of a two storied building. The roof is so constructed that he has a row of hives on each side. Br. Omar entertains the idea that the bees do well, with their hives so far from the ground. We have thought they did best to have the hives only a few inches from the ground." He directed the changing of the grade of the public highway, shifting the road ten rods east and raising it, improving the adjoining fields. Pease spent the last three years of his life as North Family elder.[20]

After Pease died in 1883, Richard Van Deusen, originally from Tyringham, came from the Church Family to be deacon at the North Family. A noted horticulturist and pomologist, he developed acres of fruit trees, including a splendid four-acre pear orchard, for the Enfield society. He also bred fine blood stock, particularly horses, and trained them. Accustomed to much interaction with the world, he apparently had a streak of vanity—he liked to drive a fine carriage drawn by handsome horses.

Isaac Augur was elder, trustee, and business manager of Hancock's Church and Second families. In 1819, at the age of four, he came to the Society with his parents, his brother William, and his sisters Sophy and Jennet (or Jeannette). His family was prominent, his father, Leveret, being a church elder and a shrewd, progressive Yankee farmer. Isaac, appointed trustee in 1856 and elder in 1861, was interested in stock raising, particularly Holsteins, and was frequently seen at agricultural shows. In 1873, Henry Blinn remarked of him, "His very presence speaks peace. We feel that we are always made better by meeting him." His sister Jennet also became trustee and then eldress.[21]

Another of Hancock's most esteemed trustees, Ira Lawson, was born in Union, Connecticut, on April 25, 1834, the son of Robert Lawson, one of the first settlers there. He joined the Believers in 1852 at age eighteen, traveled a seed route with Jefferson White at twenty-one, served as elder with David Terry at the Hancock West Family at twenty-three, and was appointed Church Family trustee at twenty-eight. He was renowned for his shrewdness with money: when he took on the trusteeship, accounts were reportedly in chaos, but when he died in 1905, the Hancock Society was wealthy. Under his supervision the Church Family began to breed and raise cattle for area markets. Along with the reconstruction of the Round Stone Barn, he directed the rebuilding of the Church Family's substantial gristmill in West Pittsfield after a fire. He was responsible for improvements to the brick dwelling such as replacing the twenty-four-pane windows with four-pane windows and piping water up into the second and third lofts. He helped dig Hancock out of the problems its seed industry faced after the Civil War and helped direct the lucrative investments of later years.

Lawson had a romantic adventure of his own, however. One June evening in 1871, at the age of thirty-seven, he left the Society with Sister Eliza Van Valen, who had lived with the Hancock Shakers since she was a baby. The couple traveled by carriage and train to an Albany hotel, where they were married. Immediately after the ceremony, however, Lawson was stricken with remorse. Appalled at himself, he vowed not to consummate the marriage and to attempt to return to the Shakers. His wife, though emphatically objecting to the switch in plans, was finally persuaded to return, and after a night of "chaste companionship" they took the eastbound train to West Pittsfield. The fact that Lawson was so quickly forgiven and reinstated to his prominent position indicates his value to the Society—and its eagerness to retain talented brethren. Eliza remained with the Shakers for another year before leaving and marrying a non-Shaker.[22]

Judging from the numerous tributes to Ira Lawson that survive in Shaker and newspaper records, he was universally liked and respected. Phidelio Collins wrote the following: "Ira R. Lawson is a wide awak go ahead yankie. Nature has endowed him with great abilities. Far above middling. What ever he undertakes always proves a sucess. But very few men can keep so many things moving and not have something come to loss as he can. He is what can truly be called a great financier. If you want to get a man to manage one hundred thousand men successfully, get Ira R. Lawson."[23]

Despite such talents, however, the trusteeship was an office that was easily abused. According to Thomas Damon, the Shakers had to begin assigning their most gifted members to the trusteeship because so much Shaker money—$200,000, in his estimate—had been lost in the first part of the century by incompetent or unscrupulous managers. Damon proposed a better bookkeeping system, annual reports to the families and the Ministry, the prohibition of any land transactions without family approval, and the entrustment of sisters' checking accounts to women. Some societies instituted some of the suggested reforms. Yet problems continued—the Enfield trustees, in particular, lost family money in far-flung enterprises—

and these would cause serious erosion of confidence by the turn of the century.[24]

As membership declined, the Hancock society could not manage its large property, especially since the community was now made up predominantly of aged people, children, and women, most of whom did not work in the fields. The Society began to sell off its land, consolidating as each family closed. In March 1867 the Tyringham society sold the North Family property to John Canon, brother of Hannah Canon Hawkins, for $12,000, and Elder Richard Van Deusen moved to Enfield three days later. That same year the society sold its West Stockbridge gristmill. Enfield's East Family closed in 1874, its members moving to the North Family.[25]

Most significant, however, was the final closing of the Tyringham Church Family, marking the first closing of any of the long-term Shaker societies. (Two more would close in the 1800s before the spate of closures in the early twentieth century.) This community had struggled along, with its numbers greatly diminished, since the exodus of 1858, probably with very low morale and barely holding on.

The New Lebanon Ministry thought of closing the Tyringham society as early as 1870. In the late 1860s the society had refused an offer of $30,000 for its entire property. According to journal entries, the New Lebanon ministry visited Tyringham in August 1870 to consult with the Hancock ministry about selling the property and moving to "a more favorable locality"— specifically, the society at Enfield, Connecticut. That October the New Lebanon elders toured Tyringham, and "it was concluded to try to sell out as soon as possible, but not to sacrifice the place."[26]

Events moved slowly, however, for five years. The Ministry elders, including Hancock's Thomas Damon, began to consider trading the property for forestlands, which were very profitable at the time as local woodlots continued to shrink. At least one diarist, however, thought that the idea of trading developed, productive farmland, with buildings, for wild lands somewhere out west was preposterous. Yet two key Tyringham leaders, Michael McCue and Hastings Storer, both relatively young and highly esteemed for their business acumen, died in 1873 and 1874, respectively. Julia Johnson, Church Family eldress, went to the world around the same time. And membership figures given by Hancock elders to Charles Nordhoff, collecting data for *Communistic Societies of the United States,* showed Tyringham having only six brethren, eleven sisters, and six hired laborers in 1873. That March and April the following people moved to Enfield from Tyringham: Calvin Parker, Addison Storer, Eunice Storer, Electa Parker, Rebecca Harris, Aaron Manchester, Edwin Davis, and, last of all, Elder

Albert Battles and Eldress Harriet Storer. It was nearly one hundred years since Ann Lee and the Shakers had arrived in America.[27]

Finally, in the winter and spring of 1876, the Tyringham property was exchanged for half of a nine-thousand-acre tract of hemlock forest in Pike County, Pennsylvania, with tanneries nearby, and the North Family of New Lebanon bought the other half. Elders Frederick M. Evans and Thomas Damon and Brothers Levi Shaw and Ira Lawson engineered the deal. The Shakers would henceforth refer to the new property as the Promised Land.[28]

It was a sad irony that the Tyringham property should be exchanged for forestland, considering that Tyringham had always been praised for its magnificent trees. But by 1858 it was clear that the Society's voracious appetite for wood demanded timber from woodlots out west. In October of that year New Lebanon's Benjamin Gates and Robert Valentine went out to Michigan to cut, haul, and saw one hundred thousand feet of timber on a woodlot owned by the Shakers, "a portion of which is to be shipped home to assist in the building of a New Dwelling house at the 2nd order."[29]

The Shakers did not exhibit a sentimental attitude toward buildings and land; when these no longer served their purpose, they would be remodeled, torn down, or moved. In the same way, a small community could be merged with a larger one. In that spirit the elders must have decided that virgin timberland was more valuable than a struggling farm.

The purchaser of the Tyringham Shaker property was Dr. Joseph Jones, previously of Honesdale, Pennsylvania. Dr. Jones was a multifaceted man: he was a medical doctor, he owned woodlands out west for investment purposes, and he now intended to be entrepreneur of a vacation resort. He wanted to capitalize on the discovery of Tyringham by the rich and famous. The lovely valley had grown in popularity during the nineteenth century, frequented by such personages as Samuel Clemens and President Grover Cleveland, an avid trout fisherman. Riverside Farm and Orchard House had distinguished guests, and many private farm houses welcomed summer boarders.

Jones renamed the Shaker village Fernside, left many of its idiosyncrasies unchanged, and operated the resort successfully throughout the 1880s. A condition of the sale was that the grass in the old Shaker graveyard be cut annually; accordingly, the original stones were removed, some were placed in the wall surrounding the plot, and smaller stones were placed flat on the ground. Ironically, considering the long-ago local hostility to the Believers, the townspeople of Tyringham were worried that the departure of the Shakers would deal a death blow to their town, which had suffered losses by fire of paper mills and other industries.[30]

Despite the difficulties of the 1860s and 1870s—the impending end of
Tyringham, the deaths of beloved leaders, the destruction by fire of so many
buildings, the spiritual devastation of the Civil War, the closing of families,
and the now-perceptible decline in membership—the mood in the Hancock Bishopric was hardly grim. As William Dean Howells wrote in the
Atlantic Monthly in 1876, regarding the community at Shirley, Massachusetts: "I should be sorry to give the notion of a gloomy asceticism in the
Shaker life. I saw nothing of this, though I saw self-restraint, discipline,
quiet, and heard sober, considered, conscientious speech. They had their
jesting, also; and those brothers and sisters who were of a humorous mind
seemed all the better liked for their gift of laughing and making laugh."[31]
One such person was Hancock brother Calvin Fairchild, left "in the night
near the house" with the Shakers as a baby in 1843, who wrote at age twenty-
six, "Good, round, hearty, side-shaking laughter is health for everybody,
for the dyspeptic it is life."[32]

Although despite exceptions the majority of men were not staying with
the Society, many women still found Shaker life profoundly satisfying, as
suggested by the building of a substantial new sisters' shop at Enfield's
North Family in 1873. Indeed, when tiny Tyringham closed it still had seven
sisters between the ages of twenty and forty, two more forty to sixty, and
six above the age of sixty. Among the Believers a young woman could find
loving friends, a decent primary education, training in useful work, and the
opportunity—almost unknown in the world—to hold a leadership position. From the ranks of Shaker sisters during the mid-1800s emerged outstanding leaders such as Jennet Augur, Elizabeth Richmond Copley, Sophia
Copley, Anna Irving, Emeline Hart, Clarissa Pease, and Wealthy Storer;
artists such as Hannah Cohoon; skillful horticulturists such as Marion
Patrick; and talented writers, poets, and historians such as Catherine Allen,
Julia Johnson, Lucy S. Bowers, and Fidella Estabrook. For the brilliant
woman, the Society offered the chance to excel.

For aged or infirm members of both sexes the Society provided a serene
retreat. Sister Esther Williams, for example, broke her back and hipbones
in an accident at the age of twenty-seven. Her legs paralyzed, she lived in
the Hancock community until she died at ninety-two, her meals brought
to her by sisters for sixty-four years. In 1869 the *Berkshire Eagle* carried her
obituary, and the writer added, "During the time she has always been so
pleasant and thankful for any little kindness as to draw the simpathy and
affection of all who have been acquainted with her."

For young women, particularly those who were orphaned or destitute,
the Society was the doorway to a better life. One spring evening in 1873 a
visitor to the Enfield Church Family met with a group of sixteen or so
young sisters, who "gave evidence of careful cultivation. Their address, their

attire and their general deportment was highly commendable. After conversing awhile, we learned that each one was provided with a book, and
had proposed to read before the company. This proved to be very interesting." Poised, accomplished, and articulate, these sisters could have
graced an upper-class parlor, in sharp contrast with the prospects faced by
penniless young girls in the world. Opportunities for women in the world
had improved little, after all, during the nineteenth century. Mill workers
were poorly and erratically paid, often for more than sixty hours of work a
week. The life of a farm woman, meanwhile, could be an exhausting dead
end, with no rest, few diversions, wretched health, and no prospects. Her
nearest neighbor might be a mile away. Her husband, with long work days
in the summer and empty days in the winter, might be a drunkard or sexually abusive.[33]

Many young girls were sent to the Shakers because of the excellent education they offered. Fourteen-year-old Hattie Belden, for example, of
Whately, Massachusetts, was indentured in 1876 by her mother, H. F. Bel-
dens to learn housekeeping. The Shakers were expected to teach her a business; provide food, lodging, and clothing; provide "a good common school
education"; and train her in "habits of frugality and virtue" until she
reached the age of eighteen. The sum of $200 would be given to her as a
marriage portion; if she should get sick between the age of eighteen and
the time of her marriage, then part of that sum could be used to care for
her. Also, the indenture form allowed her "such clothing as shall be necessary and decent for a person of her age and situation."

The Shaker girls were supervised by the younger women, who sometimes became a lifelong inspiration. Sister Emily Copley long remembered
a certain beloved sister who taught her to write hymns. "The words came
to me in my sleep," she recalled. "A sister I used to love when I was a child,
taught me. I used to see her when I was asleep." Sister Emily, in turn,
brought up many younger girls, as did her elder sister, Eldress Sophia Copley, said to have brought up nearly fifty girls. The sisters would be "up in
the morning before light, tending animals or getting breakfast, sewing, baking, building, planning, tending the sick and the aged, gathering and preserving fruits in their season, running the mills, scrubbing the floors, and
at night—'the quiet Shaker nights' . . . tired heads on soft clean pillows
sometimes dreamed wonderful dreams."[34]

Many young women did leave, though not in as great numbers as the
young men. Those that left on good terms were given a substantial amount
of clothing as their share in the community's property. Emmoretta Belden,
for example, who served for years as second eldress in Hancock's Church
Family, left December 28, 1897, with the following: five wool and seven
cotton dresses and cloth for two more; six wool and six cotton shirts; three

fine chemises, five common chemises, two linen chemises; three cotton and one flannel nightdresses; four skirtwaists; three fine and three cotton drawers and three flannel; two red and two white flannel vests; two dozen pocket hankies; four over aprons, six calico; six pairs stockings; four pair shoes ("two good—two quite poor"); some slips; two pairs rubbers; one double shawl, one summer shawl; one umbrella; one jersey; and two crocheted capes. (A young man named William Conway, on the other hand, left in 1875 with "five shirts partly worn, five shirts good as new," six pairs footings, all the boots and shoes he would take, shaving tools, and $100.)[35]

Sister Emily Copley grew resigned to the eventual departure of her charges. Asked why the Shakers could not allow young girls to marry and stay in the community, she said, "First they'd be planning to keep for themselves and then for their children. I've brought up eleven children, everything but bearing them, and they're all good and useful too, and that's something. . . . But they married and live in the world's way. Yes, it's natural."[36]

Despite the steady departure of members the Hancock and Enfield societies gleamed with prosperity. One Shaker traveler wrote in September 1872:

> Passing through Hancock recently, we were pleasantly surprised at her improved appearance. Always neat, she now looks beautiful. Meeting house modernized; the antiquated, elevated aqueduct by the roadside is no more; beautiful stone fences, with posts and boards above; large permanent gates, painted red, and fastened by spring padlocks—all looking rejuvenated. Very likely her people are being illustrated as those consecrated souls who "put their hands to work, and give their hearts to God."[37]

Building was underway in both Hancock and Enfield. In 1870 the Hancock Shakers had remodeled the meetinghouse, changing its roof from a gambrel to a gable style. Six years later they expanded their central office, or trustees' house, for the second time. The brethren erected a two-story addition, connecting the office with the wood house just east of it. On the first floor of the addition was the new kitchen, replacing the old one, which had been prone to flooding.[38]

The Hancock society's "improved appearance" was partly an effort to attract new members. For the same reason, and to survive the social turmoil of the post–Civil War era, the Society was attempting to relax some of its stricter rules. The Shaker villages looked different now, as members and elders eased the standards of plainness established by Mother Ann and the early elders.[39]

Canterbury brother Henry C. Blinn observed the Society's changing public face as he traveled through the New England communities on his way to Kentucky in May 1873. Blinn's record is worth examining closely, displaying as it does his wide-ranging curiosity and great powers of observation. He commented on everything from the quality of education in the different societies to the color of paint used in the Ministry apartments.[40]

At Enfield's North Family, Blinn found Omar Pease supervising the building of the large new sisters' shop (sometimes called a dwelling), three stories high, white frame with green blinds, and in the shape of a cross. It contained a girls' dwelling, sisters' shops, and a laundry, all topped by a slate roof and an observatory. Blinn noted the "ornamental style of painting . . . [which] is wholly new to us," referring to the interior doors with "white pannels and blue muntings." The rest of the interior woodwork was painted white, except for the faces of built-in drawers and cupboards; these were black walnut, "finished with French polish." The building, with its large windows, spacious rooms, and fixtures of Italian marble, was expected to cost $25,000.

Blinn also discussed the newly permitted practice of planting trees and shrubs in the dooryard. At Hancock he found "the Brethren ornamenting their dooryard with fruit trees. It seems that as soon as the liberty was granted to place trees & shrubs in the dooryard, the privilege has been generally accepted. . . . At Enfield Ct. we saw quite a number of trees in places that a few years ago was consecrated to grass only. Some of these were in front of the meeting house, and dwelling house. Every available spot was made use of, and now instead of no trees, it is fast becoming all trees." In Hancock the rows of fruit trees stretched from the brick dwelling to the trustees' office. Before long purely ornamental flowers also would be planted in the dooryards, just as ornaments would adorn the dresses of Shaker sisters.

In Hancock, Blinn noted an energetic attitude. "Everything shows a progressive spirit. The buildings are renewed by being painted & repaired. Some new ones have recently been erected. The fences are being renewed. Old buildings are being torn down. Rods upon rods of stone wall have been built and they are still at work, relaying or building."

Blinn described the recent changes to the Hancock meeting house: "The meeting house has recently been changed from the old style curb roof to the gable roof. It is now a beautiful two storied house with green blinds. The meeting room has not been changed. The wood work is painted blue, and they still retain the benches for believers. The spectators are provided with fast seats having good backs. The upper part of the house or Ministry's apartments are stained yellow."

Yet Blinn was not entirely happy with a remodeling of the apartments upstairs, saying, "This manner of patching old buildings and having one part finished with all the modern improvements & the remaining part left in the style of a hundred years ago is far from being congenial with our mind."

Three years after Blinn's visit to Enfield the handsome six-story brick dwelling at the Church Family was begun, partially designed by Sister Emeline Hart and constructed mostly by outside labor. It was described in 1897 as "a large substantial structure of brick with a greystone basement . . . a model of convenience throughout in every department, with steam heat, running water, good ventilation, and the most improved appliances for preparing food in their cooking and baking departments." The dining room was in the basement of the house, with the cooking rooms adjoining. Above were the music room, sitting room, library, and meeting room. The sleeping rooms, with one or two persons per room, were connected with bathrooms. An adjoining laundry featured washers and wringers run by engine.[41]

Shaker schools were not untouched by the changing times and now offered many more subjects, including history, astronomy, geometry, philosophy, drawing, algebra, and written composition. As part of the free-school system, the school district furnished equipment such as books, maps, charts, and blackboards. Shaker teachers now seemed bent more on furnishing a good education than on merely creating a model Shaker. They did not expect their students to go on to college, however, and so did not provide the classical education in Greek and Latin that was offered by local public high schools.[42]

Henry Blinn, a former teacher himself, commented on the school at Enfield (he considered it inadequate) and the one at Hancock (he called it "excellent"). About the Enfield schoolroom he said:

The place was well furnished with books & maps &c, &c. They also had a set of Lowell Mason's music charts, containing some sixty lessons. This society as yet has no school house fitted up for the children of the society, but provides for the girls in summer by occupying a private room, and then arranging for the boys in another place during the winter. Enfield should have done better by its children. It needs a room fitted up with a good desk for the teacher and comfortable seats for the pupils. They have recently remodeled one of their buildings and made a "Music Hall." The room is high posted, well lighted on every side, and arched some 2 ft. We were well pleased with this blessing for the singers, and have not the least doubt but that it will be fully appreciated."[43]

The Shaker music instruction was especially thorough, judging from a notebook shared by Hancock sisters Ann Lee Cumings and Martha Johnson in 1869. Students learned music theory, including analysis of the scale, comparison of major and minor scales, practice exercises, and dictation. They were still using Shaker notation to transcribe songs, although by 1873 this must have changed: Blinn noticed "[a] large blackboard . . . well covered with the round notes" in a room used as a "singing school" in the Hancock dwelling.[44]

During the late 1860s a movement arose to allow instruments to accompany the singing. Many Shakers were vigorously opposed to this, fearing it would distract from and dilute the spiritual gift of music. As one writer put it, "I have no doubt that the introduction of any worldly instrument into our meeting at this time, would banish every good Spirit from them, and would entirely destroy the spiritual gift of the meeting. Of course its tendency would be to make the *young* Worldly and draw *them* back into the flesh. . . . That which comes from the *World* attracts to the *World,* and that which comes from the *heavens* attracts to the *heavens.* All true Godly progress and increase in Zion must come from within."[45]

Yet this was only the culmination of the long process in which Shaker music had moved away from its beginnings. Now it had little in common with the original chants and wordless songs. The publication in 1813 of the hymnbook *Millennial Praises* had ushered in a period when hymns with written words became widely accepted. Hymns then began to appear in print with notes attached, using Shaker notation. Soon a knowledge of the principles of harmony began to seem desirable. Singing schools sprang up, wherein young Believers learned good diction and the correct position of the mouth. This often required the employment of a non-Shaker singing master. The urge to harmonize rather than sing in unison meant, as Daniel W. Patterson has pointed out, that new melodies tended to be in the easily harmonized major mode as opposed to the unusual modes characteristic of early Shaker songs. The major mode, Patterson suggests, is culturally defined as "cheerful"; thus, later Shaker music also served to represent the Society as upbeat and progressive.[46]

By 1870 Shaker music was evidently being measured against a worldly standard by Believers themselves, and many felt that the singing could never really improve in intonation and tone without instrumental accompaniment. The Ministry then authorized the purchase of the Society's first organs. Within four years the Enfield schoolroom boasted "a grand and glittering piano," and a cabinet organ graced the Church Family's singing room.[47]

Even with all these changes, the spirit behind the music was still powerful, according to an 1870 visitor to Hancock, who observed: "The singing was of a character not taught in conservatories. There were strains that reminded one of the Marseillaise, which coupled to the significant words, created the highest enthusiasm. It was a burst of human emotion that carried malcontents and barnacles along in spite of themselves, producing conviction, for the moment at least. It was a spiritual tidal-wave."[48]

In December 1871 the twelfth issue of *The Shaker* newspaper appeared, published in Watervliet. On the final page was a Shaker song, written for the first time on a staff in standard musical notation. The purpose of *The Shaker* was to disseminate Shaker ideas to the world; and to share Shaker music, it was necessary to change the system of notation so that the world could understand.

Shaker intellectual life was more vigorous than ever as the Believers expanded their dialogue with the world. *The Shaker* newspaper, directed toward both the Society and the world, was established in 1871 in Watervliet and continued under different names until 1899. Some Shakers felt that it quickly became "too Infidel, and too Aristocratic." Entire issues of the newspaper in the late 1870s and 1880s never mentioned Mother Ann nor the beginnings of the faith. Instead, the contributors were concerned with the challenges of living together, both within the Society and among mankind in general, and eagerly discussed such issues as pacifism, woman suffrage, celibacy, and education. Such articles reveal the determination felt by many progressive members to find a useful and relevant role in the changing American society.[49]

The Shaker was part of a new direction for the Society, an attempt to reach potential converts by narrowing the gap between Believers and world's people. Like the new influences heard in Shaker music, subtle changes appearing in Shaker dress, and shifts visible in architectural style, worldly elements that might attract the general reader filled *The Shaker*. The journal ran essays on domestic science, pithy sayings, witty or earnest letters, book reviews, meteorological observations, commentaries on politics and farming, and home cures. The last not only dealt with earaches or smallpox but also appealed to worldly vanity with concoctions for removing freckles, dandruff, and warts.

One editor of *The Shaker,* who was also leader of the progressives in the Society, was Elder Frederick Evans of New Lebanon's North Family. Evans demonstrated a new brand of proselytizing, writing scores of articles on all subjects for worldly journals, presiding over a convention in Boston in 1867, traveling to England on a lecture tour in 1871. An intellectual, he carried on correspondence with such luminaries as Leo Tolstoy and Henry Ward Beecher. He understood how to use the press, and his lectures in the 1880s on topics as diverse as land limitation, debt collecting, spiritualism, Mormonism, ensilage, and woman suffrage were widely covered by newspapers.

Evans was certainly effective in attracting attention. In August 1879, for example, one thousand people attended the Shaker meeting in New Lebanon to hear him preach, and 226 teams of horses were hitched outside. But though Evans's progressivism struck a chord throughout the Society, there was much resistance from conservative Believers. In fact, the burst of intellectual energy seemed largely to pass the Second Bishopric by; even though Anna Irving and Daniel Orcutt of Enfield and Betsey Johnson of Tyringham were early correspondents, the great majority of contributions to *The Shaker* bore New Lebanon and New Hampshire postmarks. In contrast to that crowded meeting in New Lebanon, the Enfield Believers were turning inward, and after 1884 they closed their meetings to the public.[50]

As the numbers of Believers dwindled and those remaining aged, they were less of a threat and more of a curiosity; the world probably considered this a peculiar but no longer bizarre sect. The Society had survived for one hundred years. Americans in general were more sophisticated now and accustomed to, if not always tolerant of, diversity. The vigorous Shaker dance, the custom that most outraged non-Believers, had been modified into a few quiet steps accompanied by fluid hand gestures. The Shaker wealth commanded respect. Other communal societies had broadened their niche. And the softening of the stricter Shaker customs may have made them more acceptable to outsiders. Yet some scholars, most notably Henri Desroche, have suggested that the Shakers lost their true direction in the last quarter of the nineteenth century with their attempt to bridge the gap between their beliefs and those of the world.[51]

Certainly it appears that way to us, with our modern point of view. With the ultimate fate of these communities in mind we cringe when we see worldly influences stealing into Shaker ways. Yet if they had not chosen to bridge the gap with the world, their alternative would have been to isolate themselves, to continue to produce only for themselves. Such a move would have been unlikely for the Shakers. Economically, they had always been a part of the larger society—neighborhood, region, and nation—around them. Consequently, they were subject to the same forces of change that worked on worldly communities.

In the 1870s and 1880s, however, there were still many reasons for optimism. The Enfield Society impressed Henry Blinn with its excellent land—"the abundance of this world fills their treasury"—and its mechanical contrivances, particularly the steam engine in the laundry. The entire Enfield community was industrious and productive, judging by the fact that, in early May, "we found that the farming business was already quite well advanced for the season. The potatoes had already been planted some two weeks, & many of the fields sowed with grain. The asparagus & lettuce were large enough for the table." Most significantly, Blinn observed several new converts in the Enfield South Family in 1873, "which gave a freshness & ray of life to the place."[52]

An eleven-year-old boy entered the Enfield Church Family in 1880 who was destined to become the last male Shaker in the Hancock Bishopric. Ricardo Belden became a general handyman in the Enfield community, able to fix anything that needed it; he eventually specialized in making and repairing clocks, particularly all-wood cuckoo clocks, refusing to guarantee his work on metal parts. Later he would take charge of driving and maintaining the Hancock Shakers' cars. He was admitted into membership in 1893 at age twenty-four.

Members still did not perceive the Society to be in a major decline but merely in a temporary slip that would be corrected soon. Eventually, the tide would turn, most Shakers believed, and a flood of eager converts would come, just as they had come to Mother Ann Lee in Niskeyuna. The Believers patiently awaited that time when God would restore the faith and perhaps not only inspire the public but also stir the Shakers themselves. As Blinn remarked, discussing the construction of the sisters' shop in the Enfield North Family in 1873, "It would seem that they had built very largely for so small a family, still who knows but that a prophetic spirit may whisper of the future."

CHAPTER TEN

Final Years of the Hancock and Enfield Shakers

To those pure realms of endless light where millions find employ
In singing praise in glory bright in everlasting joy,
Then we can join with them in praise on the celestial shore,
And loud hosannas we will raise and sing for evermore.[1]

As the nineteenth century swept like a torrent into the twentieth, the Shaker communities had to struggle to stay afloat. Often this meant casting off key values such as separation from the world or the importance of labor in order to remain relevant to a changing America. One by one the Western societies closed. In the East, small communities of a dozen or so Shakers, mostly women, paid hefty taxes on vast properties and either watched the farms slide into neglect or paid hired laborers to maintain them. "It is a great burden," Ira Lawson wrote to Elder Joseph Holden in 1900, "which Believers will have to meet so long as we owne so much land and buildings." Intertwined with all of the other troubles was the loss of the spiritual leadership of the nineteenth century.[2]

One bitter pill was the sale in January 1905 of Promised Land, the nine-thousand-acre Pennsylvania tract received in exchange for the Tyringham Shaker lands. Valued in 1875 at $120,000, the property was sold to the state for a mere $13,000. "It represents one more step in [the Shakers'] decline," reflected a reporter at the time. "The tremendous sacrifice was necessary because the property was eating up their funds in taxes and was bringing them no return." Though the property had yielded a decent income at first from timber, the Shakers had no one competent to manage or develop it.[3]

Brother Levi Shaw, who had entered the Society as a boy in 1827, was the negotiator and entrepreneur who made the first contact with Dr. Joseph Jones and persuaded him to trade his Pennsylvania woodlands to the Shakers for the Tyringham property. Both Shaw and Jones were involved with a lumber mill in Windsor, New York, that processed the lumber from the Shakers' "Promised Land." Shaw apparently managed this mill, which in 1888 burned down with an uninsured loss of $12,000.[4] In the same town was a buggy whip and carpet beater factory, owned by one Charlie Comstock. In 1899, Shaw helped finance Comstock's participation in the Klondike gold rush. The elders, however, made Shaw dissolve the partnership and hire Comstock. When Comstock was unable to repay money borrowed from the Shakers, Shaw confiscated his factory and moved it to New Lebanon, which thenceforth made whips. Six years later the Promised Land was sold at a huge loss.[5]

With its textile mills flourishing, the town of Pittsfield had grown rapidly during the second half of the nineteenth century and in February 1890, with 17,252 residents, voted to incorporate as a city. The Barker brothers' mills became the hub of a prosperous settlement, just east of the Pittsfield–Hancock border, that soon overtook the sleepy farms around the Shaker community. Various parcels of Shaker land were sold or rented to enterprising neighbors. In July 1890 the name of the railroad station was changed from "Shakers" to "West Pittsfield."[6]

Fewer obvious differences now existed between the Shakers and their neighbors. The sisters' dresses, for example, were no longer strictly unadorned: trimmings and brooches appeared in the numerous photographic portraits of the period. An organ accompanied Hancock's Sunday meeting, now held, without dancing, in the dwelling. On the walls in the office parlor hung pictures; knicknacks rested on shelves. The sisters attended political rallies and celebrated Labor Day 1899 with a picnic at Pittsfield's Lake Pontoosuc. And some even referred to one another as "Miss" instead of "Sister."[7]

With one exception, the Shaker buildings were unchanged, still presenting to the world a simple and dignified appearance. In 1895, however, the Hancock Shakers transformed their trustees' office—the only building meant to host world's people—to conform to the prevailing Victorian architectural fashion. The remodeled building sported a tower, bay windows, awnings, ornamental moldings, and pillared porches; fancy wallpaper covered the plain white walls inside. The decoration of this building with Victorian frills indicates the Shakers' acceptance of the fact that the world had irrevocably changed and that they would have to change their image in order to attract converts.

The Shakers themselves did not object to this particular departure from tradition. Even the outspoken Henry Blinn, visiting again in 1899, approved of the changes to the trustees' building. "Brother Ira, the trustee of this Society," he wrote, "has within a few years made important additions to the Trustees office, which is now a beautiful building and has been furnished with all the modern conveniences."[8]

Inside the Hancock trustees' office, visitors would gather in the salon or waiting room, cooled by water-powered fans as they awaited their turns to make transactions at the trustees' windows. Some customers might order a dozen wooden yarn swifts, still an important community product; others were tourists looking for Shaker souvenirs such as dolls, 150 of which were sold in 1905. One little boy from Barkersville was often sent by his mother to buy butter, "the best available, and when I had a nickle I would buy a little box of candied butternuts or flagroot." The sisters sold poultry, apples, pears, homemade wines, pincushions and other such "fancy work," brooms, confections, vegetables, and eggs, the last being by far the most important. At least one customer thought the Shaker sisters were undercharging for their goods: "They were the best and biggest eggs I've ever seen and I knew they were not charging enough for them." Their sales were enough to pay for "sundries" and turn a small profit.[9]

The trustees took out newspaper advertisements listing their products and promoting the Shaker life as something of a curiosity. One advised, "Don't miss visiting and seeing the Shakers and their wares." Sales were no doubt increased by the construction of a new state road through the village to the New York state line near the New Lebanon Shaker community. After the turn of the century the sisters took their fancywork and preserves on the road, setting up booths at county fairs, department stores, and seaside resorts.[10]

"A little city on the mountain," Fidella E. Estabrook called the Shaker village at the time. She and her natural sister, Fannie, had come as young women to Hancocck from South Hadley, Massachusetts, in 1880. According to Sister Fidella, main Hancock correspondent for *The Shaker Manifesto*, 1899 was a good farming year. She described abundant orchards; busy sawmills; heavy harvests of hay, sweet corn, and tomatoes; and a school of sixteen pupils visited that year by the Hancock school committee. The community had two hundred cattle; the previous year it had bought eighty calves and fifteen horses and colts and built a new stock pen. At the same time, non-farm-related brethren's industries were disappearing. The machine shop, possibly the first communal enterprise one hundred years earlier, when plenty of brethren were available to run it, was used in the late nineteenth century just for cutting and storing stove wood. In a 1902 tax assessment it was described simply as a "large red woodhouse."[11]

In Enfield, meanwhile, the once-impressive seed industry had dwindled by 1897 to practically nothing, with only a few seed packets put up every fall. Other industries, such as canned corn and beans, had taken its place. The Church Family, with its large herd of cows, no longer specialized in butter and cheese, although it continued to sell milk and cream from the door. The dairy remained a top priority: on January 12, 1897, the Enfield Church Family's second cow and ox barn, built in 1878, burned, and within the year a new cow barn was built to replace it. That July, Enfield North Family correspondent Edith E. Shufelt wrote to the *Manifesto* that it was a good farming year, with haying commenced on schedule and the cherries gathered. The Church Family had shared a "liberal feast of strawberries," she wrote. Morning services were hosted by the Church Family, she said; afternoon singing was held at the North Family.[12]

South Family elder Thomas Stroud may have epitomized the Shaker farmer of the period—thoughtful, meticulous, experimental, demanding best quality. He was noted for his model poultry houses and his greenhouses for cultivating cucumbers. Like others, he studied farming; he decided after much research, for example, to dehorn the family's fine herd of Jersey cows. His special interest, however, was in cultivating small fruits and nuts, and he planted splendid orchards and fine borders of nut trees. "Elder Thomas is a most genial man to meet," wrote a visitor in 1897, "and shows in all his work the value of an education in farming. He makes a science of it, and studies it in leisure time." South Family eldress Marion Patrick was also involved in the cultivation of fruit, especially after dairying changed from sisters' work to the work of hired men.[13]

Dedicated leaders like these were the spark that kept the Shakers going at the end of the century. But the labor force that now sustained the communities, tending the new horses and calves at Hancock and rebuilding Enfield's burned barn, was a hired one. Hired men were not a new phenomenon. In Enfield in the early 1860s it was a rare day when Anna Granger did not serve dinner to five or so laborers at the office, and by 1880 nine hired men lived at Enfield's Church and North families. They were the ages the Shaker brethren were not—between twenty and thirty.[14] Their presence had an increasingly disruptive effect on the community.

In 1900 the Hancock community was composed of two men—sixty-five-year-old Ira Lawson and fifty-three-year-old Louis Basting, both of whom would die in 1905—and forty-one women and girls, only four of whom were between thirty and sixty. Sixteen girls were under age sixteen; ten women were over sixty. At Enfield there were twenty-eight males, only three of whom (Ricardo Belden, thirty-one, Walter Shepherd, forty-five, and Thomas Stroud, fifty-five) were between thirty and sixty, and fifty-seven females, fourteen of whom were of those key ages.[15]

Fifteen hired men lived at Hancock, working under the direction of the two remaining Shaker brethren. The community had too much land and too few capable members to do the work itself, so the Believers had become indistinguishable from landed gentry sustained by hired labor. This situation resulted from the slow but sure erosion of one of Ann Lee's fundamental convictions—a belief in the joy and holiness of work. Hired men were indifferent at best to Shaker values and often directly refuted them.

The proximity of hired men had an effect on young women in particular. Edith Hall, probably the elder sister of trustee and eldress Frances Hall, was born around 1870 and came to the Hancock Shaker community at age eight. In 1888, at age eighteen, she left and then returned two years later. She signed the Hancock covenant on December 31, 1895, along with Emma Strobridge, Fidella Estabrook, and Henrietta Morgan, and became an office sister. But in 1900, according to the Hancock Day Book, she "left to get married to Comfort Sykes, 22, employed as a teamster. . . . She was given $25.00 and a large amount of clothing."

That same year Miriam Estabrook, sixteen, and Julia Lownsborough, fourteen, "ran away in the night, aided by John Drake, Jr., a hired man." The police returned the two girls; within a year both were placed in private families.[16]

Twenty-seven-year-old Emma J. Thayer left the community in the fall of 1904 to prepare for her wedding the following April to Paul J. Audette. Thayer, born in Belchertown, Massachusetts, had been placed with the Enfield South Family at age two after her parents died. She later moved to Hancock's East Family, where she became second eldress with Eldress Catherine. One of her duties was to hire and pay the laborers, among whom was Audette. A romantic newspaper account picks up her story:

> It was a case of love at first sight on both sides when they met four years ago [wrote a reporter], but neither dared speak to the other. During the last Presidential campaign [summer 1904] the Shakeress attended a Democratic rally in Pittsfield, and Audette . . . had his first conversation with the young woman. He accompanied her back to the settlement that night, and it became noised about that they were married. Miss T. became more secluded than ever. One day, as Audette was passing his lover's window, a thimble dropped to the ground. Looking up he saw Miss Thayer in the window. He immediately tore a piece of paper from a notebook, wrote a proposal of marriage, tucked it in the thimble, and tossed it to his sweetheart. Last November Miss T. forsook the Shaker religion and went to Winsted, Ct. to be with her brother, where they were married in April.[17]

By 1905 nearly all of the Hancock Church Family's labor force was hired. That year, when fire destroyed the Deacons' Shop, an unused garden seed shop was moved from the north side of the highway to occupy the spot and house the workers.[18]

Contact with hired and other worldly men was strictly limited. Stella Thorpe and her two elder sisters were left with the Shakers by their widowed father during the 1890s. While in the Shaker community, Stella had occasionally been driven by a hack driver, though she had never allowed herself to meet his eyes. Her sisters waited for Stella to turn twenty-one, and then all three left the Shaker community, finding work at an inn in nearby Lanesborough, Massachusetts. The young driver remembered Stella and followed her, and a few years later they were married at Lanesborough's Old Stone Church.[19]

Romantic intrigues were not the only problem associated with the presence of hired men. In 1912 a brand new span of bay mares was stolen, complete with harness and lumber wagons. The horses were returned a week later. "One of the thieves used to work at Hancock," commented a diarist.[20]

At Enfield, Emily Copley felt sorrow at seeing the Shaker inheritance falling to ruin, laid waste, she felt, by hired help. "Look at that fence!" she said once. "Oh if the man who built it should see it now! It was only a farm fence, once straight and fine of railing and post, now battered and broken, and sagging to its ruin." The peace of a Shaker community could now be shaken by an ugly incident. A hired laborer once threatened to strike Sister Emily if she didn't get him something from the storeroom. She faced him and cried, "You dare not strike me, you dare not!" The man "slunk away." Like the Shakers who live today at Sabbathday Lake, Maine, Copley was deeply committed to preserving the high standards and the physical legacy of the Believers of previous generations.[21]

In 1908, Elder Walter Shepherd rejected the idea of getting a milking machine for the Church Family's still substantial dairy (thirty-six cows were yielding 420 quarts a day), saying what they really needed was "intelligent and reliable help."

I still have the helper I mentioned in my last [Shepherd wrote to a friend], and he is doing very well, but he only knows a few words of English, and it is difficult to make him understand nice distinctions. On the whole our help is very unsatisfactory and always will be as long as the old man hires it. I had a fracas with a drunken milker yesterday. I quickly told him when I saw the condition he was in to go down to the men's shanty, that I would finish his cows as he was not in a condition to milk them. I waited some minutes to see if he would get up and go, and finally had to take the pail from him and push him along to the door. Well he called me for everything, and wanted to fight me. He was too drunk to stand and kept falling down back of the cows. What with one thing and another I have a pretty hard row.[22]

Yet without hired labor the Believers would have had to sell their lands, and thus the laborers made an important contribution to the Society. The Shaker lands—the fields, the imposing buildings, the feast grounds, the gardens, the streams and woodlots and burial grounds—these were not only the legacy of previous generations, but they held the Believers' history. The well dug by James Whittaker, the meetinghouse where Lucy Wright worshipped, the fields where sisters and brethren labored—these were deeply significant to the remaining Believers. More important, holding onto the property reflected their faith that Shakerism would endure and their numbers would expand again.

The "old man" referred to by Shepherd was undoubtedly Elder George Wilcox, his eighty-eight-year-old senior partner in the eldership. Wilcox had had a long and successful tenure as elder. Now, despite occasionally irresponsible behavior, he was unwilling to relinquish his position, a situation Shepherd found excruciating.

Leadership problems, whether lack of competence, trustworthiness, or compatibility, had became a major preoccupation of the Ministry by the end of the century. "Every family of Believers is so limited for help," wrote Sisters Lucy Jane Osborne and Betsey Johnson in 1883, "that the Ministry restrain us and give us only a short time" for a trip to Groveland.[23]

Many important Hancock leaders died during this period, followed soon by their elderly successors. Thomas Damon succumbed to malarial and typhoid fever in 1880; in addition to Shakers at least one hundred of his friends and acquaintances in the world attended his funeral, held at Enfield, his first Shaker home. Albert J. Battles, age seventy, succeeded Damon as Ministry elder and by 1884 was serving as both elder in the Hancock Church Family and first in the Ministry. Elder Isaac Augur died of erysipelas in July 1883. His position as trustee was taken by seventy-year-old Phidelio Collins, who died nine months later. Augustus W. Williams, longtime leader of the East Family, died in 1888 at the age of eighty-three; his associate, seventy-six-year-old William B. Pomeroy, lived only eight more years.[24]

An exception to this trend was forty-one-year-old Louis Basting, who moved in 1888 from New Lebanon to the Hancock Church Family to become head gardener and to lead meetings when Elder Albert was away. "Elder Louie," as Basting was called, was the last male minister and elder at Hancock. The 1850 horse barn was sometimes called "Elder Louie's Barn." He supervised a number of sisters' activities; in addition to taking care of the garden and selling surplus vegetables and fruit he was appointed to take charge of the poultry. He was also a poet; in 1877 he wrote a poem titled "Shaker Burials," which suggested that the Shakers should plant a tree by every grave.[25]

Meanwhile, the position of second eldress in the Hancock Ministry was changing every few years. In 1887, Hannah R. Agnew was released from the Ministry, and Caroline Helfrich, originally from Enfield, was appointed first eldress, with Emma Strobridge as second. After four years, Eldress Emma left the Ministry and moved back to Enfield to become eldress there. Emiline Pierce was appointed in her stead to assist Eldress Caroline, signing the Hancock Church Family covenant in October 1892.[26]

The following May, however, Sister Emiline suddenly left for the world.

Her abrupt departure, climaxing years of problems retaining qualified elders, may have galvanized the New Lebanon Ministry into action. Less than two weeks later, on June 8, 1893, the word came: "The Hancock Ministry is abolished. The Ministry of Mt. Lebanon take henceforth Mount Lebanon, Watervliet, Hancock, and Enfield under their charge. A. J. Battle continues trustee with Ira Lawson. C. Helfrich [Ministry eldress] and Emmaretta Belden—elder sisters in church." The New Lebanon Ministry was then composed of Joseph Holden, Harriet Bullard, and Augusta Stone. In 1898, Ira Lawson was appointed to serve as second with Holden.[27]

The Enfield society, meanwhile, was facing a different challenge—how to incorporate the members, particularly the leaders, of communities that closed. In the 1860s and 1870s, Enfield had to absorb new members from Tyringham, including that society's talented elders, Albert J. Battles, Richard Van Deusen, Harriet Storer, and Calvin Parker. When the Enfield East Family closed in 1874, its members moved to the North Family. Those changes occurred relatively smoothly—Harriet Storer, for example, became Church Family eldress instead of Second Eldress Sophia Copley—perhaps because the new residents were of the same bishopric and thus well known in Enfield.

The prosperous Enfield society had large new dwellings in both the Church Family (finished 1879) and the North Family, and its spacious fields seemed capable of accommodating additional members. After all, the North Family contained only seven men, ranging in age from sixty-one to eighty-five, and ten women, the youngest of whom was fifty. But although in earlier years the community seemed to absorb elders from outside with relative smoothness, later leaders would find it extremely difficult to establish a harmonious new hierarchy. Despite the Shaker belief in humility and self-denial, strong personalities had emerged among the elders and trustees, and individualism, as throughout the United States, was the rage.

The five-figure farm proceeds of the first half of the century had shrunk to the nickels and dimes earned by the sisters from eggs and fancy work. Lacking large incomes, the trustees invested the societies' capital in western real estate and in the nation's burgeoning new industries. Like their counterparts, stock speculators in the world, the trustees quickly became bold and sophisticated. Some, like Ira Lawson at Hancock, proved to be shrewd money managers; others, like Levi Shaw, were less successful.

Richard Van Deusen, George Wilcox, Thomas Stroud, and Albert Battles were among those trustees who invested energetically in the development of the American frontier. Van Deusen held many mortgages on land in Colorado, Kansas, and Tennessee, via various land companies. These companies were sometimes unscrupulous; a Chattanooga attorney claimed, for example, that the Lookout Mountain Company had taken advantage of the Shakers and that a certain property wasn't worth one half of the money they had loaned. Sometimes the companies were merely insolvent, like the Continental Land and Securities Company of Denver, which went bankrupt in 1891, a year after Van Deusen bought $5,000 worth of its stock.[28]

When Richard Van Deusen died in 1893, John William Richmond Copley returned to Enfield with his family to act as agent for the North Family. He, his wife (the former Kezia Lyman), his son William, and William's wife, Mabel, lived in a non-Shaker house near the former West Family. The extraordinary idea of hiring Copley, a married man, was probably conceived by his influential relatives among the Shakers. Judging by letters exchanged during the previous few years,[29] his mother, Elizabeth Richmond Copley, and Kezia's mother, North Family eldress Clarissa Lyman, were very fond of their five shared grandchildren. In addition, John Copley's sisters Emily and Sophia (the latter, first eldress in the Church Family) were trustees of the North Family sisters' funds.[30]

The Copley/Lyman influence in the North Family ended during the 1890s, however, as many of the strong female members of those two families, including the two matriarchs, died within a few years of each other. Averill Ann Copley, the baby of the family, died in 1891 at the age of thirty-nine; Amelia Lyman died in 1892 at sixty-one; Elizabeth Susannah Richmond Copley died in 1893 at fifty-one; Clarissa Lyman, the matriarch of that family, died in 1897 at the age of eighty-three; Kezia Lyman Copley died that same year at sixty; Sophia Copley died in 1898 at fifty-one; and Elizabeth Richmond Copley, the Copley matriarch, died in 1899 at eighty-two.[31]

Many members of the larger Shaker community were scandalized by the hiring of a married man and particularly by the hiring of Copley, who had so scandalously left Enfield with Kezia Lyman twenty-seven years earlier. Beneath the crisp note in the Church Family's journal—"J. W. Copley an outside salaried man is made to act as superintendent of, and foreman on the farm of said North Family"—also lay the keen awareness of the lack of qualified brethren to take on the trusteeship.[32]

Church Family elder George Wilcox was particularly disturbed by the hiring of John William Copley and proceeded to act as trustee himself. According to a note dated February 6, 1896, certain North Family properties were sold to one Amos D. Bridge, and "Eld. Geo represented to Mr. Bridge that himself, Sophia and Emily comprised all of the North Family Trustees."[33]

John Copley, in turn, distrusted Elder George Wilcox. He discovered, two years after the fact, that in March 1894 Wilcox had quietly sold ten North Family shares of Bell Telephone stock for $1,850. Yet that very April, according to Copley, the seventy-four-year-old Wilcox had claimed he had no North Family funds with which to pay taxes; taxes were finally paid that year with $2,000 paid back from a loan to the Groveland community. As late as 1895, Wilcox and Stroud exchanged $24,450 worth of Shaker securities for stocks and bonds of Lookout Mountain Consolidated Company in the names of Wilcox, Sophia Copley, and Caroline Tate. Whatever the financial problems, it seems clear that a schism was developing between members of the community and between the Church and North families.[34]

The Ministry in New Lebanon, somewhat removed from the situation and perhaps able to take an objective view, was also unhappy with the idea of a non-Shaker family living in the Enfield community. On February 19, 1897, a settlement was made with John Copley "for a time employed as farm superintendent at North Family." Copley's wife, Kezia, died that same year.[35]

By April 1897, the Shaker society at Canaan, New York, had closed, and its thirty-five members were installed in the Enfield North and Church families. The newcomers included Elder George W. Clarke, fifty-three, who had been with the Shakers for about twenty-five years and had signed the Enfield covenant on January 25, 1897. The "Canaanite" elders' order—Clarke, Eldress Miriam Offord, and Sister Angeline Brown—was transferred intact to the Enfield North Family.[36]

The next two years were spiritually difficult for the Enfield society. The Church Family seems to have absorbed its new members with relative ease, but the few remaining North Family Shakers were fiercely resentful of the large group of new arrivals to their community. Unlike the Tyringham family that came in 1875, these newcomers were of a different bishopric. They did not share a common history of visits, of shared projects, of beloved elders, or of general intermingling of members.

Central Ministry elder Joseph Holden resided at Enfield for periods of time, and in one of several despondent letters to the Sabbathday Lake society he wrote that "the spiritual elements does not seem to be as lively as one would desire but I know of no better way than to keep continually pulling for the right and condemning the wrong." In fact, in a situation that required tact and sensitivity, his management was clearly inadequate.[37]

In early 1899, just weeks after matriarch Elizabeth Copley's death, Elder Joseph assigned trusteeship positions in the North Family to Elder George Clarke and Eldress Miriam Offord of the closed Canaan community and to Caroline Tate of the Enfield Church Family. The new appointees were no "winter Shakers," each having been there for decades—Clarke had been a Believer since he was about thirty, and Offord had arrived at the Society in 1850. Tate was the daughter of Hannah Richmond Tate (niece of Thomas Richmond and Elizabeth Copley, and cousin of Emily Copley). Her mother had left her with the Shakers at the age of two, along with her two brothers. She signed the Church Family covenant in 1880.

Yet because these individuals were replacing John W. Copley and were from outside the North Family, the new appointments created a good deal of bitterness and may have increased the estrangement between families and generations that became so evident in the twentieth century. An unsigned note on Richard Van Deusen's stationery, dated January 23, 1899, seems to be marshaling facts for an argument over who had earned the right to lead. This note lists the following as members of the North Family, with their ages and number of years among the Shakers: Gilbert Avery (age 91), 69 years in the Society; John Damon (80), 72 years; Alden Lyman (63), 58 years; Elizabeth Copley (83), 45 years; Abigail S. Brooks (74), 55 years; Sarah Maria Lyman (65), 58 years; S. Emily Copley (55), 46 years; and two teenage girls, Sophia and Lizzie Hebrante.[38]

A handwritten document dated February 20, 1899, contributes the following:

Whereas George W. Clarke, Miriam Offord and Caroline Tate and others having been Fraudulently recorded in the Town Clerks Office as Trustees for the North Family Shakers of Enfield Conn. Without having been properly appointed or accepted by the North Family Members as Trustees. (The attempt to appoint and record the above parties Trustees as aforsaid was done secretly and without the knowledge or consent in any way of the North Family members.) Therefore we the members declare the same to be Null & Void as well as any action on their part as Trustees or Members of said North Family Shakers.

This unsigned statement was possibly written by Maria Lyman and Emily Copley, still members of the North Family.[39]

A similar sentiment is expressed in an undated note found attached to the bottom of a candle box at Sabbathday Lake: "Therefore we protest against the occupation or use of NF property by the citizens of another state as a high-handed act of injustice and a gross violation of the commandment which says 'Thou shall not steal.'"[40] It is not difficult to imagine how outraged these long-term Shakers felt when Avery was nudged from the eldership by Clarke, and how disregarded they felt as an entire new community filled their buildings. By 1900, the surviving members of this original North Family lived in isolation in the office, while the Canaanites inhabited the dwelling and sisters' shop.

To add to the complications, the 1890s had been the final decade for Enfield's South Family, a community that, though peaceful and productive, had steadily shrunk over the past forty years. By 1900 only six members remained: Elder Thomas Stroud (55), Eldress Marion Patrick (64), Rhoda Strowbridge (75), Maria Witham (75), Carolina Williams (50), and Mary A. Blivin (64),[41] along with eight minors. The decision was made to consolidate the South and North families and to sell the South Family buildings. In the fall of 1901 the Enfield South Family broke up, and its four last members, Marion Patrick, Thomas J. Stroud, Rhoda Strowbridge, and Maria Witham, moved into the North Family.

The Enfield society clearly needed to untangle the matter of the North Family trustees. On November 10, 1902, a meeting was held at the Enfield Church Family. Every ablebodied member of the Enfield society under age eighty attended, with the striking exception of the three remaining Copley and Lyman members: fifty-nine-year-old Emily Copley, sixty-nine-year-old Maria Lyman, and sixty-seven-year-old Alden Lyman. More than half of those present had come from the closed community in Canaan.[42]

The group declared that the only authorized North Family trustees were Church Family elder George Wilcox; Church Family eldress Caroline Tate; George Clarke and Miriam Offord, recently of Canaan; former South Family elder Thomas Stroud; and former South Family eldress Marion Patrick.[43]

Sister Maria Lyman was determined, however, to have the last word on the subject: two documents reveal, in their striking departure from Shaker communal principles, the deep hurt and resentment she felt toward the rest of the community. In a will dated February 1902, Maria Lyman bequeathed all of her property, including all rent and interest in the North Family property, to Gilbert Avery, John Damon, Alden Lyman, and Emily Copley. She requested that John W. Copley be retained as agent and counselor and directed that he be paid $600 yearly for his services. In 1910 she rewrote her will, leaving all of her property to Emily Copley for life and then to their shared nieces and nephews—Sophia Copley Watson, William E. Copley, Arthur B. Copley, Clarissa Copley Hawthorne, and John M. Copley—"in equal shares forever."[44]

Climaxing the decades-long drama of the Copley/Lyman families' relationship with the Enfield Shaker community, this will shows that, along with the vertical hierarchy of the Society, there existed a hidden horizontal structure, where natural family ties remained strong. Natural family ran counter to the Shaker structure and ideals, yet it played a vital part in cementing the community together. And when the Shaker ideals seemed to be eroding, the members of this particular blended family remembered, and gave preference to, their ties of blood.

At the turn of the twentieth century the Hancock society was composed of three families: the Church, Second (with Eldress Sophia Helfrich), and East (with Eldress Catherine Pepper) families. In 1902 the Church Family buildings included the meetinghouse, the brick dwelling, a sisters' shop and dwelling, the schoolhouse, the trustees' office, the ministry shop, the brethren's workshop, the dairy, the "old tan house," the hired men's shop, and the "old seed shop." There were an old and a new corn drying house; the "large red woodhouse," or machine shop; two old lumber houses; the poultry house; the ice house; and six barns, including the Round Stone Barn. The total value of the buildings was $10,000; that of the 1,225 acres of land, only 100 acres of which were cultivated, was $15,350.[45]

Children, few of whom would stay with the faith, were still being deposited with the Shakers by widowed or destitute parents. They attended school and Sunday school and in the evening often gathered at a "young people's meeting" where they chose a topic from the Bible to discuss.[46]

Sylvia Minott Spencer wrote a charming account of her childhood, spent with the Enfield Church Family starting around 1902.[47] By that time the family no longer worshiped in the meetinghouse but in the meeting room of the dwelling. The Church Family dwelling also contained the kitchen, bakery, dining room, parlor (with piano), and sleeping quarters. Sister Lucy Bowers taught school, and Robena Page took charge of the sisters' room. The family used the laundry not only for washing and ironing but also for canning and preserving during the summer. Sister Ann Offord presided over the office, selling sweets and small craft items to the public and serving dinners to travelers during the summer. The South Family had closed by the time little Sylvia and her older sister Irene arrived at the Society, and they visited the North Family only once or twice in the years they lived among the Shakers.

Children arrived at the Shaker societies for different reasons during this period: many were orphans, some were the children of hired hands, others were left by widowed fathers going off to the Klondike or the Spanish-American War, and some, like the Minott sisters, were boarded there. The boarders enjoyed a slightly different life-style from that of the orphans, receiving cream and sugar on their oatmeal instead of molasses and not having to work, although they most likely chose to anyway. Irene, for example, became an expert ironer by the age of ten. "Industry was really an integral part of the Shaker life," Spencer wrote, "and one could not remain with them without wanting to work too."

Spencer's memoirs glow with love for the sisters who cared for her, particularly Sister Lucy and Sister Robena. Sister Lucy Bowers in many ways epitomized the modern Shaker woman. A born historian, she kept careful records of the events of her time at Enfield and assembled invaluable lists of when individual members joined the Society and when buildings were erected. She referred to Sister Emily Copley as "Miss C.," and in later life, though still a Shaker, she wore civilian dress. Though she was practical and competent, she had a playful and gentle side, liked dogs, and was known to wade through snow to her waist in order to feed the birds. And even though she was one of the newcomers she reached across the schism and developed a fond relationship with Emily Copley.

Spencer characterized the Shaker attitude toward children as "loving though not soft care" and then went on to describe wild sledding outings with the sisters, sample cookies tasted from Sister Robena's "great sheets . . . (some with caraway seeds) cut while still warm into squares," piano lessons with Sister Lucy, sleighrides to Springfield with Sister Robena to visit her married sister, berry-picking expeditions, pea-shelling parties, and the joyous Sunday meetings. The sisters, particularly Lucy and Robena but Eldress Caroline Tate as well, doted on their young charges and revealed this through countless daily kindnesses.

At the age of ten, Irene Minott wrote to her brother, who had stayed with their father, a letter that reveals sisterly affection but not a trace of homesickness. "Do you get much time to stay outdoors or play with the other children?" she asked. "If you were down here you might, and you would be a great deal stronger by the time you went back, but seeing you are not I will be ahead of you in your strength for I am getting stronger every day and also taller." She went on to describe the children's melodeon, "which has not much music in it," and to offer to mend his stockings, "although I do not know how to mend my own very well yet unless I take great pains. . . ."[48]

Sylvia M. Spencer commented in her memoirs on the still-strict separation between the sexes, noting that of the men she "saw little except as they worked around the farm and attended services and meals." Separate staircases took brethren and sisters to their separate quarters at opposite ends of the dwelling house; separate tables seated them at mealtimes. She did remember Brother Ricardo Belden, however, whom she termed "a rather darkly handsome man . . . much admired by the girls who had not as yet learned to 'Live as the Angels of God!!'"

Unbeknownst to the happy little girls, the Shaker Society at Enfield was unraveling in many respects by the early 1900s. Even the press caught wind of the tensions: the *Springfield Republican* reported on February 26, 1905, that the community was "in a state bordering on dissolution on account of the internal dissentions that have cropped up among the inhabitants, and it will not be surprising if, in the course of a few years, the entire settlement will have passed." After an error-filled account of the history of the Enfield Shakers, the reporter discussed the influx of Believers from Canaan, adding "but matters went from bad to worse, as it is said the new settlers could not agree with the old." The article went on to mention a bill in the state legislature, "empowering selectmen of towns to appoint receivers or trustees of communities like the Shakers, when the board finds that such a course is necessary."[49]

A few days later, Walter Shepherd sent off an angry retort, declaring that the community would outlast its critics and attacking the legislative bill as "a gratuitous insult to an inoffense, honest, law-abiding people, who are among the heaviest taxpayers in town." He also discussed the situation of the alienated members of the North Family:

> We had reason seven years ago to discharge a man who was acting as manager on one of our farms. He is related to the three members who are located there and who are now in rebellion against Shaker authority. This man has seemingly succeeded in making tools of the Enfield selectmen and your correspondent. We have a good conscience in the matter, however, and are in no way dismayed, though very much annoyed.[50]

A continuing problem was the need to rely on unsatisfactory outside help for farm labor; much deeper and more troubling, however, were the intensifying frictions between leaders of different generations. No longer did this antagonism smolder beneath the surface, as a decade ago; by 1908 eruptions were so frequent that the North and Church families were quite separate. "They don't come down here at all now, either to meeting or to visit," wrote Walter Shepherd, who would become the last Church Family elder at Enfield. "The two families are not embracing each other lately. Not much."[51]

In some remarkably frank letters of the period, Walter Shepherd complained of the quality of the hired help and lamented the poor staying power of new arrivals at the community: "Yea, I remember a galaxy of constellations that have made their fleeting visits to the North family in my time. Another meteor strikes them every once in a while but it is but to rebound again into space."

His harshest words, however, were reserved for the elders, whom he accused of everything from tyranny to deceit: "The old man [Elder Brother George Wilcox, then aged eighty-eight] may outlive me and work his sweet will in spite of all we can do. God knows. He has just sold an out farm for $2,500 I understand. I have only heard of it through the hired foreman. We are not consulted or informed of such matters. We have no rights that he need respect."

Shepherd also reported that Wilcox had a habit of "filching money out of the sisters." According to the younger man, Elder George would tell the sisters he had bills to pay, would receive a blank check from them, and then would make it out for twice as much as he had requested.

Other elders fared no better in Shepherd's view. Ministry Elder Joseph Holden was called "fat and sleek . . . says to his soul take it easy for tomorrow we die." Elder George Clarke of the North Family was described as "not doing much stamping lately" due to corns and rheumatism.

A situation involving Levi Shaw was particularly trying for Shepherd and, he suggests, for the other brethren and sisters in the Church Family. Wilcox had decided that Shaw—who, Shepherd declared, was at ninety "one of the most critical of men" and "one of the anomalies of Shakerism"— should move from the North Family to the Church Family. Shepherd attributed to Wilcox the worst of motives for this plan: that Elder George wanted to get in through "foxey moves" on Shaw's rumored "7 thousand dollars of whip bonds drawing 6 pc. interest." Apparently, Wilcox repeatedly proposed that Shaw pay for his board. None of the brethren and few of the sisters had been consulted about Shaw's move, although they were all opposed to it. Levi Shaw died two months later.

These tensions and resentments resulted in a weighty depression, at least for Shepherd. Hearing of a supposedly accidental death among the Canterbury Shakers, he immediately assumed it was suicide. "I fear he got discouraged and had not the nerve to make a brake. . . . Conditions among Believers have got to be very depressing . . . I have felt the terrible effects of it myself at times. Now, nothing will disturb me. I am prepared for the worst. I shall hang on here (God willing) and rescue something, all I can, for the support of the members left."

Despite George Wilcox's erratic behavior as he approached ninety, he was the mainstay of the Enfield community, having been elder at the Church Family for more than fifty years. Without him the society began to disintegrate. Just seven months after he died (in February 1910), the Enfield Shakers offered their entire property—more than two thousand acres—for sale.[52]

The property, after a century and a quarter of Shaker cultivation, was magnificent. A 1911 newspaper article described the farms as flourishing, even with the meager number of members left to manage them. "Even now, thousands of acres were all under cultivation, with splendid orchards, berry patches, in the best of condition." The hay crop was better than any the writer had seen. The barns were still in the very best of condition; the horses were "big fine animals"; the farm implements were new and up-to-date. Despite the problems with hired help, the Church Family had hosted the Connecticut Dairymen's Association's field meeting the previous August.[53]

Walter Shepherd had taken Wilcox's position as Church Family elder. In addition to Shepherd, the Shakers still living at the Church Family after Wilcox's death were Daniel Orcutt and Frederick Schnell (both aged eighty), Caroline Tate, Lucy Bowers, Mathilda Schnell, Gertrude Whitney, and Lorena Hodgeth, along with a boarder, Mrs. I. Clark, and a "pro tem,"

Genie Page. Ricardo Belden had left but would return to the Hancock community. The North Family, meanwhile, was dissolved in 1913.[54]

Negotiations ensued during 1913 and 1914 for the sale of the Enfield property, and finally, on November 20, 1914, the real estate was sold for $100,000 to one John Phillips, to be used as a tobacco farm. In addition, the buyer paid $5,000 for all of the horses, the farming tools, and the grain in the horse barn. The remaining Shakers were to be allowed to live in the 1791 meeting house (now the infirmary building), which was to be moved to a reserved piece of land near the Shaker cemetery, a prospect they looked forward to as "the expected haven on the hill." Until the building was moved, the remaining Shakers would reside in the large brick dwelling house with the new farm manager.[55]

The temporary situation was not entirely comfortable for the remaining Shakers, according to the vividly written diary of Lucy Bowers. The new farm manager, Fritz Dressler, moved into the dwelling house with an ailing Angora cat, whose distressing condition Lucy, who loved animals, recorded in intimate detail. Dressler isolated himself in his room, with a combination lock on the door and his own personal stove, forbidden indulgences to the Shakers. All of the livestock was sold to a Hartford butcher, who, Lucy felt, then took liberties with Shaker possessions ("Butcher makes use of our man's cutter yesterday and today. Nobody dares do anything about it!"). Elder Walter bought a horse and carriage—"We wonder what he will do with them—we have no room or stable. Funny things happen."

Perhaps the most painful aspect of the Enfield closing was the dismantling of the dairy, which Sister Lucy described in poignant detail:

April 1, 1915. Three teams and eight men come to take the cows away. Hitch bull to one wagon. . . . He goes sidewise because he has to. . . . Cows are wild, run in every direction but finally fall into moderation. One remaining cow is taken by the Polanders at the west after dinner, the last distressing scene so far as our cows are concerned, for she had to be pulled every inch of the way.

This experience, caused by the sale of the dairy herd, has been severe, and has made a hole in which there is a veritable heart choke.

The following day the knife was twisted when a neighboring farm family brought over milk to sell. "Thirty quarts per day at 6¢ per quart is $10.50 a week [sic] or $42.00 per month," wrote Sister Lucy. "Some expense."

During 1914 and 1915 the sisters were occupied in carefully sorting and disposing of the contents of the buildings, well over a century's accumulation. Lucy Bowers's description reveals the meticulous attention the Shakers paid to this activity, as to every aspect of their lives: "About the middle of August 1914 we begin in earnest to clean out old garrets and cupboards, nothing is allowed to remain that can be lifted by the sisters. . . . In October we remove the bedding and furniture, all the dishes etc. from the Office,

except a few heavy pieces. Wash Office blankets. Through October, or during that month with Eldress Catharine we collect and post all the books
on the premises."

Some special treasures were "rescued" and shipped to New Lebanon and
Hancock. Other once-precious items had lost all meaning and were de-
stroyed: "Over one hundred books called 'Sacred Roll,' 'Divine Book of
Holy Wisdom,' and others are thrown out of the attic window and burned."

The furniture was crated and lovingly distributed to friends and to char-
ity—"[A] counter for Hancock and one for Lebanon N.Y., a bureau for
Libbie at Watervliet, a sewing table from the Office for Emma Strowbridge,
a center table for Sadie Neale at the Lebanon Church." The crater, one Mr.
Siebold, was paid $1.75 and given six meals and two nights' lodging, wrote
Lucy.

Ultimately, the contractor who was supposed to move the old Shaker
meetinghouse decided not to take on the job, and the dream of the "haven
on the hill" evaporated. Between 1915 and 1917 the remaining Shakers moved
from Enfield to the Hancock, Watervliet, and Mt. Lebanon church families.
Maria Lyman went to Watervliet, as did Eldress Caroline and Sister Lucy,
who lived together in their own small house, along with a little dog Lucy
adopted.[56]

A reporter visited Enfield in April 1916, and found Elder Walter Shepherd, sixty-five that year, and "Uncle Daniel" Orcutt, eighty-five, once a
'49er and now a Shaker for fifty years, just before they moved to the New
Lebanon Church Family.

"People don't want religion any more," were Orcutt's words for the
press. "They want joy rides, moving pictures, steamboat rides, amusements
of every kind."[57]

Thus, in 1917, Hancock was the sole remaining community of what had
been the Second Bishopric. Its members had suffered important losses already in the century, including the death of the beloved Ira Lawson, who
succumbed to pneumonia in April 1905.[58] "We miss him everywhere," wrote
Fidella Estabrook, "for he was a man in a thousand, able to command and
to do, kind, honest, quick to understand and to sympathize. . . . He left all
business in good condition. . . . All was accomplished by his wise thought,
for when he assumed the care there was nothing but a debt as a start." His
funeral was widely attended by local people, and the Canterbury society
sent a little pillow embroidered "Our Brother." Four months later, Louis
Basting, Hancock's last male elder, died. In 1911, Sister Fidella Estabrook
herself died, and that same year the Hancock East Family was sold, the
remaining sisters having moved to the Second Family.[59]

Ministry elder Joseph Holden, who turned eighty in September 1916, maintained his office and residence at the Second Family. As well as administering the affairs of the United Society, Holden served for a time as proprietor of the Second Family's gristmill. Holden's stationery was headed "Shaker Mills, 191–, W. Pittsfield, Mass.," offered "Wholesale and retail Flour, Grain, Meal, Feed, etc.," and proclaimed it was "Agent for the Shaker Swifts, A Reel for Winding and Doubling Yarn." The Shaker Mills continued to be an imposing landmark on the road through West Pittsfield until destroyed by fire in 1915. The mill, uninsured, was not rebuilt. Elder Joseph died in 1919 and was succeeded as Ministry elder by Walter Shepherd.[60]

Cordial relations with the world continued. In the summer of 1909 the Albany Hi-Y Walking Club stopped at the village while hiking and was invited into the kitchen, where the members had cookies and punch for 10 cents each. The following July, Mr. and Mrs. Archibald K. Sloper of Pittsfield were married in a Shaker meadow. Despite the Shaker prohibition of marriage, the Hancock sisters sent over, according to Mr. Sloper, "a freezer of ice cream made with wild strawberries, a layer cake and a red Shaker cloak for the bride."[61]

However, a new group had arrived in the Shaker community, a group that simultaneously foretold the decline of the United Society and saved it from oblivion. These were the collectors, who at the turn of the century already were beginning to see the importance of the Believers' history and the beauty and power of their "culture." The first to arouse public interest in the Shakers was John P. MacLean, who wrote *A Biography of Shaker Literature,* developed a collection that he entrusted to the Library of Congress, and also established a warm and intimate correspondence with many Shakers, including Hancock sister Fidella Estabrook. Wallace H. Cathcart assembled the largest Shaker collection for the Western Reserve Historical Society in Cleveland, Ohio. Another collector, Edward B. Wight, became deeply interested in the Shakers while an undergraduate at Williams College. He visited many communities, wrote a long term paper, complete with hand-drawn maps of the villages, and assembled a collection that was given to the college in 1931.

Faith and Edward Deming Andrews stopped off at the Hancock Church Family in 1923 in their Model-T Ford on the way home to Pittsfield from an antiques hunt, hoping to purchase some of the famous Shaker bread. When the basement door of the brick dwelling opened to them, the Andrewses remembered later, they caught a glimpse of another world: "A soft-voiced Shaker sister welcomed us warmly. We bought two loaves of bread. And in the long clean 'cook-room' we saw much besides; a trestle table, benches, rocking chairs, built-in cupboards, cooking arches, all beautiful in their simplicity. Later, eating the bread, we knew that our appetite would not be satisfied with bread alone." The couple became leading collectors and dealers of Shaker artifacts and wrote many books and articles about the United Society.[62]

At Hancock, Dr. and Mrs. Andrews became particularly close friends with Alice Smith. They often visited this gentle sister, finding her in the midst of weaving, sewing, tending the flower garden, playing the organ, or working in kitchen or washroom. Sometimes Sister Alice shared with them her own collection of precious Shaker objects, and one day she told the Andrewses that she had something special to show them. She proceeded to unwrap a beautiful, enigmatic painting inscribed "A Vision of the Heavenly Sphere." For the first time outsiders were viewing a "spirit drawing."

Sister Alice told her spellbound visitors that as a little girl she had once seen an eldress kindling a fire in the bake oven with a roll of colorful, decorative drawings, including this one. Perhaps the eldress had considered the drawings mere wastepaper, or perhaps she was intentionally destroying them, as the Shakers are suspected to have done with compromising documents. Charmed by the drawings' color and life, Sister Alice had begged the eldress to give them to her. Over the years she had studied and marveled over the rich imagery and intriguing details. To her the drawings became the most sacred of Shaker documents, and she entrusted them to Dr. and Mrs. Andrews.[63]

During the 1930s, Dr. and Mrs. Andrews exhibited their Shaker furniture and artifacts at the Whitney Museum of American Art, the Worcester Art Museum, and the Berkshire Museum. Their collection was already so substantial that they sought a permanent place for it.

Other individuals were just as avidly interested in preserving Shaker history. In 1947 the Shaker Historical Society held its first meeting, led by John A. Scott. John S. Williams established the Shaker Museum on his dairy farm in Old Chatham, New York, in 1950. Chartered by the New York State Board of Regents, it finally provided a center for those interested in the Society.

Even as public fascination with the Shakers grew, the Shaker reality was slipping away. Nearly all of the western societies had closed even before the end of Enfield, along with the community at Shirley, Massachusetts. The following twenty years saw the societies closing at Harvard, South Union, Enfield (New Hampshire), Alfred and, in 1938, Watervliet. At Hancock the Second Family had closed. Many Believers had died—Julia Sweet in 1913, Jane Gregor in 1917, Hattie E. Belden in 1918, Elizabeth Thornber in 1920, Emily Curtis in 1929, and Alice Smith in 1935. Both Eldress Caroline Helfrich and Eldress Catharine Pepper died in 1929; Fannie Estabrook became the new, and last, Church Family eldress.

The decline of the Hancock community was now becoming evident to observant visitors. The Round Stone Barn, for example, the pride of the community, was abandoned in 1932 after a state ruling prohibited keeping cows on a wooden floor. Without animal heat to keep out the frost, cracks soon gaped in the walls. As one visitor wrote, by 1937 the societies were no longer "the neatly efficient, thriving agricultural enterprises so much commented upon by nineteenth-century visitors. . . . [O]ne was left with the impression of a once-flourishing undertaking very slowly running down, with only the elderly left to carry on the Shaker way of life." By 1939, the Federal Writers' Project volume *The Berkshire Hills* observed, "There is a loneliness in the moribund community. . . . The Shaker village and Hancock town grow ever weaker, while the forest with renewed vigor marches forward over fields once laboriously cleared."[64]

Many buildings were removed or dismantled during the 1930s and 1940s to ease the Shakers' tax burden. The schoolhouse was sold and moved, becoming a private home. The meetinghouse, unused during most of the twentieth century, was taken down in 1938. As in most of the Shaker communities, the gravestones were removed from the cemetery in 1943, and a single stone monument was erected in their place. The only construction that went on was to accommodate boarded cattle: the 1910 barn for horses, hay, and wagons was extended in 1939 to include a dairy wing for thirty head of Holsteins, and in 1946 a dairy wing and two silos were added to the round barn.[65]

The Hancock Shaker school, now being taught in the brick dwelling, closed in 1942 after 140 years of existence. From 1898 until 1934 the school had been taught by Sister Elizabeth "Lizzie" Belden, who usually had about six pupils. "We would keep them for a while," she told a newspaper in 1934, "and then they long to get out into the world. We cannot persuade them to remain with us despite all our promises of a comfortable home and education." The last teacher, a non-Believer hired for $750, at one point had only one pupil.[66]

Across the New York state border the Mt. Lebanon society was already ending. In 1931 the Church and Center families had been sold to Charles Haight, to become Lebanon School and later Darrow School. Increasingly during this century, and especially since the death of Ministry elder Walter Shepherd in 1933, the leadership of the United Society had come from the still vital societies at Canterbury, New Hampshire, and Sabbathday Lake, Maine.

In 1947, Eldress Sarah Collins, gifted Mt. Lebanon chairmaker, died at age ninety-two. The six remaining members of the Mt. Lebanon community moved to Hancock that December in time to celebrate Christmas. The new arrivals were Sisters Rosetta Stephens (aged eighty-seven), Mary F. Dahm, Grace Dahm, Sadie Maynard, and Jennie Wells, and Brother Curtis White.

Despite the Shakers' continuing graciousness to visitors, an impression of vulnerability and insecurity characterizes reports of the period. At Hancock, wrote one visitor, "the buildings in the period after World War II had grown shabby and forlorn. The fields were sadly neglected. Missing was the slow movement of cows in the rich meadows. Where corn had grown tall, goldenrod now replaced it, hiding rusty barbed wire fencing. The Shakers were strong and careful administrators dedicated to an orderliness which was not carried out with equal care by superintendents or, in some cases, by nearby farmers who rented their acres." This same observer reported hearing that local men would enter the Mt. Lebanon village at night and help themselves to anything that was not locked up.⁶⁷

Trustee Frances Hall, in a 1946 letter to Eldress Emma B. King at Canterbury, attributed the financial insecurity to mishandling of Shaker money by Elder Walter Shepherd. Shepherd apparently invested income from the sale of several Shaker properties, including the society at Enfield, Connecticut, and the Church Family at Watervliet, in "poor stocks and bonds." "Eldress Ella asked me one day," Hall wrote, "if I would take the bundle to the bank and ask Mr. King if he would look over the papers and see if there were any use in keeping them. I shall never forget the surprised look on his face when he saw the amount of the investments. His remark was, 'I don't wonder Eldress Ella has heart trouble.'"⁶⁸

"We would be much better off today," the letter continued, "if the sisters had been allowed to handle some of the money, for as a rule they have been cautious and prudent." And in a final wry note, "We are not making any fancy work these days, for it takes what few there are to keep house. The members decrease, but the homes remain as large as ever."⁶⁹

Even the once fiercely independent sisters now required hired help. A nurse looked after the failing Sadie Neale, and a hired woman cooked for the family. Non-Shaker caretakers were paid to live on the premises and manage the farm, boarding cattle and renting out the fields and barns. Notwithstanding their expense, the very presence of these caretakers was a constant source of tension, if not friction, for the aging Shaker sisters.

A family named Goyette, for example, "had brought a trailer into the dooryard with three children and a baby—no sanitary conditions. Also the children yelled and raced all around the flowers under Eldress Fannie's window. When she told them not to run around they hid and made faces at her, making her more nervous and about sick." Goyette apparently refused to move the trailer when Frances requested it, and asked why she didn't go to the brick house where she belonged. Within three weeks Goyette was given notice.[70]

Despite the general atmosphere of decrepitude, a glance inside the brick Shaker garage would impress any visitor. This was the domain of Ricardo Belden. Belden, who among other things served as chauffeur and mechanic, insisted that the sisters should ride in new cars, always of the best manufacture. He would keep a car for three years and then trade it in top condition. Each new automobile had to be dark in color, curtained, and spacious enough to seat three sisters comfortably in back.[71]

Frances Hall's feeling of financial insecurity was perhaps unfounded. According to statements from just one of several Pittsfield bank accounts, the Hancock Shakers had more than $1.2 million in 1957, invested in blue-chip stocks.[72]

Checks drawn during the year 1957–58 show the expenses common to any community of elderly people. At least four people were being paid weekly wages, including Eldress Fannie's nurse, Bertha Mowry. Medical bills were a steady financial drain. Coal and fuel oil, miscellaneous repairs, trash collection, and the family automobile, then a 1953 De Soto, all required regular payments. The remaining Shakers stayed well informed about current affairs, maintaining subscriptions to *National Geographic* magazine and the *Christian Herald* and even purchasing an early television set for $383.75. And they continued to garden: $19.65 was spent on seeds in this society whose seed-raising business had once been so lucrative.[73]

The situation was difficult, however, with the handful of aging Shakers living in buildings built for hundreds, and the enormous property lying idle or being farmed by strangers. Many of the last group of Shakers died during the late 1940s and 1950s, including Freda Sipple in 1948, Curtis White in 1951, Sadie Maynard in 1953, and Jennie Wells in 1956.

Sister Frances Hall died on March 10, 1957, at the age of eighty-one, followed the next year by Sister Grace Dahm and Brother Ricardo Belden, who was buried in the Enfield Shaker cemetery. Now only the failing Eldress Fannie and Sisters Adeline Patterson and Mary Dahm remained. This may have been the catalyst that made the Central Ministry at Canterbury decide to close the Hancock society and sell the property. First, however, the Ministry ensured the future peace of the Shaker cemetery by transferring 550 acres of woodland to the state to become part of the Pittsfield State Forest. As part of the arrangement the state agreed to maintain that cemetery and the one above the former West Family.

Fortunately, the Hancock Shakers were not isolated but had many loyal and concerned friends both in the community and nationwide. Among these were Amy Bess Miller, a lifelong friend of the Shakers, and her husband Lawrence K. Miller, publisher of *The Berkshire Eagle,* as well as Dr. and Mrs. Andrews and numerous other interested, influential individuals. They founded the Hancock Shaker Village Steering Committee, whose purpose was to find a way "to preserve the physical assets of Shakerism in Berkshire County." And they began to concoct a grand scheme to achieve their goal: to create a "living museum" of the Shaker village, a museum that would simultaneously preserve Shaker buildings and artifacts and present the story of the Shakers in a vital, appealing way.[74]

In the fall of 1959 the Central Ministry put the entire property of the Hancock society on the market for $200,000. Of the 974 acres more than half were woodland, 200 were pasture, and almost 100 were cultivated fields. Eleven main buildings and ten less important ones remained, along with the pond on the ridge north of the Church Family.

Concerned about future use of the property, the Ministry placed certain restrictions on the sale. No parimutuel gambling or racetrack would be permitted; no use as a penal or correctional institution would be allowed; and no alcoholic beverages could be sold on the premises. The property must be used for a nonprofit, educational, literary, or charitable purpose only, and if it were not, ownership would revert to the Shaker Ministry.

The Millers met several times with the Ministry and its lawyers. The Shakers were intrigued and gratified by their concept and anxious for the group to succeed. On June 28, 1960, the steering committee offered $125,000 for the property. Other groups, including a nearby racetrack, were willing to pay more but could not agree to the restrictions.

The day after the group's final presentation the Ministry voted to sell them the property. Although the remaining members of the Hancock society would stay in the area, the community's assets would be transferred to the Shaker Central Trust Fund in Manchester, New Hampshire.

The closing took place on October 14, 1960. For the Shakers it was the end of a 170-year-old community rich in history and spirit. But it was a happy ending because for those who envisioned a Shaker museum on the property it was simultaneously a beginning. Ministry eldress Emma B. King said:

While there is naturally a feeling of regret at closing up a Shaker home of over a century and a half, our regret is tempered by the knowledge that our physical properties will serve some purpose of benefit to mankind after we have left them.

It is therefore a satisfaction and a joy to us that the group which will now assume these properties at Hancock will use them for the preservation of the Shaker traditions and the education of others in the Shaker crafts and industries.

Just a few weeks before the closing, on September 19, Eldress Fannie Estabrook died at age ninety and was buried at Hancock cemetery. Eldress Fannie had entered the Society in 1880, when she was ten years old. Her obituary in *The Berkshire Eagle* included a song entitled "Our Trade," written in 1872 at Hancock:

> Our tools are kind and gentle words
> Our shop is in the heart
> And here we manufacture peace
> That such we may impart.[75]

These quiet words express the legacy of the Hancock Shakers, a radiant peace and simplicity increasingly rare in the twentieth century. Sometimes visitors glimpse this quality of Shaker life and try to purchase it in the form of a beautiful object. But the shining order of Shakerism came from the spirit, from the early visionaries' belief that perfection was possible on earth. The Shakers' devotion to peace, their conviction that human beings could live together in harmony, and above all, their belief that human beings should strive for perfection—these issues are as relevant to us today as they were two hundred years ago.

 EPILOGUE

"The Substantial Work of Consecrated Hands"

Amy Bess Miller was twenty-four years old and a new mother in the summer of 1936, when she drove west along the Pittsfield–Albany road to visit the Hancock Shakers. She had known the Shakers since she was a child growing up in Worcester, Massachusetts, when her mother and aunt would take her to visit the society at Canterbury. The order and serenity of the Believers' lives had made a deep impression on the little girl. Later, while at boarding school in Pittsfield, she sometimes passed the Hancock and New Lebanon societies on field trips, and she was struck by the respect the driver felt toward the Shakers. Upon the occasion of her marriage her friends at the Canterbury society had given her a blue Shaker cloak.

She soon found that her father-in-law, Kelton B. Miller, shared her interest in the Shakers. As publisher of *The Berkshire Eagle,* Miller had received thoughtful and provocative letters to the editor from the Shakers on various political issues and had subsequently developed warm friendships with several Believers.

Now Amy Bess Miller was hoping to collect their subscription to the Pittsfield Community Fund. Eldress Fannie Estabrook and Sisters Frances Hall and Mary Dahm invited her into the front parlor of the trustees' house and proceeded to interrogate her about the community fund. Soon, however, they discovered her connection with the Canterbury Shakers, who had recently given her baby daughter a little red Shaker cloak. Sister Frances stepped out to bring some cider and cookies and came back with a check for twice the amount of their usual contribution.

Touched by the Shakers' generosity, Miller could not help noticing that the society was in a state of decline. Buildings needed painting, fences were sagging, hired workers were careless. The remaining sisters were anxious to sell off some of the furniture in the many empty rooms of the brick dwelling.

"They had so much furniture," she recalled. "Each sister had *everything*— table, chairs, bed, sewing table. The buildings were closing, so they thought why not sell things and make a little money? There was always this feeling that the sisters are helping the brothers."

Amy Bess and her husband bought Shaker furniture for their new home in Pittsfield. The grace, purity, and simplicity of the items she acquired made her curious about their makers. Soon thereafter she met Faith and Edward Deming Andrews, who were by then avid collectors. Before long she was deeply absorbed in learning about Shaker history and collecting their artifacts.

During the next twenty years it became clear that the Hancock community was coming to an end. Deeply concerned that the village be respectfully preserved, Amy Bess Miller spearheaded the campaign to purchase the property and establish Hancock Shaker Village, Inc., becoming the corporation's president in 1960.

Since then Hancock Shaker Village has been preserving the history of the Society and sharing it through its re-creation of how the Shakers lived. Reconstruction of the decaying Round Stone Barn was one of the first priorities. Other restoration projects followed, as funds to support them came in. A particularly joyous addition was a meetinghouse. Moved piece by piece from the Shaker community in Shirley, Massachusetts, it provided a spiritual centerpiece and filled the gap left by the razing of the Hancock meetinghouse in 1938.

Today thousands of visitors tour the village every month between May and October. They visit the barns, shops, and dwelling; they sample Shaker cooking and try their hands at Shaker crafts; or they watch skilled craftspeople attempt to re-create the perfection of Shaker products. Most of all, they take in the feeling that still lingers in the village, the sense of peace and serenity and faith.

Amy Bess Miller's leadership has continued to inspire those around her. When news of President John F. Kennedy's assassination reached her at Hancock Shaker Village in 1963, she called visitors and staff together in the Round Stone Barn for an impromptu memorial service. Appropriately enough, the group sang Shaker hymns as they shared their feelings of shock and grief.

Down in Tyringham, Dr. Joseph Jones apparently did well with the Fernside resort, keeping the place full of boarders and refusing other offers for the property. According to Tyringham historian Eloise S. Myers, the original William Allen house was demolished in 1889. Jones finally divided and sold his holdings that year because his other properties, his Pennsylvania woodlands, were not proving lucrative. He moved to Stockbridge and practiced medicine there.[1]

A *New York Times* reporter stayed at Fernside during its heyday twelve years after the Shakers left and described his impressions of the place.[2]

> Whether by accord or because in such a country they could not help themselves [he wrote], they placed their houses on a beautiful site. A shoulder of the mountain covered with noble trees juts out into the valley, and just this side, where many springs burst forth from the steep slope, their houses are clustered.
>
> [The houses] . . . are in the familiar Shaker style, bare and angular, but very heavily and thoroughly built. Nowhere else have I found window sashes that would slide up and down without sticking yet would stick where wanted without support. Underneath them are great stone drains that carry off the water that springs from the bedrock, and the foundations are of great squared stones laid in mortar that has become as hard as they.

Inside the buildings, Shaker features seemed already to be quaint remnants of a long-gone era:

> Around every room, a little below the ceiling, a strip of wood is set into the wall into which a row of wooden pegs is driven. These were used not only for the hats of the Shakers, but also for hanging up their chairs. The thickness of the walls was taken advantage of for the insertion of numberless little cupboards and excellently made drawers, principally for the reception of seeds. Some of the little labels still remain on these, so that your bureau drawers may be distinguished as the squash drawer, the red-onion seed drawer, etc.

The reporter described the brook, "dammed not after common fashion, with log boards, but with great stone walls, that must have cost immense labor." He noted the large seed garden and the mills for manufacture of woodenware. Although some fields remained, forest was taking over many of the acres the Believers had cleared and cultivated. Yet, like previous visitors, the reporter was impressed by the grove of "primeval" sugar maples on the right, a dozen feet in circumference—trees that may have been tapped by both Indians and Believers. "They will outlive the present generation," he wrote, "and they have seen the Shakers come and go."

The Church Family property was acquired by a group of New York professional men who called themselves the Fernside Forestry Association and who used the place for various recreational activities during the 1890s. According to newspaper reports they built a tennis court and a summer house below the seed house, tearing down a seed-drying shed to do so (although no trace has been found of these). When the club dissolved, the property ended up belonging to a New York lawyer named Robert S. Rudd, who returned it to agricultural use, raising Angora goats and sheep, adding onto the old ox barn, and reshingling and re-siding many of the other old Shaker work buildings.[3]

Meanwhile, much of the North Family property, which still had four large houses near the red mill, had gone to a neighbor, John Canon. The Canons tore down the gambrel-roofed sisters' dwelling and built a new house where a residence that burned in 1870 had stood. Mrs. M. F. Hazen purchased the former dairy/weave house, added a front gable and a porch and named it Nakomis Lodge. The South House, meanwhile, eventually fell down, and the land around it was divided and sold.

Brother Henry C. Blinn had made a nostalgic journey to the vacated Tyringham Shaker village in 1899, visiting the office, the meeting house, and the dwelling. "Everywhere," he said, "was to be seen the substantial work of consecrated hands." He commented on the little cheese house: "A little building was made in the side of the mountain, and about 10 feet square, to be used for the setting of milk and the storing of butter. A large limestone slab formed the roof, and assisted in making this a simple cold storage."[4]

Robert S. Rudd died suddenly of typhoid fever in 1903. The Church Family property was bought, sight unseen, by a Scotsman, John Dingwall, who had made a fortune mining and ranching in Mexico. A group of friends and neighbors, nervous about his intentions for such a large piece of the Hop Brook valley, got together and purchased it back from him.

To make the property pay for itself they sold lumber and two key buildings of the village. The meetinghouse, which by the turn of the century had been turned into a residence and divided up with partitions, was bought in the fall of 1925 and hauled a mile to the site of a recently burned house on the Leavenworth farm, which a few years later was acquired by playwright Sidney Howard. In the fall of 1929 the upper two and a half stories of the seed house were dismantled and moved—donated by the town, which then owned it, to a widow with nine children.

That year one of the owners of Fernside approached John S. Rudd and Alethea Rudd Truax (children of Robert S. Rudd) about buying it to save it from further degradation. The Rudd family ended up with the property, which they used as a family summer place for many years. Descendants of Robert S. Rudd still reside in the houses.[5]

After the Enfield community closed, much of its property was leased to the Consolidated Cigar Corporation, and Triphammer Pond was leased to the Hartford Ice Company. The Church, North, and East family properties were later sold to the state of Connecticut in 1931 for use as a prison farm. To this end the state removed most of the Shaker buildings but retained the 1876 dwelling to use as the central cellblock; it was demolished in the

1960s. Richard Steinert became fascinated by Shaker history during his twenty-six years as superintendent of the minimum-security prison at Enfield and offered the remaining buildings to various historical groups, without success. The 1791 Moses Johnson meetinghouse and trustees' office were burned down by prisoners, but the third meeting house remains standing. Fittingly, by mid-century the prison farm developed a prize-winning herd of milk cows. The South Family, meanwhile, is in private hands, and several of its important buildings are intact.[6]

The fate of the Shaker villages at Enfield and Tyringham makes one all the more appreciative of the careful preservation of Hancock. Enfield, in particular, is a great loss: the "palaces" that impressed nineteenth-century visitors are completely gone, remembered only in photographs, and much of the property is off limits to the public. Tyringham retains the special feeling of a Shaker village, even though two of its most important buildings were taken away. Of the three communities discussed in this work Hancock has received the most attention, partly because its history is so palpable in its many buildings still standing.

But although their buildings were beautiful, they were only shells; the essential thing was what went on within. It is an important exercise for us, today, to peer at the dim, unsmiling faces in the faded photographs and try to understand the vigorous, visionary life of the Shaker. As our own lives grow ever more different from theirs, we can still learn from them—their hope and faith, their humility, their constant struggle to live as angels.

The last word should belong to a true Believer. The town of Tyringham celebrated an "Old Home Week" in 1905. Elizabeth Thornber, called "the last surviving *faithful* Tyringham Shakeress," wrote the following words from Hancock: "I wish it was in my power to give you the history of the many, beautiful, sweet, noble lives that have lived and died at dear old Fernside. Souls that lived as pure, holy, consecrated lives as I believe it is in the power of mortals to live in this world—I can only say that, as I look back on my childhood days, I feel they were spent with saints, although I did not sense it then, as I have since, in my advanced years."[7]

Eldership Order, Hancock Ministry

Eldership Order, Hancock Ministry

First elder	Second elder	First eldress	Second eldress
1790s			
Calvin Harlow 1790–1795	Jeremiah Goodrich 1790–1793	Sarah Harrison 1791–1796	Hannah Goodrich 1791–1793
Nathaniel Deming 1795–1845	Reuben Harrison 1790–1791	Cassandana Goodrich 1796–1848	Rebecca Slosson 1793–1796
	Daniel Goodrich 1791–1793		Sarah Markham 1796–1835
	Nathaniel Deming 1793–1795		
	Daniel Goodrich 1795–1796		
	Nathan Slate 1796–1812		
1800–1809			
1810–1819	Daniel Goodrich, Jr. 1812–1818		
	Grove Wright 1818–1845		
1820s			
1830s			Cassandana Brewster 1835–1845
1840s			
Grove Wright 1845–1860	Thomas Damon 1846–1860	Cassandana Brewster 1848–1856	Clarissa Hawkins 1845–1846
			Wealthy Storer 1846–1851

First elder	Second elder	First eldress	Second eldress
1850s			
		Eunice Hastings 1856–1871	Anna Erving 1851–1854
			Sarah Harrison 1854–1871
1860s			
Thomas Damon 1860–1880	Phidelio Collins 1860–1864		Clarissa Pease 1865–1871
1870s			
		Clarissa Pease 1871–1872	Caroline Helfrich 1871–1873
		Jennet Augur 1872–1873	Emma Strowbridge 1873–1880
		Betsy Johnson 1873–1880	
1880s			
Albert Battles 1880–1893		Hannah Ann Agnew 1880–1887	Betsy Johnson 1880–1881
		Caroline Helfrich 1887–1893	Caroline Helfrich 1881–1887
			Emma Strowbridge 1887–1891
1890s			
			Emeline Pierce 1891–1893

NOTE: The Hancock Ministry was abolished in 1893.

NOTE ON SOURCES

These appendixes have been created from numerous sources including diaries and other community records, testimonies, letters, census reports, family genealogies, newspaper accounts, and town birth and death records. Outstanding sources of information were: "Members of the United Society at Hancock, Mass." (Hancock Shaker Museum); Thomas Damon's "Memoranda" (Shaker Museum, Old Chatham, N.Y.); "Center Family [Enfield] Records" (Western Reserve Historical Society); and "Grove Wright's Book" (Private Collection). Marcia Eisenberg, Magda Gabor-Hotchkiss, Robert F. W. Meader, and Stephen Paterwic helped fill in gaps.

The author welcomes any corrections or additions to the information in this appendix, and may be written at P.O. Box 692, Williamstown, MA 01267.

Eldership of Selected Families of the Hancock Bishopric

A. Church Family, Hancock

First elder	Second elder	First eldress	Second eldress
1790s			
Reuben Rathbun 1792–1799	Jonathan Southwick 1792–1799	Eunice Deming	Jennett Davis
Jonathan Southwick 1799–			
1800–1809			
			(Sarah Deming, Jr.) (d. 1813)
1810–1819			
1820s			
William Deming 1828–1848		Rebecca Clark (1829)	Dana Brewster (1829)–1835
1830s			
	Joseph Wicker 1835–1848	Sabrina Cook (1839–1845)	
1840s			
Joseph Wicker 1848–1852	Isaac Augur 1848–1856*	Anna Wright 1845–1856	Judith Collins (1846)–1852
1850s			
Simon Maybee 1852–1861	Phidelio Collins 1856–1860*	Jennet Augur 1856–1871*	Jennet Augur 1852–1856
			Lucy Jane Osborne (1856)

First elder	Second elder	First eldress	Second eldress
1860s			
Isaac Augur 1861–1864*	Henry Purdy 1860*–1884		
Phidelio Collins 1864–1883*			
1870s			
		Elvira Hulett (1871)	
1880s			
Albert J. Battles (1883)	Louis Basting 1888	Betsey Johnson (1885)	
Henry Purdy 1884–1889*		Martha Johnson (1886)	
Louis Basting 1889–1905			
1890s			
Albert Battles 1893–1895 d.		Caroline Helfrich 1893–1929*	Emmoretta Belden 1892–1897
1893–1909			
1910–1919			
1920s			
		Fannie Estabrook 1929–1960	

NOTE: The Hancock Church Family was closed in 1960.
   *Conjecture by the author.
   A date in parentheses indicates that this individual served as elder in this year, but his or her full tenure is unknown to the author.

B. Church Family, Enfield

First elder	Second elder	First eldress	Second eldress
1790s			
Eliphalet Comstock 1792–1808	Daniel Goodrich 1792–1795	Mary Wood 1792–1815	Ruth Pease 1792–1792
	Benjamin Wheelock 1795–1797		Judith Emerson 1792–1810
	Asa Tiffany 1797–1808		
1800–1809			
Asa Tiffany 1808–1812	James Slate 1808–1809		
	David Fairbanks 1809–1810		
1810–1819			
Nathan Slate 1812–1830	Jacob Wood 1810–1812	Lydia Comstock 1815–1822	Lydia Comstock 1810–1815
	Asa Tiffany 1812–1822		Agnes Munsell 1815–1816
			Lovicy Farrington 1816–1822
1820s			
	Russell Haskell 1822–1844	Lovicy Farrington 1822–1838	Elsa Parsons 1822–1851
1830s			
Daniel Clark 1830–1837		Clarissa Ely 1838–1843	
Asa Tiffany 1837–1851			
1840s			
	George Wilcox 1844–1851	Anna Erving (Irving) 1843–1851*	
1850s			
George Wilcox 1851–1910	William Kellogg 1851–1860	Averill Haskell 1851–1864	Phebe Wilcox 1851–1853
			Elsa Parsons (1853–1869)
1860s			
	Russell Haskell 1860–1880	Clarissa Pease 1864–1865*	Emeline Hart 1869–1874
		Averill Haskell 1865–1869	
		Olive Stebbins 1869–1874	

First elder	Second elder	First eldress	Second eldress
1870s			
		Emeline Hart 1874–1882	Sophia Copley 1874–1890
1880s			
	Daniel Orcutt 1880–1916	Harriet Storer 1882–1890	
1890s			
		Sophia Copley 1890–1898	Caroline Tate 1890–1898
		Caroline Tate 1898–1916	Lucy Bowers 1898–1916
1900–1916 Walter Shepherd 1910–1916			

NOTE: The Church Family was closed in 1916.
*This individual went on from this post to serve in the Ministry.

C. North Family, Enfield

First elder	Second elder	First eldress	Second eldress
1790s			
Amaziah Clark I 1794–1810	Elisha Allen 1794–1806	Lucy Markham 1794–1806	Ruth Farrington 1794–1806
1800–1819			
Elisha Allen 1810–1838	Martin Wood 1806–1808	Ruth Farrington 1806–1846	Rozina Allen 1806–1813
	Needham Allen 1808–1809		Mitta Munsell 1813–1846
	Davis Fairbanks 1809–1811		
	Amaziah Clark, Jr. 1810–1838		
1820s			
1830s			
Amaziah Clark, Jr. 1838–1852	Timothy Terry 1838–1851		
1840s			
		Mitta Munsell 1846–1849	Anna Granger 1846–1847
		Clarissa Pease 1849–1864	Mary Russell 1847–1850
1850s			
Nathan Damon 1852–1856[b]	Nathan Damon 1851–1852[a]		Zilpha Blanchard 1850–1864
Stoughton Kellogg 1852–1859	William White 1852–1853[b]		Anna Granger 1850–1853[b]
John Wilcox 1856–1867	Gilbert Avery 1853–1883		
1860s			
Robert Aitken 1867–1874		Zilpha Blanchard 1864–1874	Emily Curtis 1864–1874
1870s			
Daniel Orcutt 1874–1880		Anna Granger 1874–1893 d.	Clarissa Lyman 1874–1893
1880s			
Omar Pease 1880–1883			
Gilbert Avery 1883–1897			

First elder	Second elder	First eldress	Second eldress
1890s			
George Clarke 1897–1913	Gilbert Avery 1897–1908 d.	Clarissa Lyman 1893–1897[a] d.	Angeline Brown 1897–1913
		Miriam Offord 1897–1913	
1900–1909			
1910–1913			

NOTE: The North Family was closed in 1913.
[a]Conjectures by author.
[b]Courtesy Stephen Paterwic.
"d." indicates this individual died while serving as elder.

D. Church Family, Tyringham

First elder	Second elder	First eldress	Second eldress
1790s			
1800s			
1810s			
1820s			
Thomas Patten*			
1830s			
Eleazer Stanley* (1830)			
1840s			
Albert J. Battles 1844–1875	Calvin Parker (1846)	Molly Herrick (1864)	Desire Holt (1846)
1850s			
	Hasting Storer 1854–		
1860s			
	Calvin Parker (1860)	Wealthy Storer (1860)–1864* d.	Julia Johnson (1860)
		Harriet Storer 1864*–1875	
1870s			

NOTE: The Church Family was closed in 1875.
  *Conjecture by author.
  The abbreviation "d." indicates this individual died while serving as elder.
  A date in parentheses indicates that this individual served as elder during this year, but his or her full tenure is unknown to the author.

E. North Family, Tyringham

First elder	Second elder	First eldress	Second eldress
1790s			
1800–1809 Henry Herrick*			
1810–1819			
1820s			
1830s Leonard Allen* (1830)			
1840s Joseph Allen* Leonard Allen 1840–1846* Eleazer Stanley 1846–1851	Eleazar Stanley 1840–1846*	Phebe Wilcox (1846)	Anna Seton (1846)
1850s Calvin Parker 1851–1858 Richard Van Deusen 1858–1867	Richard Van Deusen 1851–1858		
1860s		Betsey Johnson*	

NOTE: The North Family was closed in 1867.
*Conjecture by the author.
A date in parentheses indicates that this individual served as elder during this year, but his or her full tenure is unknown to the author.

APPENDIX III

Family Trees

GOODRICH FAMILY

Benjamin
(1715–97)
m. Hannah Olmsted

- Daniel (1738–1807)
  m. Anna Baldwin
  - Daniel (1765–1835)
  - Cassandana (1769–1848)
  - at least 6 other children
- Abigail (1740–?)
  m. Hezekiah Osborne
- Benjamin (1742–?)
  m. Mary Douglas
- Samuel (1743–1776)
- Nathan (1745–1806)
  m. Hannah Fuller ——— 5 children
- David (1747–1802)
  m. Ann Robinson ——— 5 children
- Ezekiel (1749–1783)
  m. Eunice Rathbun
  - Eunice Thankful (1771–1858)
  - 3 other children
- Elizur (1751–1812)
  m. Lucy Wright
- Hezekiah (1755–1827)
- Jeremiah (1757–1810)

LYMAN FAMILY

Israel Lyman
(1772–1836)
Sarah (Sally) Moody
(1783–1848)

Alonzo
m. ?

> Eli Dyer
> (1829–57)
> **Harriet Amelia**
> (1831–92)
> **Seth Alonzo**
> (1834–68)
> **Edward Israel**
> (b. 1839)

3 daughters

son

Almon
m. **Clarissa Burnett**
(1814–1897)

> **Sarah Maria**
> (1833–1918)
> **Alden Burnett**
> (1835–1909)
> **Clarissa Kezia**
> (1837–97) ——————— 5 children
> m. **John W. R. Copley**

Harvey
(b. 1815)
m. **Mary Ann White**

Elijah

Edward Mason

Boldface type indicates that this individual was a Shaker for some part of his or her adult life.

RICHMOND–COPLEY–TATE FAMILIES

*That this individual was named David is a conjecture by the author; if so, he had a nephew as well as a son with that name. His nephew, the cousin of Thomas Richmond and Elizabeth Richmond Copley, was excommunicated by the Shakers.

Boldface type indicates that this individual was a Shaker for some part of his or her adult life.

Notes

INTRODUCTION (pp. 1–7)

1. [Rufus Bishop and Seth Y. Wells], *Testimonies of the Life, Character, Revelations and Doctrines of Our Ever Blessed Mother Ann Lee, and the Elders with Her; through Whom the Word of Eternal Life Was Opened in This Day of Christ's Second Appearing* (Hancock, Mass.: By order of the Ministry, J. Tallcott and J. Deming, Jrs., Printers, 1810), p. 66. This book is part of the Shaker Collection, Williams College Archives and Special Collections, Williamstown, Mass.

2. Dorothy M. Billings, "The Billings-Meacham Families," Empire State College, Albany, N.Y., 1984. At Hancock Shaker Village and at the Shaker Museum.

3. "Testimony of Job Bishop," in Seth Youngs Wells and Calvin Green, *Testimonies Concerning the Character and Ministry of Mother Ann Lee and the First Witnesses of the Gospel of Christ's Second Appearing; Given by Some of the Aged Brethren and Sisters of the United Society, Including a Few Sketches of Their Own Religious Experience* (Albany, N.Y.: Packard and Van Benthuysen, 1827).

4. See Stephen Marini, *Radical Sects of Contemporary New England* (Cambridge, Mass.: Harvard University Press, 1982), pp. 52–53.

5. Bishop and Wells, *Testimonies of the Life,*, pp. 12–14, 21.

6. Bishop and Wells, *Testimonies of the Life,* p. 21.

7. The following conversation is taken from Bishop and Wells, *Testimonies of the Life,* pp. 17–21.

CHAPTER ONE "Living Souls, Let's Be Marching!" (pp. 8–19)

1. Proprietary deeds, Northern Berkshire Registry of Deeds, Adams, Mass., p. 120.

2. *A History of the County of Berkshire, Massachusetts; in 2 Parts the First Being a General View of the County, the Second, an Account of the Several Towns, by Gentlemen in the County, Clergymen and Laymen* (Pittsfield, Mass.: Samuel W. Bush, 1829).

3. *The Goodrich Family in America* (Chicago: Fergus Printing Co., 1889); "Testimony of Daniel Goodrich, Jr.," in Seth Youngs Wells and Calvin Green, *Testimonies Concerning the Character and Ministry of Mother Ann Lee and the First Witnesses of the Gospel of Christ's Second Appearing; Given by Some of the Aged Brethren and Sisters*

of the United Society, Including a Few Sketches of Their Own Religious Experience (Albany, N.Y.: Packard and Van Benthuysen, 1827), p. 125.

4. Town of Hancock Records, Book 1.

5. *Rathbun—Rathbone—Rathburn Family Historian,* Oct. 1981; J. E. A. Smith, *The History of Pittsfield (Berkshire County), Massachusetts* (Boston: Lee and Shepard, 1869), vol. 1, pp. 26, 178, 362, 452–55; see also John C. Cooley, *Rathbone Genealogy* (Syracuse, N.Y.: Press of the Courier Job Print, 1898).

6. The description of the meeting in the barn is taken from Daniel Goodrich, "Copies of Manuscripts Found among the Writings of Deacon Daniel Goodrich after His Death," SA 799.1, Edward Deming Andrews Memorial Shaker Collection (hereafter Andrews Collection), Henry Francis du Pont Winterthur Museum, Winterthur, Del.

7. Remembered by Thankful Goodrich at age eighty-two, in "Manuscripts Found among the Writings of Deacon Daniel Goodrich after His Death."

8. Wells and Green, *Testimonies Concerning the Character,* Preface.

9. "Testimony of Daniel Goodrich, Jr.," in Wells and Green, *Testimonies Concerning the Character,* pp. 126–27.

10. "Testimony of Daniel Goodrich, Jr.," in Wells and Green, *Testimonies Concerning the Character,* p. 127.

11. [Rufus Bishop and Seth Y. Wells], *Testimonies of the Life, Character, Revelations and Doctrines of Our Ever Blessed Mother Ann Lee, and the Elders with Her; through Whom the Word of Eternal Life Was Opened in This Day of Christ's Second Appearing* (Hancock, Mass.: By order of the Ministry, J. Tallcott and J. Deming, Jrs., Printers, 1810), pp. 26, 27, 29-30. For more on Lafayette, see John Harlow Ott, *Hancock Shaker Village: A Guidebook and History, 2d ed.* (Hancock, Mass.: Shaker Community, Inc., 1975), p. 8, and *The Shaker,* Sept. 1872.

12. Town of Hancock Records, Book 1.

13. "Testimony of Elizabeth Wood," Shaker Collection, Western Reserve Historical Society (WRHS), Cleveland, Ohio (hereafter WRHS) VI: B-1.

14. Reuben Rathbone, *Reasons Offered for Leaving the Shakers* (Pittsfield, Mass.: Chester Smith, 1800), pp. 6–7. See also *Rathbun—Rathbone—Rathburn Family Historian,* October, 1981; John C. Cooley, *Rathbone Genealogy* (Syracuse, N.Y.: Press of the Courier Job Print, 1898); and John H. Morgan, "The Baptist-Shaker Encounter in New England," *Shaker Quarterly* 12 (Fall 1972), pp. 93–94.

15. This discussion of David Goodrich's conversion is drawn from Bishop and Wells, *Testimonies of the Life,* pp. 22–24.

16. "Testimony of Samuel Johnson," in Wells and Green, *Testimonies Concerning the Character,* pp. 103–111.

17. Bishop and Wells, *Testimonies of the Life,* pp. 24–25, 46.

18. Discussion of the life of Lucy Wright is taken from Calvin Green, "Biographic Memoir of the Life, Character, and Important Events, in the Ministration of Mother Lucy Wright" (New Lebanon, N.Y.: 1861) WRHS VI:B-27; and Sister Frances A. Carr, "Lucy Wright: The First Mother in the Revelation and Order of the First Organized Church," *Shaker Quarterly* 15, no. 3 (Fall 1987), pp. 93–100, and no. 4 (Winter 1987), pp. 128–31.

19. Green, "Biographic Memoir," p. 7.

20. Written down by Clarissa Hawkins of Hancock, in "Copies of Manuscripts Found among the Writings of Deacon Daniel Goodrich after His Death." See also Green, "Biographic Memoir," pp. 7–8.

21. "Experience of Thankful Goodrich," Shaker Manuscript Collection No. 14,

Rare Books and Manuscripts Division, New York Public Library, Astor, Lenox, and Tilden Foundations; see also Bishop and Wells, *Testimonies of the Life,* pp. 343–44, 349.

22. Quotation about Mother Ann's effect on children is from "Testimony of Samuel Johnson," in Wells and Green, *Testimonies Concerning the Character,* p. 115. Thankful Goodrich's testimony, including the following passage, is found in "Experience of Thankful Goodrich," New York Public Library. Thankful was christened Eunice when she was born on Oct. 9, 1771, and later either took her middle name or renamed herself. Her parents were Ezekiel Goodrich and the former Eunice Rathbun.

23. "Testimony of Zipporah Cary," in Wells and Green, *Testimonies Concerning the Character,* pp. 54–60.

24. "Testimony of Olive Miller," born Oct. 24, 1766, in "Copies of Manuscripts Found among the Writings of Deacon Daniel Goodrich after His Death."

25. Mocking children along the road mentioned in "Testimony of Richard Treat," in Wells and Green, *Testimonies Concerning the Character,* p. 41.

26. In Gideon Martin, "Statements against the Shakers," New Lebanon, May 30, 1825, SA 966, Andrews Collection. Gideon Martin was tax collector for a time for the southern part of Hancock.

27. Valentine Rathbun, *Some Brief Hints, of a Religious Scheme, Taught and Propagated by a Number of Europeans, Living in a Place Called Nisqueunia, in the State of New York* . . . (Hartford, Conn.: 1781), pp. 7–8, 12.

28. Bishop and Wells, *Testimonies of the Life,* p. 70; "Testimony of Richard Treat," in Wells and Green, *Testimonies Concerning the Character,* p. 44.

29. "Testimony of Richard Treat," *Testimonies Concerning the Character,* p. 43; Edward Deming Andrews, *The People Called Shaker* (Oxford: Oxford University Press, 1953), p. 33.

30. Bishop and Wells, *Testimonies of the Life,* p. 72.

31. "Testimony of Samuel Johnson," in Wells and Green, *Testimonies Concerning the Character,* pp. 103–117, esp. p. 108; "Testimony of Elizabeth Johnson," ibid., pp. 87–90, esp. p. 89.

32. Stephen J. Stein, *The Shaker Experience in America: A History of the United Society of Believers* (New Haven, Conn.: Yale University Press, 1992), p. 14.

33. History of Berkshire County, Mass., with Biographical Sketches of Its Prominent Men (New York: J. B. Beers and Co., 1885), vol. 2, p. 390.

CHAPTER TWO "The Path of Righteousness" (pp. 20–30)

1. This account of Elizabeth Wood's first experience of Mother Ann is drawn from "Testimony of Elizabeth Wood" (WRHS VI: B-1).

2. Russell Haskell, "Some Sketches of the Rise and Progress of the United Society of Christians or Christian Believers (Commonly Called Shakers) in the Town of Enfield, Ct.," 1868, Shaker Museum and Library, Old Chatham, N.Y. (NOC 16,561).

3. Williams College Shaker Collection clipping file 98, vol. 2.

4. This account is taken from Anonymous, "History of the Enfield Community with Reference to Some Changes in Ministry" (WRHS V:B-8).

5. This account of Ann Lee's third visit to Enfield is drawn from "Testimony of Elizabeth Wood" (WRHS VI: B-1).

6. Dorothy M. Billings, "The Billings-Meacham Families," Empire State College, Albany, N.Y., 1984.

7. John Warner Barber, *Connecticut Historical Collections . . . Relating to the History and Antiquities of Every Town in Connecticut with Geographical Descriptions* (New Haven, Conn.: Durrie & Peck and J. W. Barber, 1838); John C. Pease and John M. Niles, *Gazetteer of the States of Connecticut and Rhode-Island* (Hartford, Conn.: William S. Marsh, 1819).

8. Information on Joseph Meacham's family history is taken from Billings, "The Billings-Meacham Families." A description of the senior Meacham's spiritual journey can be found in John H. Morgan, "The Baptist-Shaker Encounter in New England," *Shaker Quarterly*, 12 (Fall 1972), pp. 90–92, see particularly p. 91, n.26; see also Henry Bamford Parkes, *The Fiery Puritan: Jonathan Edwards* (New York: Minton, Balch & Co., 1930), pp. 18–19; and Sydney E. Ahlstrom, *A Religious History of the American People* (New Haven, Conn.: Yale University Press, 1972).

9. "Testimony of Nathan Tiffany," in Wells and Green, *Testimonies Concerning the Character*, pp. 169–72.

10. "Testimonies of Nathan Tiffany and Richard Treat," in Wells and Green, *Testimonies Concerning the Character*, pp. 169–72 and 38–46; Bishop and Wells, *Testimonies of the Life*, pp. 74, 75.

11. Copy of order, in Haskell, "Some Sketches."

12. John A. Scott, *Tyringham: Old and New* (Pittsfield, Mass.: Sun Printing Co., 1905); and Hop Brook Community Club, *Tyringham: A Bicentennial Review* (Great Barrington, Mass.: John Raifstanger, 1976).

13. Eloise S. Myers, *Tyringham, Massachusetts: A Hinterland Settlement* (Tyringham, Mass.: 1948, 1951).

14. The following account of the persecution in Tyringham is compiled from "A True Statement of the Persecution in Tyringham to a Religious People Called Shakers in the Year of 1782 and 3," WRHS VII A-19, reel 54; and from "Elisha Parker's Book 1861," WRHS VII B-237, reel 62.

15. "Elisha Parker's Book."

16. "Elisha Parker's Book"; "A True Statement of the Persecution in Tyringham."

17. "A True Statement of the Persecution in Tyringham."

18. "Elisha Parker's Book."

19. Daniel Goodrich, "Copies of manuscripts found among the writings of Deacon Daniel Goodrich after his death," SA799.1, Andrews Collection.

20. See *Berkshire Courier*, Aug. 17, 1899.

21. "Elisha Parker's Book."

22. The description of Mother Ann Lee's sojourn in Hancock is taken from Bishop and Wells, *Testimonies of the Life*, pp. 169–71.

23. This legend is drawn from Wells and Green, *Testimonies Concerning Character*, p. 169n.

24. Benjamin S. Youngs and Calvin Green, *The Testimony of Christ's Second Appearing*, 2d ed. (Albany, N.Y.: E. & E. Hosford, 1810), p. 169n.

25. Bishop and Wells, *Testimonies of the Life*, p. 170.

26. Ibid., p. 31.

27. Ibid., p. 172.

28. "Testimony of Richard Treat," in Wells and Green, *Testimonies Concerning the Character*, p. 44.

CHAPTER THREE Creating a Community Apart (pp. 31–48)

1. Reuben Rathbone, *Reasons Offered for Leaving the Shakers* (Pittsfield, Mass.: Chester Smith, 1800), p. 8.
2. See Priscilla J. Brewer, *Shaker Communities, Shaker Lives* (Hanover, N.H.: University Press of New England, 1986), p. 22; Edward Deming Andrews, *The People Called Shaker* (Oxford: Oxford University Press, 1953), p. 48.
3. Letter to Josiah Talcott from James Whittaker, Feb. 25, 1782, at Hancock Shaker Village.
4. W. S. Warder, *A Brief Sketch of the Religious Society of People Called Shakers* (London, 1818), pp. 9–10, in Williams College Shaker Collection.
5. See Sister Frances A. Carr, "Lucy Wright: The First Mother in the Revelation and Order of the First Organized Church," *Shaker Quarterly* 15 (Fall 1987), pp. 97–100.
6. Rathbone, *Reasons Offered*, pp. 8, 9.
7. Calvin Green, "Biographic Memoir of the Life, Character, and Important Events, in the Ministration of Mother Lucy Wright," New Lebanon, N.Y., 1861) WRHS VI:B-27, pp. 8, 16–17.
8. Testimony of Jonathan Clark, in "Copies of manuscripts found among the writings of Deacon Daniel Goodrich after his death," SA 799.1, Andrews Collection. See also D. A. Buckingham, "Epitomic History of the Watervliet Shakers," *The Shaker* 7 (May 1877), p. 37.
9. Rufus Bishop, comp., *A Collection of the Writings of Father Joseph Meacham Respecting Church Order and Government* (New Lebanon, N.Y.: 1850), WRHS VII B-59, pp. 1–2.
10. Middle Berkshire Registry of Deeds, Pittsfield, Mass., Book 22, p. 437. See also Sara Wermiel, "Chronological List of Property Acquired by United Society," HSV.
11. Calvin Green, "Biography of Henry Clough," 1860 (WRHS VI:B-25).
12. John Harlow Ott, *Hancock Shaker Village: A Guidebook and History* (Hancock, Mass.: Shaker Community, Inc., 1976), p. 18; Edward Deming Andrews, *The Hancock Shakers* (Pittsfield, Mass.: Shaker Community, Inc., 1961), pp. 16–17.
13. In "Copies of manuscripts found among the writings of Deacon Daniel Goodrich after his death." See also Reuben Rathbun's description of Calvin Harlow as "a very desirable young man, and one who had the love and esteem of all the people," in Rathbone, *Reasons Offered*, p. 9.
14. Late in the following century, Christmas, taking on worldly trappings, all but eclipsed Ann Lee's birthday.
15. "Copies of manuscripts found among the writings of Deacon Daniel Goodrich after his death."
16. Ott, *Hancock Shaker Village*, pp. 32–33.
17. "Testimony of Rebecca Clark," in "Copies of manuscripts found among the writings of Deacon Daniel Goodrich after his death."
18. Letter to Joseph Meacham from Daniel Goodrich, Sr., March 1791, in "Copies of manuscripts found among the writings of Deacon Daniel Goodrich."
19. "Hancock Shaker Village" dates families were established and dissolved, HSV; Alice Mae Smith, "History of Our Home" (1917), Shaker Museum and Library, Old Chatham, N.Y. (hereafter Shaker Museum), NOC 13,377.
20. History of Berkshire County, Mass., with Biographical Sketches of Its Prominent Men (New York: J. B. Beers and Co., 1885), pp, 393–94.

21. From "Early Book of Records of Hancock Church Family 1789–1801," Shaker Museum, NOC 10,804.

22. Russell Haskell, "Some Sketches of the Rise and Progress of the United Society of Christians or Christian Believers (Commonly Called Shakers) in the Town of Enfield, Ct.," 1868 (NOC 16,561).

23. "Testimony of Elizabeth Wood" (WRHS IV: B-1).

24. Tyringham Covenants, Shaker Library at Sabbathday Lake, Me.

25. Eloise S. Myers, *Tyringham, Massachusetts: A Hinterland Settlement* (Tyringham, Mass.: 1948), p. 79.

26. "Copies of manuscripts found among the writings of Deacon Daniel Goodrich after his death."

27. Reuben Rathbone, *Reasons Offered*, pp. 9–10.

28. "Testimony of Elizabeth Wood," in 'Copies of manuscripts found among the writings of Deacon Daniel Goodrich after his death."

29. Judson Keith Deming, comp., *Genealogy of the Descendants of John Deming of Wethersfield, Ct., with Historical Notes* (Dubuque, Ia.: Mathis Mets Co., 1904), pp. 91–92.

30. Quotation from Joseph Meacham is found in Bishop, *Collection*, WRHS VII B-59, p. 91. Other information from Green, "Biography of Henry Clough" (WRHS VI:B-25) and Ruth E. Von Euw and Margot Mayo, "A Beginning List of Shakers," *Shaker Quarterly* 10 (Fall 1970), p. 78.

31. Valentine Rathbun, "About the Shakers," *The New Star* 5 (May 9, 1797), pp. 45–46.

32. "Copies of manuscripts found among the writings of Deacon Daniel Goodrich after his death."

33. Daniel W. Patterson, *The Shaker Spiritual* (Princeton, N.J.: Princeton University Press, 1979), pp. 105–6, 115–16.

34. Goodrich's description of singing at Niskeyuna is taken from "Testimony of Daniel Goodrich, Jr.," in Seth Youngs Wells and Calvin Green, *Testimonies Concerning the Character and Ministry of Mother Ann Lee and the First Witnesses of the Gospel of Christ's Second Appearing; Given by Some of the Aged Brethren and Sisters of the United Society, Including a Few Sketches of Their Own Religious Experience*, p. 127.

35. Green, "Biography of Henry Clough" (WRHS VI: B-25).

36. "Copies of manuscripts found among the writings of Deacon Daniel Goodrich after his death."

37. Rathbone, *Reasons Offered*, p. 12.

38. Green, "Biography of Henry Clough" (WRHS VI: B-25).

39. See Marjorie Procter-Smith, "Shakerism and Feminism: Reflections on Women's Religion and the Early Shakers," in *Shaker* (Old Chatham, N.Y.: Shaker Museum and Library, 1991) for development of this theme.

40. Rathbone, *Reasons Offered*, pp. 26–27.

41. Deming genealogy, p. 169.

42. Andrews, *The Hancock Shakers*, p. 15; "A nerative of deeds kept in the Trustees' office, July 1841," HSV; Myers, pp. 81–82; see also Deeds at Sabbathday Lake Library.

43. Ott, *Hancock Shaker Village*, p. 83.

44. Ibid., p. 79.

45. See Registration Form, National Register of Historic Places, for "Tyringham Shaker Settlement Historic District," August 24, 1987, at Hancock Shaker Village (HSV), Section 7, page 1.

46. Andrews, *The People Called Shaker*, p. 220.

CHAPTER FOUR "On Earth 'Tis a Heaven" (pp. 49–71)

1. Letter from Deacon Daniel Goodrich to Elder David Meacham, October 10, 1806, WRHS IV: A-19.

2. In "Copies of manuscripts found among the writings of Deacon Daniel Goodrich after his death," SA 799.1, Andrews Collection; Priscilla J. Brewer, *Shaker Communities, Shaker Lives* (Hanover, NH: University Press of New England, 1986), p. 215.

3. Population statistics from Brewer, *Shaker Communities,* p. 215.

4. "Brief Record Kept by an Unidentified Shaker" (WRHS V:B-9).

5. Map is illustrated following page 72; 1820s quotation from [Eugene Merrick Dodd], *The Round Barn: A Short History* (printed for the Friends of Hancock Shaker Village on the Occasion of the Opening of the Restored Barn, Sept. 5, 1968; Pittsfield, Mass.: Shaker Community, Inc., 1968).

6. Eric Arthur and Dudley Witney, *The Barn: A Vanishing Landmark in North America* (Greenwich, Conn.: New York Graphic Society, 1972), pp. 146–55; Dodd, *The Round Barn*; Eric Sloane, *The Age of Barns* (New York: Funk & Wagnalls, 1967), pp. 52–55; Philip C. Ziegler, *Storehouses of Time: Historical Barns of the Northeast* (Camden, Me.: Down East Books, 1985), pp. 111, 114–15.

7. Quoted in *The Pittsfield Sun,* August 14, 1834.

8. Thomas Allen, *An Historical Sketch of the County of Berkshire, and Town of Pittsfield, Written in May 1808* (Boston: Belcher and Armstrong, 1808; in Berkshire Athenaeum), p. 5.

9. This passage and the quotations in the next paragraph are taken from John C. Pease and John M. Niles, *A Gazetteer of the States of Connecticut and Rhode-Island* (Hartford, Conn.: William S. Marsh, 1819).

10. Marci Woolson, "Shaker Dress Based on Uniformity," *Shaker Messenger,* vol. 3 (Winter 1981), pp. 3–7.

11. Pittsfield Sun, Nov. 28, 1803, at Berkshire Athenaeum; Gov. Clinton letter in Collection of the United Society of Shakers, dated Dec. 16, 1803, Sabbathday Lake, Me.

12. The Shakers were thanked by the *Pittsfield Sun* in the issue of June 10, 1824; Cargill's story is related by Eloise S. Myers in *Tyringham, Massachusetts: A Hinterland Settlement* (Tyringham, Mass., 1948), p. 84.

13. "Enfield Day Book 1799–1804," Joseph Fairbanks; "Enfield Ct. Account Book 1796–1828"; both Shaker Museum, NOC 16,489.

14. "Listing of Paper Money by Serial Number and Name of Bank, Received by Shakers from Specific People 1804–1811," Shaker Museum, NOC 16,488.

15. "Enfield Day Book"; suggestion regarding Shakers holding mortgages is from Richard Steinert, interview with author, April 1988.

16. Alfred Benney, quoted in Charlotte Libov, "Cherishing the Heritage of the Shakers," *New York Times,* Feb. 7, 1988, Section 23, p. 2, said the Enfield Shakers ran the post office and "were involved with" the operation of the train station.

17. See Richard D. Birdsall, *Berkshire County: A Cultural History* (New Haven, Conn.: Yale University Press, 1959).

18. "Testimony of Cassandana Brewster," Hancock, n.d., Andrews Collection, SA 1548; "Testimony of Cassandana Brewster" in Alonzo G. Hollister, comp., *Book of Remembrance,* WRHS VII:B-109, p. 34.

19. Mother Ann's prophecy is found in "Testimony of Jemima Blanchard," in Eunice Bathrick, comp., *Testimonies and Wise Sayings, Counsel and Instruction of Mother Ann and the Elders* (Harvard, Mass., 1869, WRHS VI:B-10–13), p. 85.

20. Letter from Daniel Goodrich, Sr. to David Meacham, Oct. 10, 1806, WRHS IV:A-19.

21. Letter to Harvard Ministry, March 31, 1813, WRHS IV:A-19; "A Record of Deaths," Collection of Jean Helwig.

22. "Testimony of Lucy Davis," WRHS VI:A-2.

23. "Testimony of Betsey Haskell," WRHS VI:A-2.

24. Calvin Green, *Journal of a Trip to Savoy* (New Lebanon, N.Y.: 1821), Aug. 15–16, 1821, WRHS V:B-90.

25. Priscilla J. Brewer, "Numbers Are Not the Thing for Us to Glory In: Demographic Perspectives on the Decline of the Shakers," in *Communal Societies*, Vol. 7, 1987, p. 31; see also Brewer, *Shaker Communities*, p. 224.

26. Mann quotation is taken from Mary Mann, *Life of Horace Mann* (Boston: 1865), p. 116. Background on education is drawn from Birdsall, *Berkshire County*, chap. 5.

27. Sherman B. Barnes, "Shaker Education," in *Ohio Archeological and Historical Quarterly* 62 (Jan. 1953), 67–76.

28. Discussion of Wells's views on schooling is taken from Seth Y. Wells, "School Instructions" (1832) Andrews Collection, SA 951.

29. "Jane Osborn's mathematics notebook," Williams College Shaker Collection.

30. Wells, "School Instructions."

31. Town of Hancock comments are in the "Annual Report of the Town of Hancock, 1943," quoted in *The Berkshire Eagle*, Nov. 2, 1943; Pittsfield School Committee report quoted in Ott, *Hancock Shaker Village*, p. 113.

32. [Daniel Myrick,] "Journal Of a visit to five societies of believers viz Enfield Conn., Tyringham and Hancock Mass., New Lebanon and Watervliet New York By a company from Harvard In the Autumn of the year 1846," Sept. 23, 1846 (Williams College Shaker Collection).

33. "Grove Wright's Book," Private Collection.

34. John A. Scott, *Tyringham: Old and New* (Pittsfield, Mass.: Sun Printing Co., 1905), pp. 20–23. Maple sugaring quotation from Howard S. Russell, *A Long, Deep Furrow: Three Centuries of Farming in New England* (Hanover, N.H.: University Press of New England, 1976), p. 275.

35. Quotations are from Myrick, "Journal Of a visit," Sept. 22 and 23, 1846; other information from memories of Julia Johnson and Elizabeth Thornber, "More About the Shakers," *Berkshire Gleaner*, July 18, 1906.

36. Russell, *A Long, Deep Furrow*, p. 67.

37. Edward Deming Andrews suggests that Albert J. Battles, elder at Tyringham and in the Ministry, may have been an influential craftsman in wrought iron, having worked as a patternmaker at the old Richmond Iron Works after 1829; see Edward Deming Andrews, *The Hancock Shakers: The Shaker Community at Hancock, Mass., 1780–1960* (Pittsfield, Mass.: Shaker Community, Inc., 1961), p. 29. Of course, the Tyringham Church Family dwelling, which is especially noted for its fine ironwork, was built in 1800, nine years before Battles's birth, but he may have contributed to Hancock's 1830 brick dwelling. For graceful examples of wrought iron, see Ejner Handberg, *Shop Drawings of Shaker Iron and Tinware* (Stockbridge, Mass.: Berkshire Traveller Press, 1976), pp. 10, 18, 20, 21.

38. D. A. Buckingham, "Epitomic History of the Watervliet Shakers," *The Shaker* 7 (July 1899), p. 50; Edward Deming Andrews, *The Community Industries of the Shakers* (Albany: University of the State of New York, 1933), pp. 258–59.

39. Map is illustrated following page 72.

40. Charles R. Muller and Timothy D. Rieman, *The Shaker Chair* (Winchester, Ohio: The Canal Press, 1984), pp. 76–79.

41. Information from Caroline Helfrich in Andrews, *The Hancock Shakers,* p. 28.

42. Jerry V. Grant and Douglas R. Allen, *Shaker Furniture Makers* (Hanover, N.H.: published for Hancock Shaker Village by University Press of New England, 1989), pp. 76–90.

43. "Journal Kept by the Deaconesses at the (Church) Office, 1830–71, New Lebanon," in Andrews, *Community Industries,* p. 240.

44. See Karen K. Nickless and Pamela J. Nickless, "Trustees, Deacons, and Deaconesses: The Temporal Role of the Shaker Sisters 1820–1890," in *Communal Societies,* Vol. 7, 1987, esp. pp. 18–21. See also Andrews, *Community Industries,* p. 184.

45. [Jane Osborne], "Diary," Williams College Shaker Collection, 98, vol. 3.

46. Quotation from letter of March, 1819, WRHS IV: A-19; water-wheel information from James Houldsworth, Shaker Lane, Pittsfield, Mass.

47. *History of Berkshire County, Mass.* (New York: J. B. Beers Co., 1885), Vol. 1, p. 275.

48. Deed for purchase of Garfield property is at Middle Berkshire Registry of Deeds, Pittsfield, Mass., Book 70, p. 108. More information on the Shaker use of that land can be found in the Walling Map of 1856 at the Berkshire Athenaeum; and in Myers, *Tyringham,* p. 80; and in the National Register of Historic Buildings registration form for the Tyringham Shaker settlement, at HSV.

49. Lucy S. Bowers, "Showing When Different Houses Were Builded in the Society of Enfield Connecticut," 1911, Canterbury Shaker Library, MS 1141, pp. 66–74. See also Ricardo Belden's notes in NOC 16,155.

50. Deeds at Middle Berkshire Registry of Deeds, Pittsfield, Mass., Book 38, pp. 211, 791, 795, 797, 803, 805, 807, 809.

51. Deeds at Middle Berkshire Registry of Deeds, Pittsfield, Mass., Book 42, pp. 547, 548, 549; Book 50, p. 29; Book 53, pp. 22 and 223; Book 55, p. 620; Book 60, p. 496.

52. Deeds at Middle Berkshire Registry of Deeds, Pittsfield, Mass., Book 38, pp. 901, 903, 909; Book 39, pp. 432, 433; Book 40, p. 328; Book 42, pp. 247, 491–498. See also Sara Wermeil, "Chronological List of Property Acquired by United Society through 1821," Hancock Shaker Village Library.

53. Deed dated August 9, 1800, Canterbury Shaker Library, MS 129.

54. This discussion of Calvin Ely's life is drawn from "Diary Kept by Calvin Ely (1780–1816)" WRHS V:B-11. See also Jerry V. Grant and Douglas R. Allen, *Shaker Furniture Makers* (Pittsfield, Mass.: Hancock Shaker Village and University Press of New England, 1989), p. 34.

55. "Record of Calvin Ely's Death," WRHS VI A.

56. "Grove Wright's Book Bought May the 10th 1815," Private Collection, Armonk, N.Y.

57. Grant and Allen, *Shaker Furniture Makers,* pp. 76–90; David R. Lamson, *Two Years Experience Among the Shakers* (West Boylston, Mass.: Author, 1848), p. 61; Letter from Grove Wright to Grove Blanchard, Dec. 22, 1849 (WRHS IV: A-19).

58. "Grove Wright's Book."

59. W. S. Warder, *A Brief Sketch of the Religious Society of People Called Shakers* (London: 1818), pp. 9–10.

60. This and the following quotation are taken from "Diary Kept by Calvin Ely."

61. "Diary Kept by Calvin Ely (1780–1816)" WRHS V:B-11.

62. May 14, 1815, WRHS V:A-9.
63. See Daniel W. Patterson, "Millennial Praises: Tune Location and Authorial Attributions of the First Shaker Hymnal," *Shaker Quarterly* 18 (Fall 1990), pp. 77–93.
64. "From manuscripts found among writings of Deacon Daniel Goodrich after his death," p. 73.
65. Quotations from the ministrations of Nathaniel Deming and Cassandana Goodrich are taken from "Testimony of Lydia Holt" in "Copies of manuscripts found among the writings of Deacon Daniel Goodrich after his death."
66. William Alfred Hinds, *American Communities* (Oneida, N.Y.: Office of the American Socialist, 1878), pp. 97–98.
67. Isaac N. Youngs, "A Concise View of the Church of God and of Christ on earth: having its foundation in the faith of Christ's first and second appearing" (New London, 1856), pp. 50–52, SA 760, Andrews Collection.

CHAPTER FIVE Bearing Fruit (pp. 72–90)

1. D. A. Buckingham, "Epitomic History of the Watervliet Shakers," *The Shaker* 7 (July 1877), pp. 49–50, 59; see also Edward Deming Andrews, *The Community Industries of the Shakers* (Albany, N.Y.: University of the State of New York, 1933), pp. 66–67. By 1790 Niskeyuna's name had been changed to Watervliet.
2. Reprinted in *The Shaker Manifesto*, Feb. 1881, p. 45.
3. Number of acres in seed production at Enfield is taken from *Greenwich and Wickford Weekly Pendulum*, Aug. 12, 1854; information on Shaker seed production is from *Shaker Manifesto*, Dec. 1882, p. 276; information on New England production of onions is from Howard S. Russell, *A Long Deep Furrow: Three Centuries of Farming in New England* (Hanover, N.H.: University Press of New England, 1976), pp. 269–70.
4. On the same page, however, a notice states: "An act is now before the Senate of the State of New York providing that any married person an inhabitant of that state, who should hereafter attach him or herself to any society of *Shakers* in the State, shall be taken to be civily dead, to all in tents and purposes in the law, and that his or her property may be disposed of in the same manner as if such person were really dead, and he or she rendered forever thereafter incapable of taking any estate by inheritance." *Hampden Federalist*, May 1, 1817, p. 1.
5. See Amy Bess Miller, *Shaker Herbs: A History and Compendium* (New York: C. N. Potter, 1976), for a discussion of the development of the Shaker seed industry.
6. Quotation from *Pittsfield Sun*, Sept. 15, 1887, p. 6; see also Miller, *Shaker Herbs*, and *Berkshire Gleaner*, June 27, 1906.
7. Andrews, *Community Industries*, p. 73.
8. See Edward Deming Andrews and Faith Andrews, *Fruits of the Shaker Tree of Life* (Stockbridge, Mass.: Berkshire Traveller Press, 1975), p. 39.
9. Hancock 1813 seed list is at Shaker Museum, Old Chatham, N.Y.; 1821 seed list is at Hancock Shaker Village.
10. Pittsfield Sun, Aug. 14, 1834.
11. Williams College Shaker Collection; Andrews, *Community Industries*, p. 73.
12. "Diary of Carson Dana Benton," vol. 2, Connecticut State Library.
13. "Gardeners Journal, Hancock," Aug. 8, 1844, Shaker Museum, NOC 10, 358.
14. Discussion of the garden year is taken from Margaret Frisbee Sommer, *The Shaker Seed Industry* (Old Chatham, N.Y.: The Shaker Museum Foundation, 1972);

see also Andrews, *Community Industries*, p. 78. Quantities of seed packaged in Hancock in 1842 is taken from "Gardener's Journal" 1842–1847, Shaker Museum, NOC 10,358.

15. See 1837–1913 "Hancock Day Book," at HSV. For more on the shipping network of the time, see Russell, *A Long Deep Furrow*, pp. 141–42, 186–88.

16. Letter to Brother Daniel from Brother Morrell, Watervliet, Dec. 26, 1822, Edward Deming Andrews Memorial Collection, Henry Francis du Pont Winterthur Museum, Winterthur, Del.

17. Letter from Jefferson White, Oct. 11, 1848, to Elder Nathan Freeman of Alfred, Me., Collection of the United Society of Shakers, Sabbathday Lake, Me.

18. "Grove Wright's Book," Private Collection, Armonk, N.Y.

19. Letter from Grove Wright, Mar. 17, 1839, WRHS IV:A-19; "Grove Wright's Book." Lewis Wheeler was mentioned in an 1834 letter from Daniel Goodrich, Jr., as having removed a cancerous tumor from Enfield member Caleb Pease's neck, with the advice of physicians (WRHS IV:A-19).

20. Sister Frances A. Carr, "The Shakers as Herb Growers," *Shaker Quarterly* 3 (Summer 1963), pp. 39–43.

21. Marcia Bullard, "Shaker Industries," in *Good Housekeeping* 43 (July 1906). pp. 33–37.

22. Andrews, *Fruits*, p. 35.

23. Correspondence in Collection of the United Society of Shakers, Sabbathday Lake, Me., Nov. 15, 1826; Jan. 22, 1827.

24. Diary of Lucy Jane Osborn, Williams College Shaker Collection, 98, vol. 3. After the Civil War trains traveling between New Haven and Springfield actually passed between Enfield's Church and West families. See "Social Record," *Shaker* 6 (1876), p. 7.

25. Russell, *A Long, Deep Furrow*, pp. 189–93.

26. Property inventory in "Enfield Reports to New Lebanon Minnistry 1843–1867," Shaker Museum, NOC 10,359.

27. Letter from Urban Johns, Jan. 4, 1840, WRHS IV:A-62.

28. WRHS: B-239, p. 2. For further discussion of this document see Stephen J. Stein, "'A Candid Statement of Our Principles': Early Shaker Theology in the West," *Proceedings of the American Philosophical Society* 133 (December 1989), pp. 503–19.

29. This discussion of *The Millennial Laws* is taken from New Lebanon Ministry, *Milenial Laws, or Gospel Statutes and Ordinances Adapted to the Day of Christ's Second Appearing.* (New Lebanon, N.Y., Aug. 7, 1821), WRHS I B-37.

30. Seth Y. Wells and Calvin Green, *Testimonies Concerning the Character and Ministry of Mother Ann Lee and the First Witnesses of the Gospel of Christ's Second Appearing; Given by Some of the Aged Brethren and Sisters of the United Society* (Albany: Packard & Van Benthuysen, 1827); Mary Marshall Dyer, *A Portraiture of Shakerism* (Concord, N.H.: Printed for the author, 1822).

31. "Good Gospel fish" is the phrase of Calvin Reed, "Autobiography," New Lebanon, N.Y., n.d., WRHS VI:B-29, p. 121.

32. Letter from Hancock Ministry, Dec. 26, 1825, WRHS IV:A-19.

33. Carson Dana Benton, "Diary and Historical Notes, 1825–1859," Connecticut State Library.

34. "Covenant of West Family," Shaker Museum, NOC 10,353.

35. Gary T. Leveille, "The Pease Family: Movers and Shakers of Enfield, Connecticut," *Shaker Messenger*, Summer, 1989, p. 10.

36. Kyle Roberts, "Biographical Insights: Views of Several Shakers from the Ty-ringham Shaker Community" (Paper presented at the Berkshire Shaker Seminar, Darrow School, New Lebanon, New York, Aug. 28, 1990); U.S. Bureau of the Census, reports for 1840–1870.

37. "Van Valen Family History," at HSV, 9757 V284.

38. Quotation from "Testimony of Thomas Damon," WRHS VI A2, reel 49.

39. Letter from the Ministry, February 11, 1830, WRHS IV:A-10, reel 17.

40. Pittsfield Sun, May 8, 1823, p. 3; May 27, 1824, p. 3.

41. See Norman Thomas, The Conscientious Objector in America (New York: B. W. Huebsch, 1925), and Lillian Schlissel, ed., Conscience in America: A Documentary History of Conscientious Objection in America 1757–1967 (New York: E. P. Dutton, 1968).

42. "Declaration of the Society of People (Commonly Called Shakers) Shewing Their Reasons for Refusing to Aid or Abet the Cause of War and Bloodshed," Hartford, Conn., 1815, Williams College Shaker Collection.

43. James M. Upton, "The Shakers as Pacifists in the Period Between 1812 and the Civil War" (Louisville, K.Y., 1973; Williams College Shaker Collection).

44. Population figures from Prsicilla J. Brewer, Shaker Communities, Shaker Lives (Hanover, N.H.: University Press of New England, 1986), pp. 217, 230.

45. Letter to South Union Ministry from Elder William Deming, Jan. 8, 1832, quoted in Ott, Hancock Shaker Village, pp. 73–74. See also "Copies of manuscripts found among the writings of Deacon Daniel Goodrich after his death," SA 799.1, Andrews Collection.

46. Harriet Martineau, Society in America (New York: 1837), pp. 313–15.

47. "Letter from Amaziah Clark, Enfield North Family, August 22, 1827," WRHS IV A-9, reel 17.

48. Richard Steinert, interview with author, Enfield, Conn., April 1988; "Inventory of Property in Enfield. Reports to New Lebanon Ministry 1843–1867," Shaker Museum, NOC 10,359; see also Enfield Shaker Collection, Connecticut State Library.

CHAPTER SIX "Their Precious Mother's Word" (pp. 91–105)

1. From "A Record of Messages and Communications Given by Divine Inspiration in the Church at Hancock Commencing in 1840," Hancock Church Family, 1840–1843, SA 1066, Andrews Collection SA 1066.

2. Robert F. W. Meader, "Foreword," in Edward R. Horgan, The Shaker Holy Land, reprinted with permission from The Harvard Common Press, copyright © 1982.

3. Railroad mileage taken from Alfred D. Chandler, Jr., ed., The Railroads (New York: Harcourt, Brace & World, 1965), p. 13.

4. "Testimony of Grove Wright" in Alonzo G. Hollister, comp., Autobiography of the Saints (New Lebanon, N.Y.: 1872), p. 153; WRHS VI:B-36–37.

5. "More about the Shakers," Berkshire Gleaner, July 18, 1906, p. 1.

6. "A Short Sketch of the Illness and Death of Almira Johnson," 1844, WRHS VI:A-9; Eloise S. Myers, Tyringham, Massachusetts: A Hinterland Settlement (Tyringham, Mass.: Publisher, 1948), pp. 86, 87.

7. "More about the Shakers," p. 1.

8. Letter from Enfield, Ct., to Hancock Ministry, Feb. 28, 1838, WRHS IV:A-9; WRHS IV:A-19 (April 1839; October 1839).

9. "Orders Given by Mother Lucy," Hancock 1839–1842, Feb. 12, 1839, Andrews Collection SA 748.

10. "A Record of Messages," p. 36.

11. See Joanne H. Jastram, "The Complexities of Shaker Dances," *Shaker Messenger* 5 (Fall 1982).

12. "Testimony of Thomas Damon," WRHS VI A2, reel 49.

13. Williams College Shaker Collection, 98, vol. 7.

14. Both the "Book of Orders Given by Mother Lucy" and the letter from Mother Ann to the Ministry and Society at Hancock, "read by Father James, and copied by mortal hands, April 23, 1841" are in the Williams College Shaker Collection, 98, vol. 7. See also 98, vol. 4, no. 50.

15. "Testimony of Olive Stebbins," WRHS IV:A-2.

16. Myers, pp. 85–86, 87; "More about the Shakers," p. 1.

17. Sprague is quoted in David R. Lamson, *Two Years Experience among the Shakers* (West Boylston, Mass.: Author, 1848), p. 41.

18. Robert F. W. Meader, "Zion patefacta," *Shaker Quarterly* 2 (Spring 1962), pp. 5–17; Edward Deming Andrews, *The Hancock Shakers* (Pittsfield, Mass.: Shaker Community, Inc., 1961).

19. Shaker Library at Sabbathday Lake, Me.; Williams College Shaker Collection, 98, 18.

20. "Journal, Enfield, Ct., Probably Left by Eldress Annie Granger," WRHS V:B-13.

21. "Shaker diary, 1854, Telling of the Journey of Elder John Rankin, Brother Urban Johns, Eldress Betsy Smith and Sister Nancy E. Moore, from South Union, Ky.," Western Kentucky University Library, Bowling Green, Ky.

22. This account of the Hancock meeting is drawn from "A Record Kept of the Several Meetings Held upon Mount Sinai by the Family Orders on Days of the Feasts, 1842–1845," SA 787, Andrews Collection; spiritual garments described by David Lamson, *Two Years' Experience among the Shakers* (West Boylston, Mass.: Author, 1848), p. 58, and Marci Woolson, "Shaker Dress Based on Uniformity," *Shaker Messenger* 3 (Winter 1981), pp. 3–7.

23. Courtesy of Hale family; photocopy at Hancock Shaker Village Library.

24. Julia Johnson, "Among the Shakers: Some Peculiar Spirit Manifestations," *The Progressive Thinker,* n.d., n.p., in clipping file, Williams College Shaker Collection, p. 104.

25. "Grove Wright's Book," Private Collection.

26. Dr. & Mrs. Edward D. Andrews, Catalog for exhibit at Smith College Museum of Art, Northampton, Mass., 1960–61. See also Daniel W. Patterson, *Gift Drawing and Gift Song: A Study of Two Forms of Shaker Inspiration* (Sabbathday Lake, Me.: The United Society of Shakers, 1983).

27. See Jane F. Crosthwaite, "The Spirit Drawings of Hannah Cohoon: Window on the Shakers and Their Folk Art," p. 8, note 18, in *Communal Societies,* Vol. 7, 1987.

28. June Sprigg, *The Gift of Inspiration: Shaker and American Folk Art, 1803–1880* (New York: Hirschl and Adler Galleries, 1979).

29. The four drawings—*The Tree of Life,* or *Blazing Tree,* Oct. 9, 1845; *The Tree of Life,* July 3–Oct. 1, 1854; *A Bower of Mulberry Trees,* Sept. 13, 1854; and *A Little Basket Full of Beautiful Apples for the Ministry,* June 29, 1856—have been reproduced in color in Edward Deming Andrews and Faith Andrews, *Visions of the Heavenly Sphere: A Study in Shaker Religious Art* (Charlottesville, Va.: published for the Henry

Francis du Pont Winterthur Museum by the University Press of Virginia, 1969); text of "The Tree of Life" is taken from p. 70. See also Sprigg, *The Gift of Inspiration*; and Daniel W. Patterson, *Gift Drawing and Gift Song: A Study of Two Forms of Shaker Inspiration* (Sabbathday Lake, Me.: United Society of Shakers, 1983), pp. 47–55.

30. Ruth Wolfe, "Hannah Cohoon," in Jean Lipman and Tom Armstrong, eds., *American Folk Painters of Three Centuries* (New York; Hudson Hills Press, 1980), pp. 58–65.

31. See Edward Deming Andrews and Faith Andrews, *Fruits of the Shaker Tree of Life* (Stockbridge, Mass.: Berkshire Traveller Press, 1975), pp. 95–96, for an account of the destruction—and rescue—of some Shaker spirit drawings.

32. Edward Deming Andrews, *The People Called Shaker* (Oxford: Oxford University Press, 1953), p. 272.

33. Crosthwaite, "The Spirit Drawings," p. 14.

34. James Guimond, "The New Heavens and the New Earth: Apocalyptic and Millennial Interpretations," ed. Theodore E. Johnson, *Shaker Quarterly* 17 (Spring 1989), pp. 3–10.

35. Hancock Journal, Aug. 1 to 14, 1846 (WRHS V:B-34).

36. Letter from the Hancock Ministry, Tyringham (WRHS IV:A-65).

37. Shakers' continued interaction with departed spirits is reported by William Alfred Hinds in *American Communities* (Oneida, N.Y.: Office of the American Socialist, 1878), Williams College Shaker Collection. See also Stephen J. Stein, *The Shaker Experience in America* (New Haven, Conn.: Yale University Press, 1992), p. 199. Information on Millennial Laws is found in Theodore E. Johnson, "Rules and Orders . . . 1860," *Shaker Quarterly* 11 (Winter 1971), pp. 140–41. See also Louis Miles, "Shaker Men and Women Together and Apart," *Shaker Manifesto* 13, no. 1, 1991.

38. Letter from Grove Wright to Ministry at Harvard, Aug. 28, 1847 (WRHS IV:A-10).

39. Departure rate cited by John Harlow Ott, *Hancock Shaker Village: A Guidebook and History* (Hancock, Mass.: Shaker Community, Inc., 1976), p. 47; quoted passage from David Lamson, *Two Years' Experience*, p. 102.

40. Lamson, *Two Years' Experience*, p. 21.

41. Ibid., pp. 21, 27.

42. Ibid., pp. 61, 81.

43. Daniel W. Patterson, "Millennial Praises: Tune Location and Authorial Attributions of the First Shaker Hymnal," *Shaker Quarterly* 18 (Fall 1990), pp. 77–93. Daniel W. Patterson has suggested that songs composed by sisters tended to be hymns of fervent emotion, not of abstract theory.

44. See Brewer, *Shaker Communities*, p. 126.

CHAPTER SEVEN "This Hundred Fold Blessing" (pp. 106–127)

1. Quotations on the season from [Grove Wright], Diary, 1818–1860, Andrews Collection SA 782; "Grove Wright's Book," May 4, 1846; apple trees mentioned in Thomas Damon, "Memoranda" (Hancock, Mass., 1846–1860), Shaker Museum and Library, Old Chatham, N.Y. (NOC 13,357), Oct. 1846 and May 6, 1847; quotation on measuring onions from [Wright], Diary 1818–1860, SA 782, Andrews Collection.

2. Thomas Damon, "Memoranda," p. 7.

3. This discussion of the Tyringham community is taken from Eloise S. Myers, *Tyringham, Massachusetts: A Hinterland Settlement* (Tyringham, Mass.: 1948), pp. 85, 88.

4. Myers, *Tyringham,* p. 85.

5. Daniel Myrick's journey is described in [Daniel Myrick,] "Journal Of a visit to five societies of Believers viz Enfield Conn., Tyringham and Hancock, Mass., New Lebanon and Watervliet N.Y. By a company from Harvard in the Autumn of the year 1846," Williams College Shaker Collection.

6. David R. Lamson, *Two Years' Experience among the Shakers* (West Boylston, Mass.: Author, 1848), pp. 48–50.

7. Letter from Joseph Wicker to Grove Blanchard, Harvard Ministry, Oct. 19, 1847, WRHS IV:A-65.

8. Albert Battle's birth is recorded in Tyringham Town Hall, "Births and Deaths 1759–1848, Town of Tyringham," p. 9.

9. David Lamson's account of his meeting with Richard Van Deusen is in *Two Years' Experience,* pp. 48–50.

10. This discussion of Enfield as seen through Benton's eyes is drawn from "Diary of Carson Dana Benton," vol. 1, Connecticut State Library.

11. Guadeloupe earthquake mentioned in Hancock Day Book 1837–1913, Hancock Shaker Village.

12. Julia Johnson's young man may have been Michael McCue (or McKeough); however, no one named Michael is listed as buried in the Shaker cemetery, where Julia said her lover was interred. Johnson's and Day's stories are told in Myers, *Tyringham,* p. 85.

13. "Letters of Hannah Pease, Jedediah Dudley, and Lemuel Steele, 1836–1849," Collection of Gary Leveille.

14. This discussion is taken from the *Pittsfield Sun,* Sept. 14, Sept. 28, Oct. 26, Nov. 2, and Nov. 16, 1837.

15. The catalog is in the collection of the Harvard School of Business Administration and listed in Mary L. Richmond, *Shaker Literature: A Bibliography* (Hanover, N.H.: University Press of New England, 1977) as #33.

16. Letter from Thomas Damon to George Wilcox, April 1, 1848, WRHS IV:A-19.

17. Population figures from *Springfield Union,* March 12, 1926; Priscilla J. Brewer, *Shaker Communities, Shaker Lives* (Hanover, N.H.: University Press of New England, 1986), p. 231.

18. South Hadley, Mass., Birth Records, Book 2 (1721–1843); Sylvester Judd, *History of Hadley, Including the Early History of Hatfield, South Hadley, Amherst, and Granby* (Springfield, Mass.: H. R. Hunting & Co., 1905).

19. Sophie E. Eastman, *In Old South Hadley* (Springfield, Mass.: H. R. Hunting Co., 1912), pp. 191–92.

20. Information on Lyman family appears in "Covenant of the West Family, Enfield" (NOC #10,353); Lyman Coleman, *Genealogy of the Lyman Family in Great Britain and America* (Albany, N.Y.: J. Munsell, 1872), pp. 273–74; Francis Olcott Allen, *History of Enfield, Ct.,* vol. 3 (Lancaster, Penna.: Wickersham Printing Co., 1900); Copley Family Bible, Collection of Helen R. McGinnis.

21. Thomas Damon, "Memoranda" (Hancock, Mass., 1846–1860), Shaker Museum, NOC 13,357, pp. 171–78.

22. "Enfield Day Book," WRHS V:B-18; Canterbury MS 720.

23. Springfield, Mass., Marriage Records, 1866, p. 65; Copley Family Bible.

24. Damon, "Memoranda," Jan. 1846.

25. Canterbury MS 720; Letter from Thomas Damon to George Wilcox, Oct. 1842, WRHS IV:A-19.

26. Letter from Thomas Damon to George Wilcox, Dec. 29, 1846, WRHS IV:A-19.

27. Damon, "Memoranda," Dec. 9, 1846 and October 19, 1847. Shorthand deciphered by Priscilla J. Brewer.

28. List of inventions is found in Grove Wright, "Diary," Aug. 7, 1854; quotation about Damon's shop is from *Kentucky Ministry Travel Journal,* July 1869, WRHS V:B-228.

29. Letter from Grove Wright to Harvard Ministry, April 11, 1848, WRHS IV:A-19.

30. Eldress Dana's last trip to Tyringham is recounted in Thomas Damon, "Memoranda," Feb. 7, 1846; Damon described her as "blind and feeble" in "Memoranda," May 6, 1846; she was said to retain her mental faculties in "Letter from Hancock Ministry," Jan. 18, 1847, WRHS IV:A-65; Grove Wright's comments are taken from his letter (Letter from Grove Wright to Harvard Ministry, Mar. 18, 1848), WRHS IV:A-65.

31. Letter from Hancock Ministry, June 3, 1848, WRHS IV:A-19.

32. Testimony of Lydia Holt, "Copies of manuscripts found among the writings of Deacon Daniel Goodrich after his death," SA 799.1, Andrews Collection.

33. Letter from Grove Wright to Harvard Ministry, WRHS IV:A-19.

34. Thomas Damon commented on the Enfield North Family horse barn in "Memoranda" in May 1855; the slate roof and the dinner with melons are mentioned in "Shaker Diary, 1854, Telling of the Journey of Elder John Rankin, Brother Urban Johns, Eldress Betsy Smith and Sister Nancy E. Moore, from South Union, Kentucky," Western Kentucky University Library, Bowling Green, Ky.; other building information is from "Grove Wright's Book," WRHS V:B-8; and "Dates of Buildings Erected at Enfield," presumably Eldress Anna Granger's notes, Andrews Collection SA 775 and Shaker Museum, NOC 18,171.

35. Horse barn is mentioned in "Grove Wright's Book," June 5, 1850; Thomas Damon's comments are taken from "Letter from Thomas Damon," Feb. 1854, WRHS IV:A-19.

36. Thomas Damon, "Memoranda," August 1854.

37. David Lamson, *Two Years' Experience among the Shakers* (West Boylston, Mass.: Author, 1848), pp. 17, 29.

38. Ejner Handberg, *Shop Drawings of Shaker Furniture and Woodenware,* vol. 3 (Stockbridge, Mass.: Berkshire Traveller Press, 1977); Howard S. Russell, *A Long, Deep Furrow: Three Centuries of Farming in New England.* (Hanover, N.H.: University Press of New England, 1976).

39. Nathaniel Hawthorne, *American Notebooks,* ed. Randall Stewart (New Haven, Conn.: Yale University Press, 1932).

40. Evert A. Duyckinck, "A Visit by Evert and George Duyckinck, Hawthorne and his son Julian, and Melville," Williams College Shaker Collection. Hilliard was probably nicknamed "Father" by the visitors, as Grove Wright would have been Ministry elder at the time. After the 1820s, however, even Ministry elders were seldom referred to as Mother or Father. See Stephen Stein, *Shaker Experience in America,* pp. 123–24.

41. "Shaker diary, 1854, telling of the journey of Elder John Rankin, Brother Urban Johns, Eldress Betsy Smith, and Sister Nancy E. Moore, from South Union, Ky.," Western Kentucky University Library, Bowling Green, Ky. The machine described as the "ne plus ultra" is part of the collection of the Shaker Museum, Old Chatham, N.Y.

42. Thomas Damon, "Memoranda," Oct. 10, 1854.

43. Ibid.

44. This discussion of a farmer's life is drawn from "Farmer's Daily Record Apr. 1850–July 1852," WRHS V:B-17.

45. "Inventory of property in Enfield—Reports to the New Lebanon Ministry 1843–1867," Shaker Museum, NOC 10,359.

46. "Account of Society of Shakers," n.d., Pease manuscript, Connecticut State Library.

47. "Farmer's Daily Record," May 10, 1852.

48. "Center Family Records 1853–1861," Enfield, WRHS V:B-18; "Sojourney Truth" mentioned April 30, 1855.

49. This journey is recounted in "Harriet Amelia Lyman's Book Presented to her by Sarah Dana Burlingame Sept. 22 1856," WRHS V:B-19.

50. "Harriet Amelia Lyman's Book," July 2, 1856.

51. "A Brief Account of the Proceedings of a Week or 2 spent at the Seaside in Wickford Rhode Island August 1858," WRHS V:B-19.

52. Marcia Bullard, "Shaker Industries," *Good Housekeeping* 43 (July 1906), pp. 33–37.

CHAPTER EIGHT Challenges from Within (pp. 128–148)

1. Timothy Hopkins, *The Kelloggs in the Old World and the New* (San Francisco: Sunset Press, 1903); also, Record of Births, Town of South Hadley, Mass., Book 2, 1721–1843. There is a record of one daughter born to Ruth and Elijah Kellogg, but she died as an infant.

2. Priscilla J. Brewer, *Shaker Communities, Shaker Lives* (Hanover, N.H.: University Press of New England, 1986), p. 231.

3. David Richmond's arrival at the Enfield South Family is mentioned on June 5, 1846, in Thomas Damon, "Memoranda," Shaker Museum and Library, Old Chatham, N.Y. (NOC 13,357). David and Thomas Richmond's occupations are listed in Stephen Paterwic, "An Extract of Names, Ages and Occupations from the U.S. Census 1850–1910 for the City of Union, Conn., the Shaker Society at Enfield," at HSV.

4. Letter dated October 12, 1846, from D. Richmond and William White, Ballard Vale, Andover, Mass., to the editor, *The Day-Star*, Nov. 7, 1846, in the Collection of the United Society of Shakers, Sabbathday Lake, Me.

5. Lucy S. Bowers, "A Brief Review and Memorial Tribute to Sister Sarah Emily Copley Deceased September 9, 1911," Williams College Shaker Collection. In this document Bowers says that Elizabeth Richmond Copley had a brother Thomas and a cousin David in America. Her father (Hannah's husband) may have been named David as well.

6. Ministry quotations from "Letters from Hancock Ministry," May 14, 1852, and June 14, 1853, WRHS IV:A-19.

7. The Copley story as told by Ricardo Belden, June 1938, in Steinert collection, item 36, HSV.

8. "Center Family Records," WRHS V:B-18; Thomas Damon, "Memoranda," Shaker Museum and Library, Old Chatham, N.Y. (NOC 13,357), Jan. 20, 1852. Three women named Hannah Richmond passed through Enfield: Elizabeth Copley's mother; her sister; and a woman born in 1821 who may have been her cousin David Richmond's wife.

9. Thomas Damon, "Memoranda," p. 127; Feb. 12, 1853.

10. Discussion of the excommunication of David Richmond is taken from "Memorandum," Enfield, January 4–March 8, 1853, WRHS V:B-18; Thomas Damon, "Memoranda," Jan. 31–Mar. 1, 1853.

11. David Richmond, *An Explanatory Address* . . . (Glasgow: Hay Nisbet & Co., 1879), Williams College Shaker Collection.

12. All Copley dates are from the Copley family Bible, Collection of Helen R. McGinnis.

13. In some respects the Copley family is similar to the Offord family. According to *The Springfield Homestead*, Nov. 30, 1907, William Offord was a respected Methodist minister in England when he decided to investigate the Shakers. He crossed the ocean in 1849 to visit Enfield, joined the Society, and sent for his family. His daughter Miriam grew up to become eldress at the North Family.

14. Eloise S. Myers, *Tyringham, Massachusetts: A Hinterland Settlement* (Tyringham, Mass.: 1948), p. 84.

15. This description is taken from David R. Lamson, *Two Years' Experience among the Shakers* (West Boylston, Mass.: Author, 1848), pp. 13, 15.

16. Ibid., p. 17.

17. Ibid., pp. 29–30.

18. Ibid., p. 83.

19. Ibid., p. 27.

20. Ibid., pp. 39–40.

21. Ibid., p. 39.

22. Ibid., pp. 22, 48.

23. Letter from Grove Wright to Harvard Ministry, April 11, 1848, WRHS IV:A-19.

24. Letter from Grove Wright to Grove Blanchard, May 22, 1848, WRHS IV:A-19.

25. Thomas Damon, "Memoranda," June 21, 1849; letter from the City of Love, March 10, 1851, WRHS IV A-65.

26. Canon family information is courtesy of Carolyn Canon and Tyringham historian Clinton Elliott; Hannah Canon is presumed to be a weaver because her name appears on an item entitled "Directions for Dyeing Yarn, Wool, Flannel, and Cotton the Colors Red, Green, Black, Yellow, and Blue" (Andrews Collection SA 1057.10). The trip to Enfield is mentioned in "Names of the Brethren and Sisters Who Have Visited This Place [Enfield, Ct.] Commencing June 1837," WRHS V:B-12.

27. Hawkins is mentioned in Tyringham Town Records, 1835, 1841, 1842; information on the Hawkins family tree is courtesy of descendant Jean Helwig.

28. The quotations in this and the two following paragraphs are taken from "Letter from Grove Wright to Grove Blanchard," April 19, 1849, IV:A-19.

29. This account is drawn from Thomas Damon, "Memoranda," pp. 101–2.

30. Grove Wright's Book, April 1852; Thomas Damon, "Memoranda," May 1857; Myers, *Tyringham*, p. 84.

31. WRHS IV:A-19, March 18, 1852.

32. Grove Wright's Book, July 18, 1852.

33. "Personal Diary of Isaac Newton Youngs, 1837–59," Shaker Museum and Library, Old Chatham, N.Y. (NOC 10,509), June 1854. Two women named Mary Ann White were listed in the 1850 Federal Census. One, aged twenty-four, in the South Family, married Harvey Lyman four years later. Born in England, she may have been

William White's sister. The other, aged thirty-three, lived in the North Family and was the wife of William White.

34. Wedlock quote is taken from Thomas Damon, "Memoranda," p. 145; Lyman-White marriage record is found in City of Springfield, Mass., Marriage Records; Lyman and Woods is mentioned in *Springfield Directory and Business Advertiser* (Springfield, Mass.: Samuel Bowles & Co.), 1867 and annually until 1879; Lyman genealogy is found in Lyman Coleman, *Genealogy of the Lyman Family in Great Britain and America* (Albany, N.Y.: J. Munsell, 1872), p. 295.

35. Center Family Records 1853–1861, Enfield, WRHS V:B-18.

36. "Eldress's Journal," June 26, 1854, WRHS V:B-13.

37. Letter from Grove Wright to Harvard Ministry, June 5, 1854, WRHS IV:A-20; Brewer, *Shaker Communities*, p. 252, n. 18. Celia Sprague is listed in the 1880 United States Census for Pittsfield as a 68-year-old widow afflicted with "softening of the brain." See Stephen J. Paterwic, "Hancock Membership According to the U.S. Census," at HSV.

38. Letters to Harvard Ministry from Grove Wright, May 14, 1852, June 5, 1854, WRHS IV:A-19.

39. Letter from Grove Wright, July 15, 1854, WRHS IV:A-19.

40. "Testimony of Carsondana Benton," WRHS VI:A-2; "Harriet Amelia Lyman's Book Presented to her by Sarah Dana Burlingame Sept. 22 1856," WRHS V:B-19.

41. "Diary of Carsondana Benton," Connecticut State Library, Jan. 28, 1855.

42. Visit to the Shaker community mentioned in "Center Family Records," WRHS V:B-18.

43. "Personal Diary of Isaac N. Youngs 1837–1859," Shaker Museum, NOC 10,509.

44. "Records Kept by Order of the Church at New Lebanon," vol. 3, Shaker Museum, NOC 10,342; population figures in Brewer, *Shaker Communities*, p. 232.

45. "More about the Shakers," *Berkshire Gleaner*, July 18, 1906, p. 1.

46. That month Isaac N. Youngs wrote, "We lately hear that Desire Holt has gone to the world, from Tyringham! It is that she was gone insane [illegible]." Youngs, "Personal Diary," Shaker Museum, NOC 10,509.

47. Myers, *Tyringham*, p. 89.

48. From "Brief Inventory of the Personal Property of the Shaker Community in Tyringham after the Union of the Two Families December 1861." Andrews Collection, SA 809. "Wonderful" bull mentioned in "Center Family Records," Enfield, WRHS V:B-18, Mar. 12, 1860.

49. Information courtesy of Mrs. Beverly J. Kennedy; see also "Indenture of Nathan Bradburn," Collection of the United Society of Shakers, Sabbathday Lake, Me.

50. This case is discussed in Brewer, *Shaker Communities*, pp. 148–49.

51. This case is described in "Letter from Grove Wright," April 14, 1856, WRHS IV:A-20; see also Thomas Damon, "Memoranda," p. 169, and SA 789, Andrews Collection.

52. "Letter from Grove Wright," April 14, 1856, WRHS IV:A-20.

53. Center Family Records, WRHS V:B-18, Jan. 22, 25, and 30, 1856.

54. Letters from Grove Wright to the Harvard Ministry, Feb. 24, 1852, Sept. 18, 1853, WRHS IV:A-19.

55. Letter from Grove Wright to "Dearly beloved Ministry," Oct. 10, 1860, WRHS IV:A-19.

56. "List of changes in Ministry," WRHS V:B-8; Letter from Grove Wright to Grove Blanchard, Nov. 1, 1860, WRHS IV:A-20; letter from Tyringham, Oct. 20, 1861, WRHS IV:A-65.

57. Alonzo G. Hollister, comp., *Autobiography of the Saints* (New Lebanon, N.Y., 1872), p. 352, WRHS VI:B-37.

CHAPTER NINE "Roll Swiftly On, Remaining Years" (pp. 149–168)

1. From *The Shaker* 7 (March 1877); by Julia Johnson, W. Pittsfield.

2. *Pittsfield Sun*, Dec. 8, 1864, p. 2.

3. *Pittsfield Sun*, April 3, 1867; John Harlow Ott, *Hancock Shaker Village: A Guidebook and History* (Hancock, Mass.: Shaker Community, Inc., 1976), p. 53.

4. See map in Ott, *Hancock Shaker Village*, pp. 32–33, for locations of known Church Family buildings; see also pp. 53, 85.

5. West Family journal, New Lebanon, N.Y., 1867, Shaker Museum. See also Thomas Damon, *Memoranda*, p. 85; Priscilla J. Brewer, *Shaker Communities, Shaker Lives* (Hanover, N.H.: University Press of New England, 1986), p. 230.

6. Anna White and Leila S. Taylor, *Shakerism: Its Meaning and Message* (Columbus, Oh., Fred J. Heer, 1904), pp. 195–97.

7. Elder Thomas's report to the New Lebanon Ministry is found in "Records Kept by Order of the Church at New Lebanon," Shaker Museum, NOC 10,343, p. 91; Jefferson's 1863 report is in "Inventory of Property" in "Enfield Reports to New Lebanon Ministry 1843–1867," NOC 10,359; Hancock's drop in earnings mentioned in Ott, *Hancock Shaker Village*, p. 54.

8. Hancock, Mass., Day Book, 1837–1913, HSV.

9. Ott, *Hancock Shaker Village*, p. 96.

10. Page Smith, *The Rise of Industrial America* (New York: McGraw-Hill, 1984), p. 425.

11. Hancock inventory from "Production of Agriculture in Hancock in the County of Berkshire in the Post Office: Hancock 1860," Hancock Shaker Village Library.

12. Enfield inventory from "Inventory of Property" in "Enfield Reports to New Lebanon Ministry 1843–1867," Shaker Museum, NOC 10,359.

13. Tyringham inventory is from "Brief Inventory of the Personal Property of the Shaker Community in Tyringham after the Union of the Two Families December 1861" (Andrews collection, SA 809). Hancock inventory from "Production of Agriculture in Hancock," Hancock Shaker Village Library; Enfield inventory from "Inventory of Property"; 1873 information from "Assessor's Field Book Records, Pittsfield, Massachusetts, May 1st, 1874," pp. 376–77, Hancock Shaker Village Library.

14. Hancock agriculture, *Pittsfield Sun*, May 2, 1876, and Ott, *Hancock Shaker Village*, p. 54; Van Deusen on onions, *Shaker Manifesto*, Dec. 1882, p. 276; dried sweet corn, Ott, *Hancock Shaker Village*, p. 126.

15. *The Shaker*, vol. 7, July 1877, p. 50; Aug. 1877, p. 59.

16. Enfield 1865 labor cost, "Enfield Reports to New Lebanon Ministry 1843–1867"; population statistics, Stephen Paterwic, comp., "An Extract of Names, Ages, and Occupations from the U.S. Census 1850–1910 for the City of Union, Conn., the Shaker Society at Enfield," at HSV; see also Brewer, *Shaker Communities*, p. 231.

17. "Enfield North Family Account Book," WRHS II: A-3.

18. "Inventory of Property."

19. This discussion of Enfield economy is drawn from "Enfield Reports to the New Lebanon Ministry"; quotations on Enfield North Family holdings, pp. 79, 81.

20. Gary T. Leveille, "The Pease Family: Movers and Shakers of Enfield, Connecticut," *The Shaker Messenger,* Summer 1989, pp. 10–11; also Henry C. Blinn, "Notes by the Way while on a Journey to the State of Kentucky in the Year 1873," *Shaker Quarterly* 5 (Summer 1965), p. 19; Jessie Miriam Brainard, "Mother Ann's Children in Connecticut: The Enfield Shakers," *Connecticut Quarterly,* vol. 3, no. 4 (1897), p. 471.

21. Blinn, "Notes by the Way," p. 39.

22. Pittsfield Sun, June 15, 1871; *Springfield Republican,* Apr. 22, 1934, in Williams College Shaker Collection Scrapbook #99, Vol. 2; *Biographical Review Containing Life Sketches of Leading Citizens of Berkshire County, Massachusetts* (Boston, 1899), vol. 31, pp. 210–14.

23. Phidelio Collins, Canterbury Shaker Library, MS 177.

24. [Thomas Damon], "Considerations Illustrating the necessity of some Revisions in the Direction and Management of Temporal Concerns," Andrews Collection SA 766.

25. Letter from Albert Battles to Elder Thomas Damon, Mar. 11, 1867, Canterbury MS 129; Canterbury MS 1141, March 14, 1867.

26. "Records Kept by Order of the Church at New Lebanon," vol. 3, p. 517, Shaker Museum 10,342; *Berkshire Gleaner,* July 18, 1906.

27. Skeptical comment of diarist is found in "Records Kept by Order of the Church at New Lebanon," vol. 4, Shaker Museum, NOC 10,343, p. 36, Jan. 1875; Lucy Bowers records, Canterbury MS 1141.

28. Pittsfield Sun, May 2, 1876; "Records Kept by Order of the Church at New Lebanon," vol. 4, Shaker Museum, NOC 10,343, p. 55, Jan. 3, 1876.

29. "Records Kept by Order of the Church at New Lebanon," vol. 3, Shaker Museum, NOC 10,342.

30. "Tyringham Shakers," *Lee Valley Gleaner and Berkshire Farmers' Advocate,* February 9, 1871, at Berkshire Athenaeum.

31. William Dean Howells, "A Shaker Village," *Atlantic Monthly,* June 1876, pp. 699–710.

32. "Grove Wright's Book," April 29, 1843; Calvin Fairchild, *Sketchbook,* 1868–1869, WRHS VII B 133, Dec. 24, 1868.

33. Quotation is from Henry C. Blinn, "A Journey to Kentucky in the Year 1873," *Shaker Quarterly* 5 (Spring 1965), p. 16; see Page Smith, *Rise of Industrial America* (New York: McGraw-Hill, 1984), pp. 426–29, for more on the hardships of farm women.

34. Lucy S. Bowers, "A Brief Review & Memorial Tribute to Sister Sarah Emily Copley deceased September 9, 1911," Williams College Shaker Collection, 32, 81 B.

35. Canterbury MS 129.

36. Bowers, "A Brief Review."

37. *The Shaker,* Sept., 1872.

38. *Pittsfield Sun,* May 2, 1876.

39. The *Pittsfield Sun,* May 2, 1876, claimed the Hancock Shakers were cultivating their tillage as grain fields instead of gardens because of shrinking population, at 115 members in 1876.

40. This account of Henry Blinn's visit is taken from "Notes by the Way While on a Journey to the State of Kentucky in the Year 1873" at Shaker Museum and in *Shaker Quarterly* (Summer 1965), pp. 15–20, and (Fall 1965), pp. 37–39.

41. Eldress Bertha Lindsay, in an interview with the author, September 1988, said that Emeline Hart was involved in designing the sisters' shop. Quotation is from Jessie Miriam Brainard, "Mother Ann's Children in Connecticut," pp. 467–68.

42. Courses and materials are mentioned in *The Shaker* 6 (Aug. 1876); for more on offerings of local public high schools see "Teachers' Records" for 1880s and 1890s at House of Local History, Williamstown, Mass.

43. Blinn, "Notes by the Way," p. 18.

44. Ibid., p. 38; Williams College Shaker Collection 98/vol. 5, misc MSS.

45. "A New Years Covenant for the Sisters Under 50 Yrs. of Age" in "Collection of Canterbury Letters Regarding Music," c. 1868, WRHS IV A 7.

46. See Daniel W. Patterson, "Implications of Late Nineteenth Century Shaker Music," *Shaker Quarterly* 16 (Winter 1989–90), pp. 214–35.

47. George Noyes Miller, "Notes on the Shakers," *The Shaker* 7 (July 1877), p. 51, reprinted from *American Socialist*.

48. Quoted in *Pittsfield Sun*, Feb. 2, 1899.

49. Quotation from Philemon Stewart, *Brief Weekly Journal*, New Lebanon, 1870–1874, Andrews Collection, SA 776, Feb. 11, 1872.

50. The 1879 meeting is described in the *Pittsfield Sun*, Aug. 24, 1879. After 1871 New Lebanon was increasingly called Mt. Lebanon.

51. Henri Desroche, *The American Shakers: From Neo-Christianity to Presocialism*, ed. and trans. from the French by John K. Savacool (Amherst: University of Massachusetts Press, 1971).

52. Blinn, "Notes by the Way," p. 19.

CHAPTER TEN Final Years of the Hancock and Enfield Shakers (pp. 169–193)

1. "Let Us Sing Praises" (Hancock, 1853), in *Fifteen Shaker Songs*, selected and arranged by Conrad Held, © 1944 (Renewed) by G. Schirmer, Inc. (ASCAP). All rights reserved. Used by permission.

2. Quotation is from letter from Ira Lawson, WRHS IV:A-20, Feb. 15, 1900.

3. Quotation is from *Sun-Herald*, Jan. 28, 1905, WRHS V:B8.

4. Hancock Day Book 1837–1913 at HSV.

5. Hancock Day Book 1837–1913; for a full account of Levi Shaw's career, see Robert F. W. Meader, "Gold and the Shakers," *Shaker Quarterly* 7 (Spring 1967), pp. 5–9.

6. Henry C. Blinn, "Notes from Our Diary," *Shaker Manifesto* 28, no. 10 (Oct. 1899), pp. 146–49.

7. Lucy S. Bowers, "A Brief Review & Memorial Tribute to Sister Sarah Emily Copley deceased September 9, 1911," Williams College Shaker Collection.

8. Blinn, "Notes from Our Diary," p. 147.

9. Quotation on butter and eggs from Amy Bess Miller, *City of Peace*, p. 27; sisters' records are in Hancock Day Book.

10. The advertisement mentioned is at the Hancock Shaker Village Library and pictured in John Harlow Ott, *Hancock Shaker Village: A Guidebook and History* (Hancock, Mass.: Shaker Community, Inc., 1976), p. 106; sisters' activities are mentioned in letters from Fidella Estabrook to J. P. MacLean, Sept. 4, 1904, Jan. 22, 1905, July 23, 1905, WRHS IV:A-20; other information is from Amy Bess Miller, interviews with the author.

11. The purchase of livestock is described in *The Shaker Manifesto* 29 (July 1899), pp. 108–9; the 1902 tax assessment is in the Canterbury Shaker Library, MS 127; see also Ott, *Hancock Shaker Village*, p. 127.

12. Lucy S. Bowers, "Showing When Different Houses Were Builded in the Society at Enfield Connecticut," Canterbury Shaker Library, MS 1141.

13. Jessie Miriam Brainard, "Mother Ann's Children in Connecticut: The Enfield Shakers," *Connecticut Quarterly* 3 (1897), p. 473.

14. Stephen Paterwic, comp., "An Extract of Names, Ages, and Occupations from the U.S. Census 1850–1910 for the City of Union, Conn., the Shaker Society at Enfield," at HSV.

15. Population figures are from Priscilla J. Brewer, *Shaker Communities, Shaker Lives* (Hanover, N.H.: University Press of New England, 1986), pp. 230, 231. The following brethren lived at the Enfield Church Family in January, 1900: Elder George Wilcox (age 80), Brothers John Wilcoxe (82), Thomas Fisher (77), Daniel Orcutt (70), Frederic Schnell (70), Walter Shepherd, and Ricardo Belden, along with three boys, Harvey Stockton, Johnny Rollins, and George Healy. The following sisters lived there: Eldress Caroline L. Tate, Sisters Matilda Schnell (78), Phoebe Wilcox (78), Lucy Bowers, Fannie Tyson, Amanda Tiffany, and Robena Page. The following may have been boarders: Genie and Etta Page (a Mary Page died at Enfield in 1892 at age 21), Marion Marshall, Blanche Crossman, Georgie and Jessie Bruce, Esther Grover, Maud Pepper, Christine Schofield, Bessie Stevens, Evelyn Whitney, Mabel Lyons, Gertrude Whitney, Pearl King, Gladys Phillips, and Lillian Curtis. From "Names of Persons Living in the Chh. Family January 1901," p. 26, Canterbury Shaker Library, MS 1141.

16. Hancock Day Book.

17. *Springfield Republican*, April 14, 1905.

18. Ott, *Hancock Shaker Village*, p. 101. Possibly, this building was originally the Ministry eldresses' shop, which had been used when the seed industry was thriving.

19. Descendant Helen Dodge of Pittsfield, Mass., interview with author, November 11, 1990.

20. Hancock Day Book.

21. All quotations in this paragraph are from Lucy S. Bowers, "A Brief Memorial Tribute to Sarah Emily Copley," Williams College Shaker Collection.

22. "Letter to Moore Mason from Walter Shepherd, Shaker Station, Ct., Feb. 16, 1808 [sic]," WRHS IV:A-9, reel 17.

23. WRHS IV:A-20.

24. Church records, vol. 2, Canterbury Shaker Library, MS 1141; Hancock Day Book.

25. Hancock Day Book; Louis Basting poem in *The Shaker*, June 1877.

26. Eldress Emma had signed the Enfield covenant in 1869, followed by her sister Evelyn in 1875.

27. Hancock Day Book.

28. Lookout Mountain [Tenn.] Improvement Co.; City Real Estate Trust Co., Topeka, Kansas; and Continental Land and Securities Co. of Denver (Canterbury MSS 370, 417).

29. Collection of Helen R. McGinnis.

30. Canterbury MS. 1141. On August 14, 1893, Eldress Sophia Copley and Emily Copley were appointed trustees of the sisters' funds at the Enfield North Family.

31. Copley family Bible, Collection of Helen R. McGinnis; Steinert Collection, Hancock Shaker Village, p. 13.

32. "Record," August 6, 1893, Canterbury MS 1141.

33. This note is in the Enfield, Conn., collection at Sabbathday Lake, Me.

34. Note signed J. W. Copley, Aug. 13, 1896, in Collection of the United Society of Shakers, Sabbathday Lake, Me.; note signed UFC, Apr. 5, 1895, Canterbury MS 370.

35. Quotation is from Canterbury MS 1141.

36. Lucy S. Bowers, "Consolidations," Canterbury MS 1141, pp. 74–75; other information courtesy of Anna Mary Danton and Stephen Paterwic. Other members arriving from Canaan were Eliza Brown, 84, Angeline Brown, 50, Alice Basted, 48, Marietta Estes, 48, and Andrew Wise, 34, all of whom came among the Shakers in childhood; and Janeth Lee, 55, who had been with the Shakers about 32 years. According to the covenant at Canterbury, George M. Clarke signed on Jan. 25, 1897. Others didn't sign until Jan. 21, 1899, and they include those listed above, plus Henrietta Page, Paul Von Wagner, Miriam Offord, Angeline Brown, Hannah Wilson, Florence Staples, Janet Lee, Florence I.[?] Ashley, Edith Shufelt, Phebe Farnham, Mary Ann Manning, Mathilda Schnell, Fredk. Schnell, and Lucy S. Bowers.

37. Letter from Joseph Holden to Elder William 11/17/98, Enfield, Ct. Collection, Sabbathday Lake, Me.

38. "Complete list of all the members of the North Family Shakers of Enfield Ct." Jan. 23, 1899. Hancock Shaker Village Library.

39. Steinert Collection, Hancock Shaker Village, p. 28.

40. Candlebox, gift of Avis Howell, Shaker Library, Sabbathday Lake, Me.

41. U.S. Census, June, 1900, in Stephen J. Paterwic, "An Extract of Names, Ages, and Occupations from the U.S. Census 1850–1910 for the City of Union, Conn., the Shaker Society at Enfield," (at HSV).

42. The following were present: George Wilcox, Daniel Orcutt, Ricardo Belden, Frederic Schnell, Walter Shepherd, George Clarke, Thomas Stroud, Paul Van Wagner, Caroline Tate, Lucy Bowers, Anna Offord, Robena Page, Matilda Schnell, Miriam Offord, Angeline Brown, Marion Patrick, Hannah Wilson, Mariette Esty, Alice Braisted, Jennette Lee, and the Ministry: Joseph Holden, Ira Lawson, Harriet Bullard, and Augusta Stone; Lucy Bowers records, Canterbury Shaker Library, MS 1141.

43. Lucy Bowers records, Canterbury MS 1141.

44. Both documents are at Shaker Library, Sabbathday Lake, Me.

45. "West Pittsfield Mass. 1902: Valuation of Land and Buildings in the Town of Hancock Mass. Owned by the United Society of Shakers," Canterbury MS 129.

46. Letter from Fidella Estabrook, Jan. 22, 1905, WRHS IV:A-20.

47. This account is taken from Sylvia Minott Spencer, "Next Door to the Angels—My Memories of the Shakers," *Shaker Quarterly* (Winter 1970), pp. 124–34.

48. Letter from Irene E. Minott, Enfield, to [Ivan?] C. Minott, May 15, 1904, Collection of the United Society of Shakers, Sabbathday Lake, Me.

49. "News from Down the River: The Passing of the Shakers," *The Springfield Republican*, Feb. 26, 1905, in clipping file, Williams College Shaker Collection.

50. [Walter Shepherd], "A Reply from Shaker Station," *The Springfield Republican*, March 5, 1905.

51. The quotations in this discussion of Walter Shepherd are taken from "Letter to Moore Mason from Walter Shepherd, Shaker Station, Ct., Feb. 16, 1808 [sic]," and "Letter from Walter Shepherd, April 8, 1908," WRHS IV:A-9.

52. *Hartford Times*, Sept. 26, 1910.

53. *New York Times*, July 23, 1911.

54. "Names of Persons Living in the Church Family March 1910," Enfield, Ct., Canterbury Shaker Village Library, MS 1141; Canterbury MS 370.

55. This quotation and the following discussion of the end of the Enfield Shaker community are from [Lucy S. Bowers], "Wanamaker Diaries Kept by Unknown," # DC 18639, Shaker Heritage Society Collection, Manuscripts and Special Collections, New York State Library.

56. See clipping scrapbook, Shaker Library, Sabbathday Lake, Me.

57. *Springfield Republican*, April 30, 1916.

58. Obituary in *Pittsfield Sun*, April 5, 1905.

59. "Funeral of Ira Lawson," *Pittsfield Sun*, April 5, 1905; letter from Fidella Estabrook, July 23, 1905, WRHS IV:A-20; Hancock Day Book.

60. Canterbury MS 1192.

61. Both stories are from Amy Bess Miller, *Hancock Shaker Village/The City of Peace* (Hancock, Mass.: Hancock Shaker Village, 1984), p. 31.

62. Edward Deming Andrews, and Faith Andrews, *Fruits of the Shaker Tree of Life* (Stockbridge, Mass.: Berkshire Traveller Press, 1975).

63. Ibid., pp. 93–96.

64. Miller, *Hancock Shaker Village/The City of Peace*, p. 16; Mary Richmond, comp., *Shaker Literature: A Bibliography* (Hancock, Mass.: Shaker Community, Inc., 1977; distributed by University Press of New England, Hanover, N.H.); Federal Writers' Project, *The Berkshire Hills* (New York: Funk & Wagnalls Co., 1939), p. 55.

65. Ott, *Hancock Shaker Village*, p. 111.

66. Quotation from Springfield *Sun Union & Republican*, Feb. 11, 1934; see also *Berkshire Eagle*, April 3, 1937, and Hancock Town Report of 1943.

67. Miller, *Hancock Shaker Village/The City of Peace*, pp. 16, 19.

68. Letter to Eldress Emma B. King from Sister Frances Hall, Dec. 29, 1946, Canterbury MS 381.

69. Ibid.

70. Letter to Eldress Emma B. King from Fannie Estabrook and Frances Hall, July 14, 1949, Canterbury MS 428.

71. Amy Bess Miller, interview with author, October 1989.

72. Canterbury MS 348.

73. Ibid.

74. Hancock Shaker Village Steering Committee consisted of Mr. and Mrs. Lawrence K. Miller, Donald B. Miller, Lawrence R. Connor, Mr. and Mrs. David V. Andrews, Dr. and Mrs. Edward D. Andrews, Dorothy Miller Cahill (curator of collections at the Museum of Modern Art in Manhattan and a Shaker collector), Mrs. Davis T. Dunbar, Mrs. John A. Gilchrist (an architectural historian), Prof. Henry Russell Hitchcock, Jean Lipman, Mr. and Mrs. Carl P. Rollins, Mr. and Mrs. Milton C. Rose, Frank O. Spinney (then director of Old Sturbridge Village), and Mrs. and Mrs. Carl A. Weyerhauser.

Others who became involved included Loring Conant, director of the Trustees of Public Reservations; S. Lane Faison, director of the Williams College Art Museum; Philip Guyol, director of the New Hampshire Historical Society; Richard H. Howland, president of the National Trust for Historic Preservation; Bertram Little, director of the Society for the Preservation of New England Antiquities; and Nina Little, author and historian.

This and the following information about the sale are from Miller, *Hancock Shaker Village/The City of Peace*, p. 20, and from interviews with A. B. Miller.

75. *Berkshire Eagle*, September 20, 1960.

EPILOGUE (pp. 194–198)

1. "More About the Shakers," *Berkshire Gleaner,* July 18, 1906.
2. This account is taken from "Down in Tyringham, As a N.Y. Correspondent Saw Things," subtitled "A Suggestion of Switzerland about the Place," *Pittsfield Sun,* Sept. 15, 1887, p. 6, reprinted from the *New York Times.*
3. "Letter from John A. Scott," *Berkshire Gleaner,* July 4, 1906, p. 1.
4. Henry C. Blinn, "Notes from Our Diary," Sept. 1, 1899, in *The Shaker Manifesto* 19 (Nov. 1899), pp. 248–53.
5. E. R. Fawcett, interviews with author, June 1989 and August 1992.
6. Richard Steinert, interview with author, Enfield, Conn., April 1989.
7. Eloise S. Myers, *Tyringham, Massachusetts: A Hinterland Settlement* (Tyringham, Mass.: 1948), p. 85.

Index

UNIVERSITY PRESS OF NEW ENGLAND

publishes books under its own imprint and is the publisher for Brandeis University Press, Brown University Press, Clark University Press, University of Connecticut, Dartmouth College, Middlebury College Press, University of New Hampshire, University of Rhode Island, Tufts University, University of Vermont, and Wesleyan University Press.

LIBRARY OF CONGRESS CATALOGING-IN-PUBLICATION DATA

Burns, Deborah.

  Shaker cities of Peace, Love, and Union : a history of the Hancock Bishopric / Deborah E. Burns.

    p.   cm.

  Includes bibliographical references and index.

  ISBN 0–87451–612–9. — ISBN 0–87451–613–7 (pbk.)

  1. Shakers. Hancock Bishopric—History.   2. Shakers. Hancock Bishopric—Biography.   I. Title.

  BX9768.H2B87   1993

  289′.8′097441—dc20   92–59965

1941